W9-AEG-435

The Great Labor Uprising of 1877

BY PHILIP S. FONER

History of the Labor Movement in the United States (4 vols.)
The Life and Writings of Frederick Douglass (5 vols.)
A History of Cuba and Its Relations with the United States
  (2 vols.)
The Complete Writings of Thomas Paine (2 vols.)
Business and Slavery: The New York Merchants and
  the Irrepressible Conflict
W. E. B. Du Bois Speaks (2 vols.)
The Fur and Leather Workers Union
Jack London: American Rebel
Mark Twain: Social Critic
The Jews in American History: 1654-1865
The Case of Joe Hill
The Letters of Joe Hill
The Bolshevik Revolution: Its Impact on
  American Radicals, Liberals, and Labor
American Labor and the War in Indochina
Helen Keller: Her Socialist Years
The Autobiographies of the Haymarket Martyrs
The Black Panthers Speak
The Basic Writings of Thomas Jefferson
The Voice of Black America: Major Speeches of
  Negroes in the United States, 1797-1973 (2 vols.)
The Spanish-Cuban-American War and the Birth of
  American Imperialism, 1895-1902 (2 vols.)
When Karl Marx Died: Comments in 1883
Organized Labor and the Black Worker, 1619-1973
American Labor Songs of the Nineteenth Century
Labor and the American Revolution
We the Other People: Alternative Declarations of Independence
  by Labor Groups, Farmers, Women's Rights Advocates,
  Socialists, and Blacks
Formation of the Workingmen's Party of the United States
The Democratic-Republican Societies, 1790-1800
Inside the Monster: José Martí on the
  United States and American Imperialism
Our America: José Martí on Latin America and
  the Struggle for Cuban Independence
The Factory Girls
The Great Labor Uprising of 1877
American Socialism and Black Americans:
  From the Age of Jackson to World War II

The Great Labor Uprising of 1877

Philip S. Foner

PATHFINDER

New York   London   Montréal   Sydney

Copyright © 1977 by Philip S. Foner
All rights reserved

ISBN 0-913460-56-7 cloth; ISBN 0-913460-57-5 paper
Library of Congress Catalog Card No. 77-80725
Manufactured in the United States of America

First edition, 1977
Third printing, 1991

A Pathfinder book published by the Anchor Foundation

Cover: Assault by troops on strikers in Baltimore, as depicted in
Harper's Weekly.

Distributed by Pathfinder
410 West Street, New York, NY 10014, U.S.A.

Pathfinder distributors around the world:
Australia (and Asia and the Pacific):
   Pathfinder, 19 Terry St., Surry Hills, Sydney, N.S.W. 2010
Britain (and Europe, Africa, and the Middle East):
   Pathfinder, 47 The Cut, London, SE1 8LL
Canada:
   Pathfinder, 6566, boul. St-Laurent, Montréal, Québec, H2S 3C6
Iceland:
   Pathfinder, Klapparstíg 26, 2d floor, 121 Reykjavík
New Zealand:
   Pathfinder, 157a Symonds Street, Auckland
Sweden:
   Pathfinder, Vikingagatan 10, S-113 42, Stockholm
United States (and Caribbean and Latin America):
   Pathfinder, 410 West Street, New York, NY 10014

Contents

Preface

In 1876, as the nation prepared to celebrate the centennial of American independence, an economic depression was entering its fourth year; millions of Americans were unemployed, and for those who were still working, wages—already at starvation levels—were being cut in half. In New York City, where one-quarter of the work force was without jobs, meetings of the unemployed, called to "consider how we are to get work, food, clothing, and shelter," were brutally attacked by the police. After one such onslaught, at which men, women, and children were beaten without any warning, John Swinton, the editor of the *New York Sun,* warned:

> The power of money has become supreme over everything. It has secured for the class who control it all the special privileges and special legislation which it needs to secure its complete and absolute domination. . . . This Power must be kept in check. It must be broken or it will utterly crush the people. . . .[1]

Little wonder, then, that the *National Labor Tribune,* a weekly published in Pittsburgh, questioned whether the approaching one hundredth birthday of the nation's independence would have any meaning for American workers. At one time, it said, it might have been possible to celebrate, for America was then "the star of the political Bethlehem which shone radiantly out in the dark night of political misrule in Europe. The masses of the old world gazed upon her as their escape." Men in America could be "their own rulers"; "none could or should become their masters." But industrialization had created a nightmare:

> The dreams have not been realized. . . . The working people of this country . . . suddenly find capital as rigid as an absolute monarch. . . . Capital has now the same control over us that the aristocracy of England had at the time of the Revolution. We have the greatest work to do ever given to men. As our forefathers had the regal power and its proud

7

aristocracy to control and limit, so have we, now, the combined power of capital, protected by monopolies, defended by government and press, to limit and control.

> The workers should remember,
>   That we are in a land that's free,
> We have shaken off the British yoke,
>   And left her tyranny.[2]

According to the *Chicago Workingman's Advocate,* the centennial pointed up the need for "another revolution, as essential today as that inaugurated in 1776."[3]

In the hot mid-July of 1877, exactly one year after the celebration of America's one hundredth birthday, with the nation prostrate, a general railroad strike developed into a national conflagration that brought the country closer to a social revolution than at any other time in its century of existence except for the Civil War.

On Tuesday, July 16, 1877, railroad workers at Martinsburg, West Virginia, went out on strike against still another wage cut imposed by the Baltimore & Ohio Railroad. As the militia was mobilized and violence broke out, the strike extended up the B & O line and spread rapidly to other lines. Other workers came to the support of the railroad strikers, and by the weekend angry crowds of workers were attacking the railroads and fighting with militia in the cities of West Virginia, Pennsylvania, and Ohio. The local militia generally sided with the strikers, and, for the first time since Andrew Jackson's administration, federal troops were called in to suppress a strike.

Almost before the public was aware of what was happening, the huge contagion had spread as far as Chicago, St. Louis, Kansas City, and then on to San Francisco. Within a few days, one hundred thousand men were on strike in the first nationwide labor upheaval in history. All the main railway lines were affected, and even the employees of some Canadian roads joined the strike. Headlines blared out: "The Movement Rapidly Extending In All Directions" and "The People Excited and Agitated From Ocean to Ocean."

The railroad strikes served as a fuse, carrying the spark of rebellion to other workingmen, who, if they were working, were suffering from wage cuts, and to the unemployed multitudes in the great cities. In several cities, the original strike on the railroads expanded to many other industries, and in St. Louis it spread into such a systematically organized and complete shutdown of all industry that it became the first truly general strike in history.

Although the Great Strike was spontaneous and unorganized— it had nothing in the nature of central leadership and direction— this first nationwide rebellion of labor frightened the authorities and the upper classes as nothing before in our history. On July 24, John Hay, soon to become assistant secretary of state, wrote in alarm to his wealthy father-in-law: "Any hour the mob chooses it can destroy any city in the country—that is the simple truth."[4]

Even the Harmonists, in their utopian community at Economy, some sixteen miles south of Pittsburgh—one of the storm centers—wondered "whether this reign of terror marked the beginning of the harvest-time spoken of in Scripture . . . when 'the Heavens and earth, which are now by that same sword of God kept in store, reserved unto fire against the Day of Judgment and perdition of ungodly men.' "[5] A contemporary labor paper called the Great Strike "the Beginning of a Revolution," and predicted that "the occurrences during the last portion of July, 1877, will, in the future history of this country, be designated as the beginning of the second American Revolution, which inaugurated the independence of Labor from Capital."[6] Joseph A. Dacus, the St. Louis newspaperman whose *Annals of the Great Strikes in the United States* is one of the three contemporary "potboilers" published on the subject within a year, noted that the upheaval startled the entire world, drowned out the noise of the war in the Balkans and elsewhere, and drew "exclusive attention to the social ferment on this side of the Atlantic unparalleled in the annals of time."[7] John Swinton, the socially conscious journalist who, like Dacus, saw the strike at first hand, called it so unprecedented that there was "nothing like it in any history whatsoever."[8]

The Great Strike has been discussed in histories of the labor movement in the United States, in general histories of the nation, in histories of the railroad industry, and in works devoted to strike struggles. Its full story throughout the nation, however, was not made available until 1959, when Robert V. Bruce's painstakingly researched *1877: Year of Violence* was published. That work, which was the product of three years of research in more than one hundred libraries, is a major contribution to the history of American industrial society. Nevertheless, it is marred by several weaknesses. For one thing, by dealing with the strikes' events chronologically, instead of by railroad lines or cities, Bruce leaves the reader bewildered as to the continuity of the strike in any one area. One must constantly turn from one chapter to another for an understanding of the outbreak of a particular strike, its development, and for its final outcome. In between, the picture tends to become confused by the discussion of events on other railroads and in other cities.

In the present work, I have followed a topical organization, but, in order to retain the dramatic impact of the Great Strike's development day by day, I have included as an appendix a chronology of its events.

Since Bruce's work was published, several monographs, dissertations, and articles appearing in scholarly journals have shed additional light on both the national and local aspects of the tremendous struggle, and have pointed up weaknesses in his interpretation. These studies, together with my own research into contemporary sources, have convinced me that there is need for another all-inclusive book on this subject, especially as we approach the centennial of the great labor upheaval.

During the Great Strike, the major part of the country's transportation system and thousands of industries dependent on it were brought to a halt. In addition to the four major trunk lines—the Baltimore & Ohio, the Pennsylvania, the Erie, and the New York Central & Hudson—scores of other lines were compelled to cease operations: for example, to mention just a few, the Delaware, Lackawanna & Western, the Indianapolis & St. Louis, the Cincinnati, Hamilton & Dayton, the Ohio & Mississippi, the Missouri, Kansas & Texas, the Texas & Pacific, the Union Pacific, the Northern Pacific, the Northern Central, the Wabash, the Chicago, Burlington & Quincy, the Canadian Southern, the Grand Trunk of Canada, the Great Western of Canada, the Central of New Jersey, and the Louisville & Nashville. It is impossible to deal with the events on all of the lines and in all of the cities through which these lines ran. I have, therefore, restricted myself to a discussion of the events on those lines and in those cities which were the key areas of struggle.

Since the writings of the British historians George Rudé, Eric Thompson, and Eric J. Hobsbawm have begun to have an impact on our scholarship,[9] there has been an increasing tendency on both sides of the Atlantic, in discussing popular uprisings (even those since the Industrial Revolution), to use the words *crowds* and *crowd actions* instead of *mobs,* with the latter's unfavorable implication. It is becoming widely accepted that in most cases these actions were not mindless riots, but rather reflections of the economic, political, and social grievances, needs, and aspirations of the particular group of participants. Throughout this work, therefore, I have avoided the use of the term *mob* (except as employed by contemporaries), and have used instead the word *crowd*.

In any work on the Great Strike of 1877, one must seek to avoid the tendency to view it as a riot rather than as a strike,[10] or if as a strike, as only a railroad strike.[11] More serious, perhaps, is the tendency to view it as just another labor action born out of the frustrations of a depression, and one that disintegrated into random mob violence. Norman J. Ware was one of the first writers on the Great Strike who saw the inadequacy of such a view and who referred to the great upheaval as a social rebellion—"amounting almost to a revolution without revolutionizing intent." Ware also understood that the strike marked the presence, for the first time, of a distinct labor consciousness and raised in a credible way, for the first time, the possibility of a viable class analysis of American society.[12] Bruce, on the other hand, continued the tradition of viewing the uprising as a series of strikes that gave way to violence and lawlessness, and of persistently referring to "the mob" as ever ready to engage in such activities.[13] (It is a tribute to Samuel Yellen that, writing thirty years before George Rudé, he took conscious note of this pitfall and avoided the indiscriminate use of the words *the mob* and *tramps*.)[14] However, Bruce does pick out the faces in "the mob" and does convey a clear sense of the goals, behavior, and underlying beliefs of the crowd as a whole—the elements that Rudé suggests are key to a proper understanding of mass actions.[15]

Still another tendency that one must avoid is that of viewing the Great Strike as a full-blown insurrection which, but for a quirk of fate, would have produced a socialist America; or to insist that 1877 was a "mass strike" leading to virtual insurrection and with revolutionary potential.[16] That there were distinct insurrectionary and revolutionary elements in the Great Strike will become abundantly clear below. But it will also become evident that this characteristic did not apply in many areas affected by the strikes, and that at no point did the workers have either the power or the leadership to have transformed the strikes into a revolutionary seizure of the economy or the state.

The historian Herbert Gutman has recently alluded to the "little understood 1877 railroad strikes and riots."[17] It is my hope and belief that the present work will help to make them better understood.

In the preparation of this work, I have had the assistance of the staffs of many libraries and historical societies, both here and abroad. I wish to take this opportunity to thank Mr. Watt P. Marchman, director of the Hayes Memorial Library in Fremont, Ohio, for his assistance in the use of the Rutherford B. Hayes Papers; Anne-Mitte Kurkeby, of the University of Copenhagen Library, and Per Pio, of Det Kongelige Bibliotek in Copenhagen, for assistance in tracking down data in Denmark relating to Laurence Gronlund; Dorothy B. Swanson, of the Tamiment Institute Library of New York University, for assistance in obtaining contemporary labor papers; Harriet Williams, of the Lincoln University Library, for assistance in obtaining a wide variety of material through interlibrary loans; and the staffs of the New York Public Library, Columbia University Library, West Virginia Historical Society, University of West Virginia Library, Library of Congress, University of Kentucky Library, Louisville Public Library, Kentucky Historical Society, University of Toledo Library, Toledo Public Library, Cincinnati Historical Society, University of Cincinnati Library, the Bancroft Library of the University of California at Berkeley, University of Pittsburgh Library, Western Pennsylvania Historical Society, Chicago Historical Society, Chicago Public Library, Missouri Historical Society, St. Louis Public Library, San Francisco Public Library, State Historical Society of Wisconsin in Madison, Hornellsville Public Library, Buffalo Public Library, Enoch Pratt Free Library in Baltimore, Maryland Historical Society, Historical Society of Pennsylvania, Library Company of Philadelphia, Free Library in Philadelphia, Reading Public Library, Albright College Library in Reading, and the New York and New Jersey Historical Societies, National Archives, State Library of Pennsylvania in Harrisburg, the Terre Haute Public Library, and Princeton University Library.

I wish to thank Ray V. Brown, Christopher Hoyt, Kenneth Kann, and Nicholas Salvatore for furnishing me with copies of their unpublished studies of the strike.

I also wish to thank my brother, Henry Foner, for reading the entire manuscript and making valuable suggestions.

Philip S. Foner
Lincoln University, Pennsylvania
August 1977

I

Prologue

In *Chapters of Erie,* that pointed commentary on American business ethics, Charles Francis Adams, Jr., viewed with alarm the organized lawlessness that had grown up in this country since Appomattox, sheltered by the mantle of the law. The problem was not the ex-soldier, trained to kill, but rather the ex-administrator, who for the first time controlled the destinies of large numbers of men and large amounts of capital. Adams felt that the evil geniuses were "certain single men at the head of vast combinations of private wealth," and after delineating a general type of war-propelled millionaires, he selected two—Jay Gould and Jim Fisk—as specific examples. These speculators, under the guise of benefitting communities, had established networks of railroads without any regard for genuine need. Lines were promoted in regions where there was no competition, so that exorbitant rates could be charged. When these ventures proved unsuccessful, the speculators unloaded their securities on the residents of the towns the lines were supposed to serve, thereby relieving themselves of the obligation of paying for their mistakes.[1]

The activities of Gould and Fisk were typical of railroad financing. Fattened on government land grants and monopoly routes, the railroads tracked across the continent at a pace that astounded even their most ardent promoters. In 1850, only 2,201 miles of track were in use, but during the next ten years, this figure more than tripled. In the four years between 1869 and 1873 alone, more than 24,000 miles were built. By 1877, the railroad network consisted of over 79,000 miles. Overall, the industry represented an investment of almost $5 billion, nearly half of which ($2.26 billion) consisted of bonded debt. By way of comparison, the national debt that same year stood at $2.1 billion.

About fifty corporations, each operating between two hundred and a thousand miles of road, made up the bulk of the nation's railway system. Of them, the Pennsylvania stood first and was the nation's greatest single private enterprise. Capitalized in 1873 at $39 million, it owned, operated, or otherwise controlled 6,600 miles of line and employed about 200,000 men. No other industry in the country even approached this scale of operation.

The railroads were not only the country's largest businesses; they were fast becoming economically indispensable. All land transportation of persons and goods, except that of a purely local nature, went by rail. By the 1870s the railroads had overtaken canals and natural waterways as carriers of the nation's freight. As early as 1871, only 34 percent of the total freight tonnage passing through St. Louis was carried on the Mississippi River; by 1877, the figure had dropped to 10 percent. In 1872, the 10 million tons of freight carried by the Erie and New York Central railroads to New York City was nearly three times the 3.7 million tons borne over the Erie Canal. Four-fifths of all the grain received at eastern seaports in 1876 came by rail. In the same year, nearly all passengers, the nation's mail, its troops and their supplies, and from perhaps two-thirds to three-fourths of all freight—indeed most of the nation's commerce—moved over the railroad network.

Although several adherents of the "new economic history" argue that the railroads were not indispensable to American growth, it would be difficult to find anyone at that time who shared this view. The *Chicago Tribune* echoed contemporary opinion in an editorial entitled "The Value of Railroad Transportation" in its issue of July 23, 1877. It called the railroad system "the very heart and life of the modern system of commercial existence." Henry Poor, publisher of *Poor's Manual for Railroads*, went as far as to say that it was responsible for feeding the entire population of the United States.[2]

But as the railroads expanded, so, too, did their economic power. Entire regions lay in their grip. Communities either flourished or disappeared at their whim. The railroad companies frequently owned the coal fields and the iron mines. In some states, they were in complete control of the political machinery, and they were notorious for their rapport with high federal officials.[3] Railroad promoters and lobbyists swarmed into the state houses and the halls of Congress in search of charters, franchises, subsidies, and land grants, while fighting to prevent investigations, regulation, and new taxes. They were almost perpetually at war with the farmers and small-town merchants, who justifiably feared the power of the railroads to destroy their economic operations. They were always seeking legislative favors, offering as inducements the free pass, the political contribution, and, on occasion, the outright bribe. They also held out such considerations as legal fees to be paid, construction contracts to be let, and a variety of positions to be filled. In almost every community, they had at their beck and call a veritable army of talented attorneys, whose livelihood depended on the railroads. When these "railroad lawyers" later became judges, legislators, governors, or cabinet members, they carried their pro-railroad points of view with them into their new positions. As Clifton K. Yearley, Jr., notes in his study of the Baltimore & Ohio Railroad: "Merely in the process of operating the road its president exerted influence as great as that of any other individual in Maryland."[4]

Even presidents of the United States sometimes owed their election directly to railroad political influence. An outstanding example of this was the disputed election of 1876 between Republican Rutherford B. Hayes and Democrat Samuel J. Tilden. The dispute centered on the voting in Louisiana, Florida, and South Carolina, where state election boards, dominated by Republicans and buttressed by federal troops, alleged fraud and intimidation of Black voters and threw out enough Democratic votes to create Republican majorities. Historians generally agree that the Louisiana and South Carolina elections were too corrupt to be even understood by ordinary human beings, but that Tilden did carry Florida, and its electoral votes would have assured him of the presidency. However, the election was decided in Hayes's favor by a special electoral commission set up by Congress, and its decision was accepted largely because of the defection of southern Democrats from Tilden to Hayes. The actual determination was made by Thomas A. Scott, president of the Pennsylvania Railroad, who, in return for assurances of support for a Texas Pacific Railroad, obtained the votes of the southern congressmen for Hayes.[5] It is hardly an accident that on March 2, 1877, when Hayes received the telegram confirming his election, he was en route to Washington in Tom Scott's own luxurious private car.[6] The *New York Sun* had good reason to ascribe "Mr. Hayes' residence in the White House" to "the Texas Pacific enterprise" and "Col. Scott's influence."[7]

As for the other principal force in the railroad industry—the workmen—they had little power, either economic or political.

Railroad workers had conducted militant struggles against the companies since the first strike on the roads, which was on the Baltimore & Ohio and lasted from June 20 to 30, 1831,[8] but these had always been sporadic outbursts and never resulted in the establishment of effective unions. In fact, as late as 1873 the railwaymen had almost no unions at all. The track hands, switchmen, and brakemen were entirely without unions. A small number of machinists employed in certain repair shops belonged to the Machinists' and Blacksmiths' International Union, but the majority of the shopmen and stationary hands were without a union of any kind. A minority of skilled workers were organized according to function into three brotherhoods: The Brotherhood of Locomotive Engineers, the Brotherhood of Locomotive Firemen, and the Brotherhood of Railway Conductors, but the last two hardly operated as unions. The Brotherhood of Locomotive Firemen had been founded for "the protection and elevation mentally, morally and socially" of all firemen "for the purpose of working their way up to a higher position," and the organization placed its entire emphasis on its membership's proper moral conduct as the way to achieve improvements in their conditions. The *Locomotive Firemen's Magazine,* the Brotherhood's official journal, stressed the continued uplift of members through self-education in railroad technology, the rooting out of intemperance and loose moral conduct, and the protection of railroad workers' families through sick benefits and death insurance. Judging from the statements of its leadership and the pages of its official journal, the Brotherhood of Locomotive Firemen devoted more time to screening the railroad corporations' personnel than to representing them. "It is part of our business to secure all good members work," the *Locomotive Firemen's Magazine* editorialized, "and the many assurances from railroad officers that they will give us the preference is, in itself, a work of honor to us as locomotive firemen. . . . To place such men upon the locomotive engine as have received their education through the order, is merely to give the public a class of men who trust can be reposed in."[9]

Only one effective union existed among the railroad workers in 1873: the Brotherhood of Locomotive Engineers, with a membership of 10,000 employed on nearly every major trunk line, with well-enforced written contracts on a number of lines, with a lively monthly magazine, and with a well-managed accident and insurance program. But the Brotherhood was led by Grand Chief

Engineer Charles Wilson, a conservative trade unionist who would not countenance the idea that union engineers should cooperate with other, nonrailroad workers in joint actions on economic and political issues. Even on issues affecting the engineers, Wilson opposed strikes. Instead, he stressed that workers and employers shared a common interest, and let it be known that local lodges could not strike without his permission or they would be expelled. Under Wilson's leadership, the Brotherhood worked closely with the American Railway Association, an employers' organization.

There was hardly any recognition of the unions by the railroad companies for purposes of collective bargaining. Sometimes, as in the case of the Brotherhood of Locomotive Engineers, companies negotiated wages and work rules for the sake of convenience, or out of necessity, but never as a matter of right, and always with the thought in mind of abrogating the agreements when it suited their purposes.[10]

The fact that there was no effective railroad unionism should not be taken to mean that there was any lack of grievances on the part of the railwaymen. The official organ of the Brotherhood of Locomotive Engineers put it succinctly in the form of a question:

Are not railway employees in this year of grace, 1873, enduring a tyranny compared with which British taxation in colonial days was as nothing, and of which the crack of the slave whip is only a fair type?[11]

The facts substantiated this conclusion, and as the depression deepened, they grew even starker. It was not unusual for a railroad worker to be unemployed, and therefore unpaid, for as many as four days of the week, while the company expected him to be prepared to work at all times. When the men were able to work, they were often required to "lay over" at high-priced company hotels at the opposite end of the line until they could find a job that took them home. The alternative was to pay one's own fare back on a company passenger train at the regular rates, because most companies did not issue free passes. (One worker on the Lake Shore line in Collinwood, Ohio, was paid sixteen cents in wages to take a train to Cleveland, but then had to report back to his superior at Collinwood at a cost of twenty-five cents in fare.) Workers who paid seventy-five cents a day for board and food while waiting for return trains—and they often had to wait from two to four days—had nothing to show for their work upon their return. Indeed, they often ended up in debt, and when they finally fell so far into debt that their wages were garnisheed, they were forthwith discharged.

At the end of a month, the average railroad worker, with the exception of engineers, took home a little more than half of what he would have made had he been able to work the full thirty days. The average wage of a brakeman or fireman on four major eastern trunk lines in the spring of 1877 was $1.99 per trip, which would have netted him $59.70 if he had worked thirty trips per month. Yet, because of the lack of work, the average brakeman or fireman took home only $30.00 per month, or $10.50 less than the average unskilled worker. A worker on the Baltimore & Ohio described his condition and that of his fellow workers:

> We eat our hard bread and tainted meat two days old on the sooty cars up the road, and when we come home, find our children gnawing bones and our wives complaining that they cannot even buy hominy and molasses for food.[12]

To add to this, wages were paid at irregular intervals, and workingmen had to wait as long as three months to receive their pay. The Erie Railroad, for example, frequently waited six or eight weeks before paying its employees. The same company, however, did not hesitate to demand that its trackmen, who lived in company shanties along the side of the tracks, should pay ground rent of $20 to $25 a year or vacate their homes. Some companies made their workmen trade in company-owned stores, where prices were higher and the quality poorer than in nearby establishments.[13]

By a dozen different stratagems, the railroads forced their workmen to perform unpaid labor. Engine hostlers were eliminated, and firemen were obliged to spend a couple of hours cleaning the engine each trip, for which they were not paid. Engineers and firemen on the Pennsylvania system were compelled to pay the repair cost on engines, regardless of the cause. "If you don't pay the damages," complaining engineers were told, "we'll discharge you." Many engineers lost as much as three months of work every year because company officials did not supply them with new engines while their cabs were being repaired. In addition, engineers were paid only for the time they operated the engine. "If I fall sick and am even absent for an hour from the engine I am docked the time," complained one engineer, "while the

company can throw me off just as many hours as they choose."
"We get paid so much a day for every day we are on a run," said
another. "They pay us by the run, not by the day. . . . A day is
twelve hours and from our point of view there are fourteen days
in the week."[14] A reporter for the *New York Times* explained:

> The time figured upon the schedule of trains by no means represents
> the time required of them [the engineers] as a day's work. There are
> numberless things required when they are not on the road. The general
> care of the locomotive, the keeping in order of the headlights, the packing
> of the boxes, etc., devolve upon them, and consume a great deal of time.
> Many necessary failures in making regular trips, chargeable in no way to
> the men, are counted against them as if the fault were not the road's fault.
> They also suffer great loss, as they are kept idle while their engines
> undergo repair in the work shops.[15]

Railroading in the 1870s was a far more hazardous occupation
than it is today; most of the safety devices now in use were either
unknown then, or else little used and in imperfect form. It was
still the era of the clumsy handbrake, which threw so many
railroaders to their death, and of the treacherous link-and-pin
coupling, which maimed so many more. Crews were constantly
being reduced, and at a time when trains were controlled entirely
by manual means, this meant added dangers. And the railroad
executives seldom offered their maimed employees more than
sympathy. Nor did the courts, which began to view labor as a
commodity whose value was determined in the marketplace. In
the case of a railroad worker who claimed that his employer was
liable for injuries suffered on the job, the court ruled that since
wages for railroad workers were higher than the average, there
was no liability. The market itself compensated for increased
risk.[16]

When to all this is added the railroad companies' arbitrary
classification of engineers and firemen—men with long experience often received lower wages than those just hired—and their
discriminatory promotion policies, the desperation felt by the
workers is understandable. And to cap the climax came a series
of wage cuts during the great depression of the 1870s—which
was, itself, to a considerable extent the result of railroad over-
expansion following the Civil War, and of the wild speculation
and ruinous rate wars in which the private empires of the
railroad tycoons battled each other.

The failure of the banking house of Jay Cooke & Company on September 18, 1873, ushered in six long and terrible lean years for the American working class. By 1875, there were as many as three million unemployed, and two-fifths of those employed were working no more than six or seven months a year, while less than one-fifth worked regularly. The wages of those still working had been cut as much as 45 percent, often to little more than a dollar a day.[17]

During the grim years from 1873 to 1877, the post–Civil War pace of railroad construction was brought to an abrupt halt. While over 34,000 miles of track were laid between 1865 and 1873, only 6,000 miles were laid between 1873 and 1877—a decline of more than 50 percent in the rate of construction. Moreover, in the four years after 1873, railroads defaulted on over eight hundred million dollars in bonds, and the value of their stocks dropped to half of what it had been in 1872. During the one-month period from September 15 to October 15, 1873, the usually stable stock of the New York Central & Hudson River Company dropped twenty-one points, signifying a loss of nineteen million dollars. Every January, Henry Poor published figures showing the decrease in dividends from one year to the next: from 1874 to 1875, the reduction was $5,638,720; from 1875 to 1876, it was $6,254,540; and from 1876 to 1877, it was $9,483,356. By July 1877, no dividends were being paid on any railroad in Arkansas, Colorado, Florida, Kansas, Mississippi, Missouri, Nebraska, Oregon, Texas, or Vermont.

Still, many major railroad companies continued to pay dividends throughout the depression. The New York Central paid 8 percent in cash dividends in 1873 and 1874, and 10 percent in 1875, while the Pennsylvania and the Baltimore & Ohio paid 10 percent every year from 1873 to 1876. These and other railroad companies did not hesitate to pass the burden of their financial losses on to their employees, instead of to their stockholders. Between 1873 and 1877, railroad workers suffered reductions in their wages ranging on the average between 21 and 37 percent, while food prices dropped only 5 percent. John Garrett, president of the Baltimore & Ohio Railroad, lowered the wages of his men to 50 percent of what they had formerly been; yet not once did he either lower a dividend payment or fail to make one.[18]

Railroad workers were not even given adequate advance notice of impending wage cuts. Officials of the East Tennessee, Virginia & Georgia Railroad told their workers of a 20 percent wage cut a day before it went into effect. The Pennsylvania Railroad did not even bother to notify the Brotherhood of Locomotive Engineers that wages were to be cut, despite the existence of a written agreement between the company and the union stipulating that the wage scale could not be altered by either side without prior notice or joint consultation. When the union sent a special committee to J. M. McCullough, the system's western superintendent, to express the Brotherhood's protest, McCullough fired its members and issued an order forbidding leaves of absence to other engineers who sought to discuss the matter with him. And when enraged engineers threatened to strike, McCullough, well aware of the thousands of unemployed railroad men, replied bluntly: "Strike and be ------."[19]

Other rail officials echoed this callous viewpoint. The superintendent of the Harlem division of the New York Central lines told reporters that "if the engineers should strike, their places could be easily supplied, and the public not feel the change."[20]

Nevertheless, strike the railroad workers did—in a series of outbursts between November 1873 and July 1874. On over eighteen railroads—the East Tennessee, Virginia & Georgia; the Philadelphia & Reading; the Pennsylvania Central; the New Jersey Southern; the New York & Oswego Midland; the various eastern divisions of the Erie railroad system; the Boston & Worcester; the Delaware, Lackawanna & Western; the Louisville Short Line; the Allegheny Valley; and the Chicago & Alton—workers walked off their jobs for a period of a week or two in opposition to the wage cuts, demanding the wages due them, and opposing such employer practices as blacklisting and the ironclad oaths.[21]

While the 1873-74 strikes were neither as dramatic nor as important as the nationwide railroad strike in 1877, in several respects they foreshadowed the violent outburst three years later. For one thing, they revealed that although the railroad workers were mostly without trade union organization or experience, they had the power to disrupt traffic on many roads. Newspapers told of workers removing coupling pins from many freight cars so that they could not be moved; of workers tearing up sections of track, disabling locomotives, and cutting telegraph wires; of notches tampered with and water tanks ruined; of coaches and freight cars uncoupled; of nonstrikers pulled from cabs; of engines and boilers tampered with; and of soap placed in tanks from which the locomotives took water, "rendering the water unfit for making steam."[22]

Then, too, in every community affected by the walkouts, there was widespread sympathy for the railroad strikers. A dispatch to the *New York Times* from Pottsville, Pennsylvania, describing the strike on the coal trains of the Philadelphia & Reading Railroad against a 10 percent reduction in wages, noted that even though the miners were thrown out of work by the stoppage of all transportation, "they seem to sympathize with them [the railroad workers], thus making the movement stronger and more important than it otherwise would be."[23] Community support for the strikers expressed itself in many ways. Nonstriking workers brought provisions to the strikers; local trade unions passed resolutions praising the strikers' "pluck against acts of tyranny" and urging them "to resist the unjust demands of this [railroad] monopoly to the bitter end"; in a few instances, they voted funds for the relief of the men on strike. Among the nonlaboring population as well, there was substantial backing for the strikers, which reflected the widespread resentment against the stranglehold the railroads had on the economic life of the nation. In fact, when militias were sent to put down "violence" by strikers, they met so hostile a reception from local citizens that they let it be known that they wanted to go home. When Governor John Hartranft of Pennsylvania agreed to send troops against the Erie strikers, leading local citizens in Scranton, including a justice of the peace, a town burgess, an assistant postmaster, and a physician, publicly assailed his decision. A petition signed by a majority of the city's prominent residents charged Hartranft with "supporting the interests of a corporation against our own citizens who ask nothing but their hard-earned wages." The petitioners asked him to withdraw the soldiers "in the name of humanity." Moreover, after the state troops arrived, many merchants refused to sell them provisions, and some soldiers suffered "for want of food." A prominent officer in the state militia told Governor Hartranft that the strikers had "the sympathy of nearly if not all the Citizens of the town." He could have added the members of the militia as well, for many of the militiamen were reported to be in sympathy with the strikers.[24]

The 1873-74 strikes foreshadowed the great uprising of 1877 in still another way. Despite popular support, the strikers of 1873-74 were unable to win any of their demands. The sympathy of the people counted for naught when massive unemployment made it possible for the railroad managers to bring in new workers. And where this proved insufficient to break a strike, the state militia did the job for the railroads, over the protests of prominent citizens and even of militiamen who sympathized with the strikers. In cases where the local militia could not be trusted, soldiers and even police from towns miles away were brought in. A detachment of St. Louis police traveled over a hundred miles to Moberly, to put down the strike of engineers and firemen.[25] In the case of the Erie shopmen's strike, economic coercion was added to military and police power. The company let it be known that unless the men returned on its terms, the shops would be moved to Elmira, New York. A number of businessmen thereupon deserted the strikers and lined up behind the company. "They see," explained the *Scranton Republican,* "that unless they keep the shops running their business will be ruined."[26]

The railroad managers were not content to simply defeat the strikers. All of them refused to rehire the strike leaders, and sent their names "through the length and breadth of the country." Representatives of twenty southern companies went further and decided not to rehire workers guilty of "interference with others willing to work." They then drew up a list of proscribed workers and circulated it throughout the region.[27]

In addition to blacklists, the railroads instituted the ironclad oath on a wide scale. In most cases, before workers could return, they had to pledge never to join a union or go out on strike. Newspapers featured the following dispatch from Knoxville, Tennessee:

Late strikers of East Tennessee, Virginia and Georgia Railway, including engineers, machinists and blacksmiths have withdrawn from their Unions. Engineers in a published card acknowledge their error and say they have determined to withdraw from the organization known as Brotherhood of Locomotive Engineers. Machinists and Blacksmiths also signed a published card to same effect, withdrawing from the Society, and Blacksmith's Union. In tomorrow's *Daily Press and Herald* Vice President Jaques publishes the following to the public: "To prevent any misapprehension as to the true position of the engineers on the East Tennessee, Virginia and Georgia Railway I will state that they have withdrawn from the organization known as the Brotherhood of Locomotive Engineers and the charter of the Knoxville Division No. 115, has been delivered to me to be forwarded to Charles Wilson, Grand Chief Engineer, Cleveland, Ohio.

An ironclad oath signed by twenty-two railroad engineers read in part:

We now acknowledge that we have been beaten and that we were in error. . . . We have withdrawn from the organization known as the

"Brotherhood of Engineers," and if you think it proper to employ us again, we will work for you as faithfully as we ever did before, notwithstanding the reduction in wages.[28]

Despite the setbacks they had suffered, the engineers emerged from their 1873-74 strike struggles stronger and even more militant than before. They were enraged by Grand Chief Engineer Wilson's strikebreaking role during the strikes on the East Tennessee, Virginia & Georgia Railroad and on the Pennsylvania line, and they succeeded in removing him from office by the nearly unanimous vote of delegates to a special Brotherhood convention. "Reform" candidate Peter M. Arthur replaced Wilson, and pledged a militant response to any effort of the arrogant management to demand further concessions from the engineers.[29]

This new policy paid off. In October 1876, the Brotherhood won a victory over the Central of New Jersey by forcing the company to rescind a wage cut. Two months later, it defeated the Grand Trunk Railway of Canada when that line violated its agreements and dismissed the Brotherhood's leaders. On December 29, 1876, the engineers stopped every train west of Montreal and completely closed the single track road. While sympathizers held the roundhouses, strikebreakers were turned back. On January 3, 1877, the Grand Trunk yielded, reinstated the dismissed Brotherhood leaders, and even reimbursed Grand Chief Engineer Arthur for travel expenses he had incurred during the strike.[30]

It must be kept in mind that these victories over the Jersey Central and Grand Trunk took place at the very depth of the depression. In 1877, the number of unemployed rose to a peak of perhaps five million—with a population less than one-third of that today. Many of the jobless drifted across America, with no means of support except occasional charity; they lived in shacks and searched the garbage heaps for food. John McIntosh, the socialist poet, summed up conditions in his ballad, "The Tramp":

> We canvassed the city through and through,
> Nothing to work at, nothing to do;
> The wheels of the engines go no more,
> Bolted and barred is the old shop door;
> Grocers look blue over unpaid bills,
> Paupers increase and the poorhouse fills.[31]

A correspondent wrote to the *New Orleans Daily Picayune:*

Mr. Editor, God only knows what will become of our poor workingmen who have families or even single men, who are out of employment by thousands in our city; if something soon don't turn up to give relief. Sir, if you believe me, death is staring us in the face. . . . My family are, at this time, without the food necessary to keep life together. It is hard to be compelled to starve in this plentiful world; I cannot find any employment to provide the requisite food to sustain life. I am willing to perform any occupation that my strength will permit me so as to enable me to get food for my suffering family.[32]

Those lucky enough to work saw their wages drop as multitudes waited to do their jobs for even less. A Cincinnati cigar worker with a wife and three children was asked how he lived on earnings of $5 a week. "I don't live," he replied. "I am literally starving. We get meat once a week, the rest of the week we have dry bread and black coffee."[33]

Unlike the crises of 1837 and 1857, the long depression of the 1870s did not wipe out the labor movement, but organized labor was in a state of considerable disarray. Of thirty national unions in existence at the time of the panic, only nine remained by the spring of 1877, with a total membership of about fifty thousand— a negligible fraction of the total nonagricultural working population. Everywhere, local unions and trades' assemblies faded away, and employers took advantage of the situation by initiating vigorous anti-union drives that further decimated the ranks of the unions.[34]

Under these circumstances, it is understandable that victories such as those scored by the Brotherhood of Locomotive Engineers stood out in bold relief. With a membership listed at 14,000 in 192 branches,[35] with its treasury well-filled and its mutual insurance system the best of any union's, the Brotherhood seemed to be the only bright spot in an otherwise gloomy labor picture.

Its confidence restored, the Brotherhood next took on the Boston & Maine. Early in 1876, that railroad had cut wages 10 percent for all its employees. However, when the road ended the year with a surplus after paying stockholders the usual 6 percent dividend, and on top of this raised the salaries of its president and superintendent in January 1877, the Brotherhood of Locomotive Engineers demanded a raise of 10 cents per day for the road's sixty-seven engineers. The request was contemptuously rejected, and on February 12, after a four-hour ultimatum, the Brotherhood's engineers stopped trains wherever they happened to be.

Once again, the pattern of 1873-74 proceeded to unfold. Public sympathy was expressed for the strikers; commuters even told reporters that they would rather walk than see the men defeated. The company recruited strikebreakers from crowds of unemployed; the Boston police came at the railway's bidding and cleared the Boston & Maine's station of strike sympathizers. In the end, the Brotherhood ran out of money; the striking engineers were all replaced by scabs, and the strikers were blacklisted throughout the industry.[36]

Encouraged by the defeat handed to the Brotherhood by the Boston & Maine, the railroad corporations set out to completely destroy the one union that still operated effectively in the industry. A campaign was launched to picture the Brotherhood as a dangerous enemy to public peace and safety, and, with the railroad lobby in full gear, laws were passed in New Jersey, Massachusetts, Illinois, Delaware, Pennsylvania, Connecticut, and Michigan making it a criminal offense for an engineer to abandon his train "at any place other than the scheduled or otherwise appointed destination. . . ." Charles Francis Adams, then head of the Massachusetts Board of Railroad Commissioners, became so consumed by the desire to destroy the Brotherhood that he sent out a resounding appeal to the country's railroad presidents to cooperate in smashing the union. "The Brotherhood," he wrote, ". . . has got to be broken up. . . . It has become a mere common nuisance . . . a standing public menace. . . . The only question is how to proceed so as to break it up most quietly and most effectually."

At least one railroad president took his advice immediately. Franklin B. Gowen, president of the Philadelphia & Reading, gave his engineers the alternative of remaining with the company and leaving the Brotherhood, or of remaining with the Brotherhood and leaving the company. Those who stayed with the Reading might, if they chose, enjoy the benefits of a proposed company-managed insurance system in place of that operated by the Brotherhood. All the money an employee paid in, however, could be forfeited if he quit his job or went on strike.[37]

Gowen, of course, needed neither the Boston & Maine nor Charles Francis Adams to teach him how to break a union. He made a deliberate, concerted, and successful attempt to destroy the first important union in the coal fields—the Workingmen's Benevolent Association, formed after much difficulty in the Schuylkill and Lehigh regions of Pennsylvania in 1867, and uniting a working force made up of various nationalities: Americans, Germans, Irish, English, Welsh, and Scots. Gowen succeeded in destroying "the old WBA"—as it was nostalgically called—by stockpiling coal and then shutting the mines dependent upon his railroad, with the cooperation of other operators, for more than six months in 1874-75—an event known as the "Long Strike."[38] He then followed up the defeat of the union with a fierce, vindictive prosecution of various militant miners whom he succeeded in branding as organized terrorist groups, known as "Molly Maguires," and whom he connected with coal unionism.

Twenty miners went to the gallows in the wake of the "Long Strike," after being convicted in trials that took place in an atmosphere of religious, social, and economic bigotry, and that lacked even the elements of due process. They were prosecuted by Gowen and General Albright, who wore his full military regalia to emphasize his patriotism. The fate of the doomed miners was preordained by a rabid press and by designating juries that excluded Catholics. In his study, *From the Molly Maguires to the United Mine Workers,* Harold W. Aurand writes:

> The Molly Maguire investigation and trials were one of the most astounding surrenders of sovereignty in American history. A private corporation initiated the investigation through a private detective agency; a private police force arrested the alleged offenders; the coal company attorneys prosecuted them. The state provided only the courtroom and the hangman.[39]

Even though "reform" Grand Chief Engineer Arthur had already demonstrated the conservative pattern that was to characterize his twenty-five-year reign as head of the Brotherhood by preventing thirteen potential strikes by its members in 1876, he decided that it was necessary to mobilize the Brotherhood's full resources to meet Gowen's new challenge to unionism, and supported the Philadelphia & Reading engineers when they voted to strike. When the Reading's superintendent turned down a request for arbitration, the Brotherhood called a strike for midnight on Saturday, April 14, 1877. Half of the Reading's engineers quit work, taking care first to bring their trains to their destination, since a new law had just been passed in Pennsylvania punishing the obstruction or abandonment of trains.[40]

The Brotherhood suffered a serious defeat, as Gowen hired any unemployed worker ready to try his hand at running an engine in order to stave off starvation. Although the pile of burned-out engines and wrecked cars mounted, within a week, trains were running again. Its treasury almost exhausted, the Brotherhood called off the strike.[41]

On June 21, 1877, Gowen's triumph was complete: the first ten of the "Molly Maguires" were hanged in pairs.[42]

On April 9, 1877, the *New York Times* editorialized jubilantly:

> The Brotherhood of Locomotive Engineers is destroyed as a dictatorial body; neither railroad nor engineer will fear it henceforth or regard its ukases. . . . Both steps in the action of the Reading Company—the stand against the union and the plan of substitution as to its benefits—are an example which should be imitated by employers generally.

The Reading's insurance plan was not the only antilabor device initiated by the railroads. Around the middle of May 1877, representatives of the four great eastern trunk lines (companies that had through routes between Chicago and various eastern points) met in Chicago and concluded a pooling agreement—the first of its kind—to end the rate war that had been increasing in intensity since 1874.[43] Although Thomas Scott, president of the Pennsylvania Railroad, later denied it, it became clear that the agreement also included a decision to reduce the wages of the railroad workers by at least another 10 percent.[44]

On May 15, the Missouri Pacific led the way by cutting engineers' pay by 12 percent. Nine days later, the Pennsylvania followed up by announcing a 10 percent reduction to take effect June 1 for all employees earning more than a dollar a day—the second such cut since the onset of the great crisis. At the same time, the Pennsylvania ordered that freight trains be made up of thirty-four cars instead of seventeen—the dreaded "doubleheaders." Other lines—the Lehigh Valley Railroad, the Lackawanna, the Michigan Southern, the Indianapolis & St. Louis, the Vandalia, the New York Central & Hudson River, and the Northern Central—also ordered a 10 percent reduction in wages for July 1. Only three roads—the Baltimore & Ohio, the Northern Pacific, and the Chicago, Burlington & Quincy—did not immediately join the wage-cutting drive. They waited until after July 1.[45]

The notices threw the railroad workers, already earning barely enough to support their families, into utter despair. In an appeal to the managers of the Pennsylvania, the railwaymen pleaded:

We respectfully call your attention to our grievances, in connection with your road, on which many of us have been employed for years. Our wages have been from time to time reduced, so that many of us do not earn an average of 75 cents per day. We have sympathized fully with your directors in all their past efforts to further the interests of your company, and accepted the situation so long as it guaranteed us a bare living, but in the last move was guaranteed to many of us a pauper's grave. . . .[46]

A grievance committee of thirty railwaymen met with President Scott in his Philadelphia office and presented their plea to him. But Scott argued that the railroad was actually being kept in operation "simply that men might be employed," without even "an iota of profit to the owners." The committee thereupon decided to accept the latest wage cut.[47] Except for about one hundred longshoremen employed by the Pennsylvania at its New York docks, who walked out in protest against the June 1 cut (which brought their wages down to thirteen and a half cents an hour), the workers on all the lines accepted the pay cuts without quitting their jobs. And the longshoremen returned to work after three weeks, accepting a compromise offer of fourteen cents an hour. The railroad managers could nod agreement at the statement in the *Commercial and Financial Chronicle* that "this year [1877] . . . labor is under control for the first time since the war."[48]

What neither the managers nor the *Chronicle* yet knew was that some railroad workers were secretly organizing to fight back. Immediately after the Pennsylvania Railroad announced its wage cut, the trainmen on the Pittsburgh, Fort Wayne & Chicago (a subsidiary of the Pennsylvania) began talking of the need for a new organization "to get the trainmen—composing engineers, conductors, brakemen, and firemen, in the three grand trunk lines of the country—into one solid body." Only a short time before they met, the engineers on the railroad had struck and left their locomotives, but had been defeated when the firemen took their places. Such a lack of labor unity, they were determined, had to be remedied immediately if the railroad workers were not to be completely trampled underfoot by a united management.[49]

On Saturday evening, June 2, 1877, the talk became a reality when a group of men on the road met at Dietrich's Hall in Allegheny City, across the river from Pittsburgh, and formed the Trainmen's Union, a secret, oathbound organization. The founders knew that the three grand trunk lines were going

through with the wage cuts; they were convinced that the only
way to defeat them was "to combine into one body all the men."
They decided that after they had succeeded in organizing three-
fourths of the railroaders, and should the "railroad magnates"
not accede to their demands by rescinding the wage cut and the
doubleheader policy, and by resolving long-standing grievances,
they would strike on a predesignated day, "leave the trains
standing just where they were, and go home."[50]

The organizer of the founding meeting and the first man to
take the Trainmen's Union's oath was twenty-five-year-old
Robert Adams Ammon. The son of a prosperous Pittsburgh
insurance executive, he had been expelled at the age of sixteen
from Capital University, in Columbus, Ohio, had served for a
while with the United States cavalry as a bugler, had traveled
about from China to South America, and had finally settled down
as a brakeman on the Pittsburgh, Fort Wayne & Chicago
Railroad. Ammon earned twenty-nine dollars a month as a
brakeman, but since he had an additional income of forty dollars
a month for his work in the insurance business, he was better off
than most railroad workers. Still, as he explained, the fact that he
had this additional income "was the only way I could live."[51]

Chosen as "grand organizer" of the new, all-encompassing
railway union, and with expenses furnished by the organization,
Ammon traveled over the Fort Wayne road, the Baltimore &
Ohio, the Cleveland & Pittsburgh, the Lake Shore, and other
lines, organizing lodges and swearing in members. By mid-June,
the Trainmen's Union included thousands of trunk line railroad
workers of all crafts and activities, from Baltimore to Chicago.
Not only was it the first union in American history to combine all
railroad workers, but it included so many engineers—the
aristocrats of the industry—that Grand Chief Engineer Arthur of
the Brotherhood of Locomotive Engineers let it be known that
there was nothing in the constitution or bylaws of the Brotherhood that prevented its members from also joining the Trainmen's Union.[52]

Alerted to the existence of the union by Ammon's organizing
drive, the various railroad managements began discharging any
of the new members whose identity they could learn from
detectives and informers. On June 24, Ammon himself was
discharged by the Fort Wayne management. That same day, the
Trainmen's Union set June 27 at twelve o'clock as the deadline
for a general railroad strike, unless the roads yielded to its

demands. Delegates were immediately sent over all the different trunk lines to notify the lodges of the ultimatum and to urge them to get ready to strike.[53]

On June 25, a union committee presented formal demands to the Pittsburgh railroad officials, who refused to receive them. There was, however, another response. The five members of the committee were fired in a body, and, as if by a prepared signal, other Trainmen's Union members on various lines were handed their discharge papers. From this point on, events moved swiftly toward an almost inevitable fiasco. At a council of war in Dietrich's Hall on the evening before the strike was to take place, a split developed over the decision to walk out. Some of the men "who were the first to go into the thing" balked, "kicked up a rumpus, and it came near ending in a row," as Ammon later reported. He continued:

. . . Two of them went out on No. 11 west, and took the news out west, that there would be no strike the next day. We were all ready on the 17th, at twelve o'clock noon, to go out on strike, but we got telegrams from everywhere asking if we were going on a strike, or whether we were not going on a strike. So the thing got mixed up, and they stopped the telegraph wires, so we couldn't get a word over. We had some trains stopped at Pittsburgh, but I had them all moved out on the track again, as I thought we had better let the thing go, than make a failure of it, and wait for some better time, with a better organization, or some time when we could get things in better shape.[54]

The "they" who stopped the telegraph wires were, of course, the railroad officials, and several of the men who balked at striking were their agents, planted in the Trainmen's Union.[55] As one student of the Great Strike points out: ". . . The combination on the part of the railroad officials to pool profits and stop the rate wars was regarded as good business, but the combination on the part of the trainmen at Pittsburgh to stop the wage reduction was regarded as a conspiracy against public interest."[56]

The men who had been sent out to notify the various lodges of the strike "beat their way back" to Pittsburgh. The Trainmen's Union remained in existence on paper, but it stopped holding meetings. Still, the grievances that had brought the railroad workers together in a unified movement remained unresolved, and the very existence of the Trainmen's Union, ineffective though it proved to be at first, revealed that the railroad men were prepared to act in one form or another to redress those grievances.

During his organizing tour for the Trainmen's Union, Ammon stopped off at Martinsburg, West Virginia, and initiated railroad men there who worked on the Baltimore & Ohio. While he was there, he heard a number of the new members vow that if President John W. Garrett of the Baltimore & Ohio, who had already cut wages 10 percent in November 1876, resorted to another wage cut rather than reduce dividends below the 10 percent the line was paying annually on its stock, the men would strike. "They talked most loud at Martinsburg, but I thought it was all wind," Ammon recalled later. "I didn't think they would strike at all."[57]

Evidently Garrett shared this view. At his suggestion, the B & O directors, at their regular meeting, decreed another 10 percent reduction in wages to take effect on Monday, July 16, for all employees earning more than a dollar a day.[58] As events soon demonstrated, both the president of the Baltimore & Ohio Railroad and the head of the Trainmen's Union seriously underestimated the determination of the B & O workers to resist the new wage cut.

II

The Strike on the
Baltimore & Ohio Railroad

"The most extensive and deplorable workingmen's strike which
ever took place in this, or indeed in any other country began a
week ago Monday among the freight hands of the Baltimore &
Ohio Railroad at Martinsburg, West Virginia, the location of
extensive repair-shops and terminus of one of the regular
divisions of the road." So began the story of the Great Strike in
the *Nation* of July 26, 1877.

Actually, "the most extensive . . . strike ever to take place in
this or any other country," started at Camden Junction, two
miles from Baltimore, a critical point through which all trains
leaving Baltimore for Washington or the West passed. But it
could have started anywhere along the 2,700-mile length of the B
& O, extending from Baltimore, the home of the company's main
offices, to Cumberland (Maryland), Wheeling, Martinsburg, and
Keyser (West Virginia), and Newark (Ohio), then to St. Louis on
its southwestern tip and Chicago on its northwestern tip. During
the preceding three years, workers at these various points had
suffered reductions of 50 percent of what they had earned before
the panic; as a whole, they had sustained cuts averaging 30
percent more than the general average of reductions in railroad
wages throughout the country. They were the lowest-paid men on
any railroad in the country, except for the workers on the New
York Central line. B & O firemen had watched their wages drop
from $55 per month in 1873 to $30 in 1877; brakemen from $70 to
$30, and conductors from $90 to $50. All of them had been
subjected to the usual abuses in their most aggravated forms—
long hours, increased workloads, high prices at company hotels,
poor working conditions, the petty tyranny of officious supervi-
sors, and lack of employment for several days out of the week.
Moreover, they had been forced to take a similar reduction just
eight months before the latest 10 percent wage cut was
announced. The July 11 announcement resulted in wages of
ninety cents per day, and, as the firemen and brakemen pointed

out, in order to merely survive at these wages, they would either have to "steal or starve."[1] The *Baltimore Sun* conceded that "the story of their struggles to live is very sad," adding: "Many of them declare they might as well starve without work as starve and work."[2]

The *Sun* had helped to light the fuse that was soon to burst into flame by publishing on July 15 the report of President Garrett on the earnings of the B & O. In it, Garrett took occasion to congratulate the board of directors upon the substantial nature of the business done in the previous twelve months. He went on to point out that the road's earnings showed the usual balance over and above expenses; in short, affairs were "entirely satisfactory." Before adjourning for the summer, the directors had voted the usual dividend of 10 percent to the stockholders.

Then, as if to rub salt into the workers' wounds, the following day the *Sun* published the news that the 10 percent reduction in wages had been ordered to take effect immediately, and that President Garrett was confident that everyone, both workers and townspeople all along the line, would "cheerfully recognize" that the reduction was a necessity.[3]

Shortly before noon on Monday, July 16—the day the B & O wage cut was to become effective—the fireman on Engine 32 deserted his train at Camden Junction. Other firemen soon joined him. While company agents quickly hired scabs, the strikers remained in the area to persuade other firemen to leave their trains idle. The railroad immediately called for a large police contingent, and Mayor Ferdinand C. Latrobe, who, together with his family, had long been associated with the B & O, promptly responded and also ordered the arrest of the strike leaders at Camden Junction. Three strikers were arrested for "inciting a riot," a charge that even the police acknowledged was ridiculous by deferring their trial. Meanwhile, additional police were stationed along the route from Camden Station to Relay, the city limits.

When the police tried to operate outside the city limits, however, their authority was questioned by a Howard County judge. But the B & O was not to be put off by the courts in its efforts to crush the strike in its infancy. On the basis of authority conferred by laws of Maryland in 1860, the B & O president commissioned the police as special railway constables, and they returned to their posts outside the city limits.[4]

The railroad's first vice-president, John King, Jr., met with

Governor John Lee Carroll, but the latter felt that no troops were needed at this point. The next day, July 17, 38 engineers joined with the striking firemen, and that evening 140 members of the Baltimore Boxmakers' and Sawyers' Union and 800 tin can makers, unable to secure their wage demands, also threw in their lot with the railroad workers. However, no attempts were made to halt the trains. Passenger trains went out unmolested, and fifteen freight trains moved out onto the line in three convoys.[5]

Martinsburg, West Virginia, which was six hours from Baltimore on the B & O, was an important relay station, where engines and crewmen changed off. Late Monday evening, July 16, Martinsburg became the second and more serious center of strike activity. The Trainmen's Union included practically all the railroad workers in Martinsburg, while the local citizens and the town paper were fully behind the railroad workers in any stand they might take against the latest wage cut.[6] The *Martinsburg Statesman* accused Garrett of "putting wages down to the starvation point," and urged the men "to resist."[7]

And resist they did! On July 16, more than a score of firemen assembled around the depot, seized and uncoupled engines, ran them into the roundhouse, and announced to road officials that no more trains would leave Martinsburg in either direction until the wage cut was rescinded. A. P. Schutt, the town mayor, who had close ties with the B & O (he owned the Berkeley House, Martinsburg's main hotel, which derived the major part of its business from the railroad), ordered the arrest of the strike leaders, but the pro-strike sympathies of the townspeople nullified his efforts. Schutt then tried to start the trains with new men, but again he was thwarted.[8]

By morning, the brakemen on the freight trains had joined the firemen, and although passenger trains were not interfered with, all freight was halted. The *Wheeling Intelligencer* announced on its front page: "At Martinsburg the strikers have absolute control and refuse to allow any freight trains to move." It added that "the strike is a serious affair. . . . These reductions in wages come with a special severity at a time like the present when the necessities of life have actually gone up in cost."[9]

Reports from Martinsburg gave no evidence of casualties or property damage, to say nothing of a "riot." Nevertheless, B & O Vice-President King telegraphed Governor Henry M. Mathews of West Virginia that a "riot" was in progress in Martinsburg which local authorities were "powerless to suppress." He requested that the governor call out the militia to protect B & O property and enable the company to get its trains running on schedule.

Without making any further inquiry, Mathews ordered into action the Beverly Light Guards, a company of volunteer militiamen from the Martinsburg area, the majority of whom were railroad workers. He instructed Colonel C. J. Faulkner, the officer in charge, to "prevent any interference by rioters with the men at work, and prevent the obstruction of trains."[10]

A scab engineer, with militia protection, started to run a freight train through the yards. When twenty-eight-year-old William P. Vandergriff, one of the strikers, attempted to cut the train off and, in the process, exchanged fire with a militiaman, he was shot by several of the soldiers at point-blank range. Three balls entered his body, one breaking his left arm. Later that day, Vandergriff's arm was amputated, and after nine days of agony he died, leaving behind a pregnant wife "without pecuniary means." The *Martinsburg Statesman* called Vandergriff "a victim to Gov. Mathews' Order," and commented bitterly: "We believe he died a martyr to what he believed to be a compulsory duty. He was shot down in sight of the lowly home whose inmates he was trying to shield from starvation."[11]

Meanwhile, at the first wounding of a striker, the would-be strikebreaker deserted the engine, and no one could be found to take his place. "It is impossible for me to do anything further with my company," Colonel Faulkner wired Mathews. "Most of them are railroad men and they will not respond. The force is too formidable for me to cope with."[12] He thereupon dismissed his men until further notice.

President Gurrett and other B & O officials pressured Governor Mathews to call upon the president of the United States for federal troops. "The loss of an hour," Garrett wired, "would most seriously affect us and imperil vast interests." But Mathews balked at seeking federal assistance until he had exhausted "all means within the State to suppress the riot." The governor then sent a company of sixty-five militiamen from Moorefield—"none of them railroad men"—to Martinsburg. "I send arms and ammunition with them," he announced, "and the force will be increased as they go on. If that force is not sufficient, I will then use other means—the riot shall be stopped."[13]

The fact that there was still no evidence of a "riot" did not seem to matter to Governor Mathews. Certainly there had been no violence, no damage to or even tampering with company property, and no injuries since the first and only shooting in Martinsburg. It is significant that while the governor was unwilling to go along with the B & O officials in requesting federal troops, Vice-President King telegraphed the Washington agent of the B & O that the governor might soon change his mind, and suggested that the secretary of war be informed of the situation so that he might be ready to respond promptly with the necessary forces.[14]

While the company and the governor had been trying unsuccessfully to crush the strike at Martinsburg, it had spread to other points along the line in West Virginia: Keyser, Piedmont, Grafton, and Wheeling. At Keyser, white and Black railroad workers met and voted to join the strike. They had "soberly considered the step," and finally decided that "at the present state of wages which the company had imposed upon us, we cannot live and provide our wives and children with the necessities of life."[15]

A reporter for the *Wheeling Intelligencer* described the strikers at various railroad points in the state as "a respectable body of men . . . [who] in their towns receive every encouragement."[16] A resident of Keyser agreed and assured the Wheeling paper that nearly everyone in the communities affected believed that "the whole thing grows out of too much pay and speculation among the head men—big salaries, wine suppers, free passes and presents to Congressmen for their votes," while the men whose labor made all this possible lived on the very edge of starvation.[17] The *Baltimore Sun* reprinted the letter and cited it as evidence of the fact that the railroaders had the support of their fellow-townspeople:

There is no disguising the fact that the strikers in all their lawful acts have the fullest sympathy of the community. The 10 per cent reduction after two previous reductions was ill-advised. The company for years has boasted of its great earnings and paid enormous dividends. One must therefore ask if wages that do not now permit over $5 per week to go to the housing, clothing, and feeding of a family are more than sufficient as a remuneration for experienced labor, full of danger and responsibility?

The *Sun* concluded with an observation that was to appear frequently in other communities as the Great Strike developed:

The singular part of the disturbance is the very active part taken by the women, who are the wives or mothers of the firemen. They looked famished and wild, and declare for starvation rather than have their people work for the reduced wages. Better to starve outright, they say, than to die by slow starvation.[18]

At Martinsburg, meanwhile, the situation was at a standstill. The B & O officials offered no compromise to the strikers. The state militia remained on alert, but did nothing to "further exasperate the strikers." The latter were resorting to "moral suasion" to win over the members of the militia and the railroad shopmen in the machine and engine shops, who were still on the job. In the latter case they were successful, but not with the militia. A half dozen or more of the strike leaders called on Captain Miller in his quarters and asked what he planned to do. "They referred to the almost starving condition of men whose wages were now proposed to be further cut down; that flour was ten dollars a barrel, etc." Miller replied brusquely that he "had nothing to do with the price of flour," that he had come to Martinsburg to see that the trains passed unmolested, and that he was determined to carry out orders "if his entire company was used up in the attempt.[19]

Despite Miller's bluster, it was clear that the Martinsburg railroad men, aided by their fellow-townspeople, had effected a thoroughly successful strike. They had completely stopped the movement of freight trains through the town even when the trains were offered military protection. But the situation was still nothing resembling a riot, and a far, far cry from an insurrection. No property had been damaged, nor had any blood been shed since the first day of the strike.

However, this state of affairs hardly suited Colonel Robert M. Delaplain, the governor's aide and deputy in command of the militia. He dashed off a telegram to Governor Mathews in which he noted the intensity of the pro-strike sentiment in Martinsburg, declaring that no one could be found willing to run a locomotive, even with militia protection, and that "the odds" were "largely against our small force." The wire contained no information of new violence or disorder. Nevertheless, it ended: "Captain Faulkner thinks that two hundred U.S. Marines could not be in excess of the requirement. . . ."[20]

This time, Mathews did not hesitate to respond favorably to the suggestion that he call in federal troops. He did so without having first put Martinsburg in a state of emergency or under martial law, without calling up additional volunteers to supplement the existing militia, and without calling the legislature into special session to deal with the emergency—in short, without making any further use of powers at his command. Indeed, Mathews later conceded in a report to the legislature that before federal troops were requested, "one militiaman had been wounded, one striker killed, and a total of $8,823.41 expended on the attempt to break the strike."[21]

On July 18, Mathews telegraphed President Hayes:

Owing to unlawful combinations and domestic violence now existing at Martinsburg, and at other points along the line of the Baltimore and Ohio Railroad, it is impossible with any force at my command to execute the laws of the State.

I therefore call upon your Excellency for the assistance of the United States military to protect the law abiding people of the State against domestic violence and to maintain the supremacy of the law.

The Legislature is not now in session and could not be assembled in time to take any action in the emergency. A force of from two to three hundred should be sent without delay to Martinsburg where my aide Col. Delaplain will meet and confer with the officer in command.[22]

A reporter for the *New York World* wrote his paper from Martinsburg:

It has been well observed that if the rights of the strikers had been infringed or violated instead of that of the Railroad corporations, it is probable that Governor Mathews would have hesitated a long while before he would have thought it his duty to call on the president.[23]

Needless to say, the president of the B & O took a different view. Upon learning that federal troops had been requested, he wired congratulations to Mathews. He then sent President Hayes a long wire urging "that the application . . . be immediately granted." Garrett cited the impossibility of moving freights and the open intimidation of and attacks upon "loyal employees." The state had done all it could "to suppress the insurrection," he wrote, and traffic on the B & O—"this great national highway"— could be "restored for public use" only by bringing in federal troops. Unless this action was taken immediately, "the greatest consequences" were inevitable for both the B & O and "all the other lines in the country which like ourselves have been obliged to introduce measures of economy in these trying times for the preservation of the effectiveness of railroad property."

The B & O president even suggested how the federal forces could be used most effectively to break the strike. He recommended that soldiers be transported from Fort McHenry in Baltimore and from Washington, since these were "points near to the scenes of the disturbance . . . from which movements can be made with the greatest promptness and rapidity."[24]

The Great Strike of 1877 was the first instance in which the regular army entered into a labor disturbance on a national scale. Prior to that time, the army had had some experience with labor troubles. In 1834, Andrew Jackson ordered regulars into Maryland to end a strike of Irish workers on the Chesapeake & Ohio Canal, and during the Civil War, department commanders used troops to end strikes, including the one by engineers on the Reading Railroad and those by workers in St. Louis, Louisville, Cold Springs (N.Y.), and in the turbulent Pennsylvania coal fields.[25] However, the decision as to whether or not federal troops should be dispatched rested entirely with the president. Statute law empowered him to respond to state requests for assistance in suppressing "domestic violence," but did not compel him to grant such requests. In each instance, the president was obliged to weigh the merits of the application. In his inaugural address, President Hayes had spoken out strongly "against interfering in the domestic affairs of states," and while he was referring to Reconstruction in the Southern states, it was not difficult for many in the labor movement to expect that he would apply this principle to a situation such as that in West Virginia.[26]

However, as we have seen, Hayes owed his accession to the presidency, in large part, to Tom Scott and his associates, and he had surrounded himself with cabinet members who were closely linked to corporations in general and to the railroads in particular. Secretary of State William M. Evarts was a leading New York corporation and railroad lawyer who "usually ranged on the side of capital rather than labor," who had defended the railroads in key cases involving rate regulation, and who, as lawyer for the manufacturers in the famous Jacobs case, helped to invalidate a New York law outlawing the manufacture of cigars in tenement houses. Other cabinet members who had close railroad associations were Attorney General Charles Devens, Secretary of the Navy Richard W. Thompson, and Secretary of War George W. McCrary. Gerald G. Eggert observes that McCrary "appears to have owed his cabinet appointment to the influence of such railroad leaders as General Grenville M. Dodge, Tom Scott, and Jay Gould."[27]

On July 17, the press carried the news that Attorney General Devens and Secretary of State Evarts had left Washington on a visit to the mining regions of eastern Pennsylvania. Omitted from the dispatch, however, was the fact that the cabinet members were the guests of the railroads and were to make the tour in the private car of Pennsylvania Railroad President Tom Scott.[28]

Hayes himself had previously responded favorably to a request for troops to break a strike. In 1876, as governor of Ohio, he had sent state militia to Massillon to break a coal miners' strike. Responding to a letter of congratulations from Congressman John A. Garfield, Hayes wrote: "We shall crush out the lawbreakers if the courts and juries do not fail." He did succeed in crushing the strike, thereby earning the gratitude of both the Ohio coal operator and of political boss Marcus A. Hanna, who, on the occasion of Hayes's nomination to the presidency, wrote that the man who "took the position as did our Gov.[ernor] during our recent mining troubles at Massillon and by such action maintained the supremacy of the law giving us again control of our property," deserved to be the next president of the United States. Republicans hailed Hayes as the "law and order" candidate.[29]

As Hayes received Governor Mathews's request for federal troops, he must have pondered the fact that the army had been reduced to a peacetime total of 25,000 men, and that all but a skeleton force were stationed beyond the Mississippi River, guarding the Mexican border or fighting the Indians. But Mathews had requested only two to three hundred men. More serious, however, was the fact that army enlisted men, whose wages were already in arrears, were receiving no pay because Congress had adjourned without voting an army appropriations bill for the fiscal year that began July 1. Could such soldiers be relied on to act against workers whose chief complaint was that their wages had been cut to the starvation level?[30]

After consultation with the chief executive, Secretary of War McCrary telegraphed Mathews that the president was "averse to intervention unless it is clearly shown that the state is unable to suppress insurrection," and asked for details as to the size of the militia and the number of "insurgents." Neither Hayes nor his secretary of war seemed to doubt that it was an "insurrection," even though no source other than Mathews and Garrett had referred to the strike in those terms.

Mathews replied that he had "no doubt" that within ten days he could organize a force of West Virginians of sufficient size "to suppress any riot," but he feared in the meantime the destruction of "much property," and the loss of "valuable lives."

Hayes's reaction now was swift. Without seeking further information, he issued a proclamation at four o'clock in the afternoon of July 18, ordering all "lawless elements" in West Virginia to desist and disperse before noon on Thursday, July 19. He also instructed General William H. French to proceed to Martinsburg with the Second United States Artillery to enforce his proclamation. Following along the lines of Garrett's suggestion, the adjutant general wired the commanding officers of the Washington Arsenal and Fort McHenry in Baltimore to send every available man to Martinsburg as soon as possible. A special train to transport the troops was provided by the Baltimore & Ohio, which later presented a bill to the federal government.[31]

"Coming into Martinsburg with the United States troops, the SUN representative was surprised at the quietness of the town," wrote the correspondent for the New York paper. The train had been stopped at Harper's Ferry to wait for daylight, out of fear that the tracks had been tampered with by the strikers. But in the morning, nothing was found to be wrong, and the train continued to the outskirts of Martinsburg. Scouts were sent ahead and reported that "everything was as quiet as a Sunday." Fifteen hundred freight cars and one hundred engines were lined up on the tracks and were being watched by hundreds of strikers. A hundred or more striking canal boatmen were also in the crowd, encouraging the railroad men in the hope that they might win better terms from the canal companies if the strikers won. There was no sign of drunkenness anywhere.

Late that morning, the sheriff's deputies and the town police passed out copies of President Hayes's proclamation commanding "all persons engaged in said unlawful insurrectionary proceedings to disperse and retire to their respective abodes on or before twelve o'clock noon on the 19th day of July instant. . . ." But when twelve o'clock came, there was no "riotous crowd" to be dispersed, and the proclamation aroused little interest.[32]

That afternoon, a coal train was readied to leave for Baltimore under the protection of the state militia and federal troops. The engineer and fireman were on hand to take out the first train to leave Martinsburg since the strike started, when an incident occurred that was widely reported. Here is how one reporter described it:

> The wife and daughter of Engineer Bedford climbed to the foot board, and pleaded, tears in their eyes, that he would not go. . . . The women were heroines immediately, and were applauded by other wives and children who had gathered around the engine. Bedford turned to the officials, saying that he could not go.[33]

Later that afternoon, a replacement for Bedford was found, and a train consisting of twenty coal cars was started, with six soldiers on the engine and a dozen in the last car. A guard of three armed men walked at double-quick in front of the engine. At the East Street crossing, half a dozen men and two women were standing by the side of the track with clubs in their hands. The soldiers loaded their guns and the men and women got out of the way. It took the train ten hours to make the trip to Baltimore!

A westward bound freight train left soon after with twenty regulars ahead of the engine and still more troops stationed throughout the train. When the train reached the west end of the town, one hundred armed strikers tried to stop it. The fireman thereupon seized his meal bucket and quit. Several B & O officials pleaded with him to return, offering him premium pay. While they were arguing, his wife, mother, and two brothers pushed by the armed guards and took him away with them. The crowd set up a cheer. At this point, the sheriff, assisted by the entire militia, rushed to the scene, seized Dick Zepp, the twenty-year-old engineer who was said to be the leader of the Martinsburg strike, and arrested him. As he was being taken away, his brother George, a B & O fireman who was not in sympathy with the strike, came running down the track with a big navy revolver in his hand. His mother was following him and pleading with him not to go on the engine. But George Zepp shouted, "I'm going if it costs my life," joined the engineer in the cab, and the train moved out.[34]

This was the last train to leave that day. "The firemen are not discouraged," wrote the *New York Sun* reporter as the day ended. But warrants had been issued for the arrest of ten strikers, charging them with "exciting a riot," and more discouraging was the news that evening that "a large number of engineers and firemen from the Baltimore division" would be in Martinsburg by morning, ready to take out the strikebound freight trains.[35] On the morning of July 20, the strikebreakers from Baltimore arrived and moved out the freight trains without interference. By evening, the clogged yard had been largely cleared. "The riot here may be regarded as suppressed," Delaplain wired Mathews gleefully. B & O officials summoned reporters to the company's headquarters and gave them the news that "the backbone of the strike has been broken."[36]

But elsewhere along the B & O line, the strike was anything but broken. "I might as well die by the bullet as to starve to death by inches," strikers told reporters at different points on the B & O line. At Keyser, they met and unanimously determined to stand firm until the end, and concluded:

Resolved, that we, the men of the Third Division, have soberly and calmly considered the step we have taken, and declare that at the present state of wages which the company have imposed upon us, we cannot live and provide our wives and children with the necessaries of life, and that we only ask for wages that will enable us to provide such necessaries.[37]

On Friday, July 20, the same day that the strike at Martinsburg was reported broken, a manifesto was posted at Westernport, Maryland, and copies put up at stations along the B & O line. The eloquent and fiery document, described as "the first manifesto issued by the railway strikers," read:

WE SHALL CONQUER OR WE SHALL DIE

Strike and live! Bread we must have! Remain and perish! Be it understood, if the Baltimore & Ohio Railroad Company does not meet the demands of the employees at an early date, the officials will hazard their lives and endanger their property, for we shall run their trains and locomotives into the river; we shall blow up their bridges; we shall tear up their railroads; we shall consume their shops with fire and ravage their hotels with desperation. A company that has from time to time so unmercifully cut our wages and finally has reduced us to starvation, for such we have, has lost all sympathy. We have humbled ourselves from time to time to unjust demands until our children cry for bread. A company that knows all this, we should ask in the name of high heaven what more do they want—our blood? They can get our lives. We are willing to sacrifice them, not for the company, but for our rights. Call out your armed hosts if you want them. Shield yourselves if you can, and remember that no foe, however dreaded, can repel us for a moment. Our determination may seem frail, but let it come. They may think our cause is weak. Fifteen thousand noble miners, who have been insulted and put upon by this self same company, are at our backs. The merchants and community at large along the whole line of the road are on our side, and the working classes of every State in the Union are in our favor, and we feel confident that the God of the poor and the oppressed of the earth is with us. Therefore let the clashing of arms be heard; let the fiery elements be poured out if they think it right, but in heed of our right and in defence of our families, we shall conquer or we shall die.[38]

On the same day that the manifesto was posted, at Cumberland, Maryland, disgruntled miners, Chesapeake & Ohio canal men, railroad strikers, and unemployed workers uncoupled cars from a westbound freight train. Railroad officials managed to get the cars coupled again, and the train moved on. At Keyser, West Virginia, it was run onto a side track, and the crew was taken off by force. At three o'clock that afternoon, B & O officials met with Governor John Carroll of Maryland. President Garrett demanded that the Maryland National Guard be called out, and by 3:30 p.m. the governor had ordered Brigadier General James R. Herbert to prepare Baltimore's Fiftieth and Sixth militia regiments to go to Cumberland. As Edward Hungerford, historian of the Baltimore & Ohio Railroad, explains: ". . . The word of the President of the B & O was law to Governors, [and] all state officials."[39]

On July 18, the *Baltimore Sun* had proudly commented that, in contrast to the "serious disturbance . . . in West Virginia," the strikers in Baltimore "maintained perfect order." Two days later, it was still congratulating the city on the fact that "the striking firemen remained quiet." Other Baltimore papers extended similar congratulations and expressed the hope that conditions in Baltimore would continue at the same level.[40]

But, like the Baltimore press, Governor Carroll had underestimated the sympathies of the Baltimore working class community for the strikers. "The working people everywhere are with us," a leader of the railroad strikers told a reporter for the *Philadelphia Inquirer,* and he went on:

They know what it is to bring up a family on ninety cents a day, to live on beans and corn meal week in and week out, to run in debt at the stores until you cannot get trusted any longer, to see the wife breaking down under privation and distress, and the children growing sharp and fierce like wolves day after day because they don't get enough to eat.[41]

The depression had brought misery to Baltimore's workers, just as it had to those in other cities. It had reduced the number of local trade unions from fifteen to four, and produced a larger number of unemployed. Mayor Latrobe had shown no interest in dealing with the unemployment problem and had initiated public works programs only after the Democratic Club reminded him of the "degradation of the working man and his family." There were other signs of general discontent at the time the railroad workers went on strike. Seven hundred canmakers struck for more pay, and there was a flurry of small strikes started by the factory workers immediately thereafter.

The Baltimore & Ohio Railroad, moreover, was a very unpopular institution. Garrett, who had been its president since 1858, was generally disliked. People resented his power, hated the way in which he treated his workers, disliked his subordinate officials even more than him, and, in the words of the *Baltimore News,* were "simply tired of hearing nothing but 'The B. and O. said this, and the B. and O. said that.'" Among the city's workers, it was commonly felt that the B & O could well afford to reduce dividends instead of wages, and treat its workers at least civilly. This feeling was intensified on Friday morning, July 20—the very day the militiamen were to be called into service on the company's request—when the newspapers carried the notice inserted by Vice-President King that the company was abandoning its policy of "half a loaf of bread is better than none at all," that all strikers should consider themselves dismissed, and that in the eyes of the company, therefore, they were "trespassers."[42]

What happened that Friday night, therefore, was the product of years of accumulated resentment in Baltimore's working class circles.

There were two methods available for calling out the militia: to summon the soldiers by messengers or by sounding the militia call from the firehouse and the City Hall. Governor Carroll was opposed to ringing the City Hall bell—"Big Sam"—and the smaller fire bells; he feared the emergency call would arouse the populace. But General Herbert argued that time was of the essence, and in the end he prevailed. At about 6 p.m. on Friday, June 20, for the first time in Baltimore's history, "Big Sam" on the City Hall and the fire bells all rang the militia call: 1—5—1. At the same time, trains were prepared in Camden Station to rush the militia to Cumberland.

But the regiments never got to Cumberland. The bells pealed

out just as most of Baltimore's men and boys were leaving work. (As in other cities, it was common in Baltimore for a child of nine or ten to put in a fourteen-hour day in a shop or mill.) Crowds of the angry and curious swarmed to the armories. At Camden Station, before the emergency military call, only a handful of people were congregated; after the call, thousands had assembled in less than half an hour.

Fayette and Front Streets, in front of the Sixth Regiment Armory, had been torn up for the laying of gaspipes while buildings in the area were in the process of being erected. Rocks and cobblestones—or, as the *Baltimore Sun* put it, "the material of warfare"—were in piles a few feet apart. As soon as darkness fell, a crowd of youths, men, and some women began throwing stones at the sentries in the street and at the guard in the vestibule, who retreated to the drill room in the rear of the armory. When the anger of the crowd seemed to subside, the order was given to the 120 men who had answered the roll call to march to the trains in two groups. A band and fife corps was supposed to have led the march, but it was decided to dispense with this display. Twenty rounds of ammunition were distributed to each of the men, who carried breech-loading rifles.

As the militiamen set out, they were greeted by a shower of stones and "cries and cheers for the strikers." Driven back into the armory, the soldiers again attempted to march, this time supported by a squad of police, but again they were driven back into the armory. The third time, the militiamen came out of the door firing into the crowd. An on-the-spot reporter wrote: "The streets were quickly deserted and the detachment passed by The Sun office, still firing random shots over their shoulders with apparent recklessness." Bullets shivered the glass in windows along the streets of Baltimore as the militia passed by. Dead and wounded were carried into nearby saloons and drug stores, whose floors quickly "looked like a butcher's pen."

Of the 120 soldiers who had left the armory, only 59 remained when all three companies reached the Camden depot. (The others went home.) By that time, the "second Battle of Bunker Hill," as it was called, was over. Eleven lay dead and about forty were wounded. (The number of wounded remained undetermined because many were quickly carried off by relatives or friends.) All were civilians. A number of the dead were bystanders shot while trying to shield themselves from the fire of the military. One was fourteen-year-old Willie Hourand, whom the *Baltimore News* described as "one of the brightest" of its newsboys. He was the sole support of an invalid mother.

At Camden Station, trains were waiting, engines fully steamed, scabs at their posts, ready to go. While the soldiers were loading, an enraged crowd of about fifteen thousand circled to the rear of the station and attacked the telegraph office on Lee Street. The occupants fled, and the crowd wrecked the building. They then crossed the tracks to the train shed and stoned the engine, which was just about ready to pull out with the soldiers. The crew quickly deserted their posts, and the strikers tore up some of the tracks, making it impossible for the militiamen to leave. Actually, President Garrett and Governor Carroll had decided that the militia was more urgently needed in Baltimore than in Cumberland. The orders were revoked, and the militiamen—that is, those who had not departed—remained in the train sheds at Camden Station.

Outside, the crowd had applied torches to several wooden passenger coaches, and the flames were reaching to the sky. Firemen who responded to calls were stoned, and some hoses were cut. But with difficulty, and with the aid of the police, they succeeded in extinguishing the flames.[43]

Inside Camden Station, B & O officials goaded Governor Carroll into calling on President Hayes for help. "The rioters," he wired frantically, "have taken possession of the Baltimore & Ohio Railroad depot, set fire to same, and driven off all firemen who attempted to extinguish the flames." Hayes responded immediately. Shortly after 11:30, he ordered General William Barry, commander of Fort McHenry in Baltimore, to gather all the men he could find and proceed to the Camden depot at once. Then for good measure, he ordered down three companies of regulars from New York Harbor and told General Winfield S. Hancock, commander of the Military Division of the Atlantic, to supervise operations.

Meanwhile, both the crowd and the flames had cooled down. The rioters started drifting home after the fire was finally put out. At around midnight, Carroll wired Hayes that the troops would not be necessary; but the president sent them anyway.[44]

On Saturday, July 21, quiet reigned in Baltimore. "The striking firemen, engineers and other train hands were, as usual, standing quietly in small groups along the lower portions of Light Street." Their committees were waiting, they told a reporter for the *Sun*,

. . . to hear any proposal from the company, and are ready and anxious to work for fair wages. . . . They say that they had nothing whatever to do with the riotous proceedings Friday night, and have never used violence to person or property of any kind, but have only endeavored to prevent the running of trains by the company. They deprecate all riotous proceedings, and it is not believed they were instrumental in, counseled or provoked the unexpected outbreak which characterized Friday night.[45]

By early Sunday morning, July 22, only a few knots of curious people were outside the Camden depot, and Governor Carroll announced that the riot was over. But Baltimore was now a "military garrison" with between 1,200 and 2,000 federal soldiers in or near the city, while local forces had been swelled by citizen recruits. Seven hundred soldiers guarded the B & O property at Camden Station with two Gatling guns and several field pieces, while other troops were being kept busy opening the line. The Baltimore police were engaged in rounding up men suspected of having been involved in the events of July 20—none of whom were strikers.[46]

Most newspapers in Baltimore and nearby cities confirmed the *Sun*'s report that the strikers had not been involved in the June 20 riots, but this gained the strikers nothing but some editorial praise.[47] The B & O officials blamed them for being indirectly responsible, and showed not the slightest willingness to compromise. Vice-President King reiterated his statement that the strikers could consider themselves dismissed and that the company regarded them as "trespassers."[48]

The difficulties of the Baltimore & Ohio Railroad, however, were not yet over. Freight traffic along the main line was still paralyzed, and the company was still losing "thousands of dollars . . . every hour."[49] The strikers stuck doggedly to their task of trying to get back their 10 percent and obtain several improvements as well. On July 26, committees representing the engineers, firemen, brakemen, and conductors met and drew up a set of resolutions which were unanimously adopted by the strikers. They called for the establishment of two classes of enginemen, at a daily wage of $3.50 for first class and $3.00 for second class; for a minimum wage of $2.50 per day for firemen and brakemen; that when engines arrived at their destination, men be available to take sand and to clean, fire, and house them; that a quarter-day's pay be given each railroad worker called to duty and not furnished work, or laid over; that there be an allowance of an additional half-day's pay for Sunday operation; that half a day be allowed every worker for fetching and returning engines; that the time for the run from Martinsburg to Cumberland and return be two days; and finally

That no man shall be discharged for any act done or participation had in the late strikes, and that all men who have drawn their time shall be immediately reinstated in their positions.

The resolutions were presented to the B & O as "suggestions for an amicable adjustment," and a four-man committee representing the engineers, freight firemen, freight conductors, and brakemen also presented them to Governor Carroll with a request for his endorsement. In introducing the resolutions to the governor, engineer J. H. Elder, committee chairman, stressed that the strike had only one objective: "to obtain wages which would enable them to live," and that in seeking this goal, the strikers had not engaged in violence "and would not counsel such a thing." After listening to a reading of the resolutions, the governor stated that he had no power to remedy their "troubles," and advised them to devote themselves to persuading "a number of sympathizers who are lawless men . . . to desist from all violence." They could be sure, he added, that whether or not they succeeded in this endeavor, he intended to see that the laws were enforced and violence stamped out "at any cost." Once again, the committee disclaimed any connection with rioters or the destruction of property, and emphasized that the strikers "had simply demanded living rates for work, and had abstained from labor until those rates were allowed." But Governor Carroll was not satisfied. It was not enough, he said, for the strikers to abstain "from riotous proceedings":

You are responsible for the violence that has been done, whether you were actually engaged in it or not. You on your part must drive away from you the evil-disposed people who have done so much harm, and discountenance in the plainest way everything tending to violence.

The governor then made it clear that he was not merely talking of the destruction of railroad property, but the very strike itself, for "interference with men who work is equally a violation of law with rioting."[50]

Thus, all the committee obtained from the governor was a

lecture on violence. He had not a word to say about the murder of eleven Baltimore citizens by the militiamen.

The following day, the strikers heard an even longer lecture by William Keyser, second vice-president of the B & O. Keyser addressed the strikers at their meeting in Cross Street Institute, where they gathered to hear the company's reply to their proposal for an "amicable settlement." The reply, in the form of a letter to the strikers' committee signed by John King, Jr., and William Keyser (the first and second vice-presidents), was couched in temperate language. The B & O stood fast by the 10 percent reduction in wages, describing it as having been "forced upon the company by the exigencies of the times, the great depression in business, and the severe competition of rival lines, and it cannot be changed." But the company agreed to arrange matters so that all of its employees would be able "to obtain a full average month's work, so that . . . you can earn more wages than you now receive." Again, the company was willing to remedy the situation which subjected its trainmen to great inconvenience and expense because they were kept from their homes when trains were delayed on the road, by providing them with passes "which will enable the men to come to their homes and return to their trains, under proper restrictions." This far the company was prepared to go, and no further; it expressed the hope that the strikers' committee and the strikers themselves "will see the wisdom and justice of accepting promptly the company's terms, and thus the strike will end and work will be resumed."

Keyser's tone in speaking to the strikers after the reading of the company's letter was one of arrogance and contempt, in contrast with that of the written document. While the letter had indicated a desire that the men return to work, and said nothing about reprisals, Keyser denounced the strikers, saying they had been "the cause of this great disturbance, and will be rigidly held accountable for it." The strikers, he declared, had stopped work, prevented others from working, and injured the company by whom they were employed and the community and country in which they lived—all because of the order calling for a 10 percent cut in pay. However, Keyser went on, the president of the road had also had his pay cut 10 percent—since the order applied to all whose pay exceeded one dollar a day—but he had not seen fit to act lawlessly and encourage others to do so. He had accepted the pay cut:

You, however, a minority of less than ten per cent of the employees, have seen fit to assume the attitude that you will neither accept the reduction or allow others to fill your places.

The position is wholly untenable, and one which for a moment could not be conceded. If it were, all discipline, all law, and all order would be sapped at their foundations, and the principle would be established that a small minority of men, discontented with their real or imaginary grievances, could assume the position that the great mass of their colleagues should be forced into compulsory idleness on their account.

It is not necessary to comment on the ridiculous comparison between President Garrett's pay and that of the strikers, but Keyser failed to clarify just how the demand to rescind the 10 percent pay would destroy "all discipline, all law, and all order," when the company was able to grant two of the other strikers' demands—a full month's work and the right to use passes— without such dire effects. Instead, Keyser devoted the remainder of his lecture to a tirade in which he held the B & O strikers responsible for having convulsed the country and forced the state militias and federal troops into action, thereby compelling men to leave their "homes and their families, and from peaceful pursuits to shoulder their arms in order to protect the property of this company and the city from the lawlessness your acts have engendered; worse than all this, you have aroused a spirit which, unless curbed and quelled, strikes at the very fundamental root of the liberty and life of this country." He continued with the timeworn argument used by employers from the days of the first labor strikers:

The company asks no man to work if he is dissatisfied with his pay, and I say to you that if you can do better elsewhere or in any other vocation, it is an injustice to yourselves and to your families to remain longer in the service. . . .

However, should they think they could stay and force the company to rescind the 10 percent wage cut, they would quickly find that they were beating their heads against a stone wall. And if they tried to achieve this goal by preventing the movement of the B & O's trains, they would face the most serious consequences: "You may rest assured that the entire power of the State and the general government will be exerted to maintain law and order."[51]

It is a tribute to the strikers' courage and militancy that, even in Keyser's presence, not one striker advocated accepting the company's proposition and all insisted that the men stand by their demands. A vote was taken and the company's proposal was unanimously rejected. Keyser then withdrew from the meeting, but upon leaving the hall he told reporters that what had just happened was of no importance. He had just returned from a visit to areas on the line in West Virginia and western Maryland, and the company, with the aid of the state militia and federal troops, was beginning to run both freight and passenger trains. The men could vote to stay out if they wished, but normal service would soon be restored since "the company has all the men it wants."[52]

Keyser's statement was basically true. Bonuses of fifty dollars had been offered to men willing to run the trains, while any striker approaching men on the trains was immediately arrested. To be sure, crowds of strikers and sympathizers along the B & O line fought bitterly, but they were helpless against soldiers who did not hesitate to fire into crowds.

General William Getty, who took over command of the Second U.S. Artillery from General French,[53] carried through the process of crushing the strike. Starting at Cumberland, he deployed detachments of his men in every city along the main line, broke through the blockades, and forced strikers to surrender possession of the company's property. It required three days of fighting to open the road between Keyser and Grafton. By August 1, after sixteen days on strike, the strikers began drifting back to work all along the line. The strike on the Baltimore & Ohio was over, and the press carried King's announcement that the main line was open for traffic.[54]

Days before this, however, the strike on the B & O had been relegated to the inside pages of the nation's newspapers by the startling events taking place in other cities. It was these events that Keyser had in mind when he told the Baltimore strikers that they were responsible for having "aroused a spirit" that "strikes at the very life of this country." He had spelled it out:

You have seen the results of the terrible riots at Pittsburgh and the enormous destruction of property, to be paid for by the already over-burdened taxpayers; you have seen innocent men and women shot down in our own streets; you have seen riot and bloodshed in Chicago and Cincinnati, Reading and other prominent cities of the land. Is not this sufficient to cause you to pause and reflect before you go still further in this reckless career?[55]

The *Martinsburg Statesman* conceded that Keyser's description of what was taking place in the fourth week in July was fairly accurate. But it differed with the B & O vice-president as to who was responsible. In its opinion, the strike that had started on the Baltimore & Ohio Railroad and "become general throughout the country," with such bloody repercussions, should teach "heartless and selfish railway corporations that there is a point in oppression beyond which it is not safe to go."[56]

III

The Strike on the Pennsylvania and Philadelphia & Reading Railroads

Pittsburgh, Pennsylvania, was the western terminus of the Pennsylvania Railroad's main line, which began in Philadelphia, and the starting point for the company's major branch lines—the Pittsburgh & Cleveland Railroad, the Pittsburgh, Fort Wayne & Chicago Railroad and the "Pan Handle" Railroad, otherwise known as the Pittsburgh, Cincinnati, Chicago & St. Louis line. In 1876, about eight million dollars' worth of freight traffic passed through Pittsburgh, averaging slightly more than twenty thousand dollars per day. The Baltimore & Ohio and Erie companies had entrances into the city, but these were circuitous routes to the west; for all practical purposes, therefore, the Pennsylvania company held a monopoly over the city's commerce.

By 1877, hatred of the Pennsylvania Railroad had permeated all classes in Pittsburgh. A local physician observed that the city's businessmen "were bitter enemies of the road on account of the discrimination in freights that existed." Thus, it was frequently cheaper for a Pittsburgh merchant to ship goods to California via Boston than to ship them directly, and cheaper for a Chicago merchant to ship goods to Philadelphia than to Pittsburgh, even though they had to pass through Pittsburgh en route.[1]

The lot of the Pennsylvania Railroad's workers was not much different from those on the B & O. To be sure, until June 1877 they had suffered only one wage cut, but they had been forced to tolerate an unusual amount of abuse. "Little under-officials treated us like dogs," observed Robert Ammon, who felt that abuse was the primary cause of the strike in Pittsburgh and Allegheny City. When a worker "signed up," he had to agree to the following rules, among others:

The regular compensation of employes covers all risk or liability to accident.

If an employe is disabled by sickness or any other cause, the right to claim compensation is not recognized.[2]

On top of this, the company refused to equip its freight trains with safety devices, and during the depression it made work on the main line more hazardous by doubling the size of its trains and reducing the number of men who worked on them. All westbound freights and eastbound coal trains, for example, had been made doubleheaders. This not only meant more work and heightened danger, but it also meant that nearly half the conductors, flagmen, and brakemen would be discharged. The following dialogue took place when a company official was asked how many men he was able to do without when he doubled up a train:

A. If there were ten single trains and I doubled up, I saved five conductors and five flagmen and ten brakemen.

Q. What became of those men?

A. They were suspended.

Q. But by suspension do you mean discharged, or do you mean suspension temporarily?

A. They were given to understand that there was no more work.[3]

On July 16, Robert Pitcairn, general superintendent of the Pennsylvania's western division, posted a notice saying that beginning Thursday, July 19, all eastbound trains going as far as Altoona would henceforth be doubleheaders. Since all eastbound coal trains had long been doubleheaders, the order did not require much of a change in the workers' schedules. Pitcairn probably felt that it would hardly make any difference, and would only result in the usual amount of grumbling. ("The men were always complaining about something," he later said.) In the end, he felt, everything would go smoothly and he would be congratulated for having saved the Pennsylvania the wages of the brakemen, flagmen, and conductors who would soon be dismissed because of the laborsaving device.

But coming as it did so soon after the most recent reduction in wages, and on the day that the B & O workers quit their jobs, the notice was too much for the men to tolerate. As Ammon observed later: ". . . It was the wrong time to put on the double-headers just following the strike at Martinsburg. That just started the whole thing."[4]

In the early morning of July 19, freight trains left Pittsburgh as doubleheaders, but at 8:40 a.m. two brakemen and one flagman refused to go out on a doubleheader, and the train did not leave. The conductor notified the dispatcher that the men had struck, but when the dispatcher tried to find other men who would go out, all the trainmen refused. The dispatcher then tried to make up crews from the yard men, but the strikers prevented the engine from being coupled.

At this point, the strikers began using the same tactics developed on the Baltimore & Ohio. They took control of the switches over which the trains would have to move, and refused to let any of them pass out. Meanwhile, large groups of men, including striking miners from Wilkensburg and unemployed workers from Pittsburgh, assembled on the tracks and prevented the movement of freight trains, allowing only passenger and mail trains to pass. One or two attempts were made to start freight trains, but when an engine began moving, some of the crowd would step in front of it, swinging their hands, and the engineer would leave. When one engineer appeared to persist, he was told that he had "better not go . . . that they did not want to hurt him but would not let him through." He left the engine. When a company man warned a striker that he would regret what he was doing, the reply came: "It is a question of bread or blood, and if I go to the penitentiary I can get bread and water, and that is about all I can get now."[5]

Pitcairn, having heard no complaints about his doubleheader order, had left Pittsburgh for Philadelphia two hours before the strike began, leaving his assistant, David Watt, in charge. When news of the strike reached Watt, he went to see Pittsburgh's mayor, William McCarthy, and asked him if he would come to the station with ten constables and speak to the strikers. McCarthy argued that since a recent lack of funds had forced the city to reduce its police force to eleven men, only nine of whom worked during the daytime, he could not spare them. As for going to the station himself, the mayor explained that he could not see that a disturbance requiring only ten men also required "the city to go there in the person of the mayor." However, in the end, McCarthy instructed Detective Charles McGovern to ask for volunteers and to accompany Watt to the station. After considerable difficulty, ten men were secured and left with Watt and McGovern.[6]

When they got to Twenty-eighth Street, they found the strikers in possession of the main yard switch, and after a run-in with a striker, Watt was struck in the eye. The striker was arrested and taken to the Twelfth Ward's police station. Watt wired Mayor McCarthy for fifty more policemen, but only six or seven arrived. Leaving McGovern in charge at Twenty-eighth Street, Watt went to the company's stock yards at Torrens, accompanied by his assistant, David Garrett. There they found that the strikers would not permit a loaded cattle train to leave, and after failing to persuade them they got the train out by trickery. That was the last train to leave Pittsburgh for over a week.[7]

Watt tried to get more police assigned, but he learned that the mayor had left town to visit his sick wife, and that nobody else would act with authority in his absence. He was advised to go to the sheriff. A little after midnight, by which time the crowd numbered about five hundred, Hugh M. Fife, sheriff of Allegheny County, spurred into action by the company, urged the strikers and their sympathizers to disperse and go to their homes. The sheriff, in turn, was told to go to *his* home, and that no freight trains would leave until the difficulty with the company was settled. Sheriff Fife thereupon threw up his hands and withdrew.[8]

By the next morning, more than nine hundred loaded cars stood idle. The strike was completely effective, and, although large crowds of unemployed workers and curious onlookers roamed the streets, order prevailed. A mass meeting of the Trainmen's Union (which had sprung to life again) was attended by representatives of each class of railroad workers—engineers (who, although at first in sympathy with the strike, had up to then been unwilling to join for fear of being dismissed), firemen, conductors, and brakemen. Resolutions were unanimously adopted, and a committee consisting of five members, one from each branch, was elected to present them to the company. The resolutions affirmed the strikers' determination not to go back to work until the wage reduction was rescinded, the doubleheader edict withdrawn, the new classification system abolished, and all strikers reemployed. After interviewing the men as they left Phoenix Hall, a reporter for the *National Labor Tribune,* published in Pittsburgh, wrote: "These men merely want to live—and do not want their wives and little ones to starve, which they must certainly do if they are compelled to accept the terms of the company and go to work."[9]

"There is no disguising the matter. The people of this city sympathize with the strikers. They are incensed beyond measure with the cold, corrupt legislation which has fostered the colder and more corrupt organization known as the Pennsylvania Railroad." This observation by the *Pittsburgh Critic* was later endorsed by a legislative committee that investigated the strike. "A large portion of the people," the committee pointed out, "also believed that the railroad company was not dealing fairly by its men in making the last reduction in wages, and the tradesmen with whom the trainmen dealt also had a direct sympathy with the men in this reduction, for its results would affect their pockets." The committee continued:

> The workers in the different mills, manufacturers, mines, and other industries in Pittsburgh and vicinity, were also strongly in sympathy with the railroad strikers, considering the cause of the railroad men their cause, as their wages had also been reduced for the same causes as were those of the railroad men, and they were not only willing but anxious to make a common fight against the corporations.

On Friday, July 20, the committee appointed at the Trainmen's Union's mass meeting met Alexander Cassatt and James Pitcairn, representing the company, and presented them with the strikers' demands. Cassatt, the third vice-president of the company, interpreted the document as an attempt on the part of the strikers to usurp control of the railroad. "They proposed taking the road out of our hands," he later said, horrified over the memory of the incident. Pitcairn was equally shocked. "I told them I could not possibly send such a paper to Mr. Scott," he recollected. "It was everything. . . . I have got the paper. . . . There are about four, or five, or six demands."[10]

An attempt was made by some of Pittsburgh's leading citizens to induce the company to at least make a counteroffer so that a compromise might be worked out, but the railroad officials would not even listen. The workers had taken the law into their own hands, they insisted, and it was up to the authorities to uphold the law. That was the long and short of it.[11]

Clearly, the Pennsylvania's management was growing impatient. Sensing that the people of Pittsburgh did indeed support the strikers they began to maneuver for outside help. After Sheriff Fife's perfunctory and futile call to the crowd to disperse, John Scott, the general solicitor of the Pennsylvania, drew up a telegram which the sheriff signed, and which was sent to Adjutant General James W. Latta. (Governor John F. Hartranft was junketing in far-off Wyoming Territory at railroad expense, and had given his adjutant general explicit instructions that if any disturbance occurred during his absence, he was to assume the powers ordinarily vested in the office of the state's chief executive.) After going on at some length about "intimidation" and "violence," and "molesting and obstructing," Sheriff Fife's wire (composed by Scott) concluded:

As the sheriff of the county, I have endeavored to suppress the riot, and have not adequate means at my command to do so, and I, therefore, request you to exercise your authority in calling out the military to suppress the same.

Latta immediately ordered General A. J. Pearson to call out one regiment of the Sixth Division located in Pittsburgh. Pearson was able to muster only 250 of his 326 men, but fearing that the majority of these militiamen sympathized with the strikers, he telegraphed Latta warning of this danger, and suggested that troops from Philadelphia be dispatched to Pittsburgh. The latter, in the governor's name, at once telegraphed Major General Brinton, commanding the First Division of the National Guard in Philadelphia, to prepare his command to move to Pittsburgh. At two o'clock in the morning of July 21, six hundred militiamen left Philadelphia for Pittsburgh, stopping off in Harrisburg for two Gatling guns and ammunition.[12]

Company officials were overjoyed. Tom Scott boasted that he would settle "this business with Philadelphia troops." He was confident that the militiamen, fresh from the influence of the banking and mercantile center, would not fraternize with the "mob."[13]

"The insane policy of calling Philadelphia troops to quell domestic quarrel is reprehensible beyond degree," a Pittsburgh paper commented.[14] But even this was an understatement. The folly of using any troops in such a volatile situation was only compounded by the request for militia troops from Philadelphia. The animosity that existed between Pennsylvania's two major cities was hardly a secret, and Pittsburghers felt many grievances against Philadelphia, not the least of which was the fact that the home office of the Pennsylvania Railroad was located there.[15] Their anger was further aroused by reports that *en route* to their city, the militiamen had boasted that they were going to clean up the workingmen's town. Even the *Army Journal* admitted that the Philadelphians were spoiling for a fight.[16]

Saturday, July 21, a day long to be remembered by Pittsburghers, dawned bright and beautiful. The strikers had remained stationed along the line during the entire night. Early the next morning, they were joined by rolling-mill men, mechanics, the unemployed, and women and children. Regiments of the Pittsburgh militia were stationed near the strikers and their sympathizers. The soldiers joked and fraternized with the crowd. Most of the time their arms were stacked. The strikers let them know that they would resist any attempt to start a freight train out under the doubleheader order.

It was the custom for the different mills and shops in Pittsburgh and its vicinity to shut down at about noon on Saturday. Fearing that the sudden increase in the crowd following such shutdowns would create complications, several Pittsburgh manufacturers approached Vice-President Cassatt and urged him not to attempt to open the road that afternoon, but rather to wait until Monday afternoon, when the mills would be operating. They pointed out that it was natural that the local militia "should sympathize with the strikers" and therefore could not be depended upon in case of a riot. To call in the Philadelphia troops under these circumstances, they insisted, was fraught with the utmost danger.

But Cassat refused to delay. The company, he said, had already lost a great deal of time, and it was the duty of the government to open the road regardless of the consequences.[17]

Following this conversation, a meeting of the strikers was organized. Dr. E. Donnelly, the main speaker, urged the strikers to be prudent in their reaction to the troops from Philadelphia, and not to resort to violence:

> They are not, you may say, your brothers. . . . These men will come here strangers to you, and they will come here regarding you as we regarded the rebels during the rebellion, and there will be no friendly feeling between you and them. For this reason, I implore you, for God's sake, to stand back when they arrive. . . . I have been informed by the men who are leading the strike that they will exercise the greatest caution and forbearance when the soldiers arrive, and I entreat you to stand back and let them manage the thing in their own way.

The speech was greeted with cheers, and before the meeting adjourned, the strikers adopted resolutions assuring the community that no effort would be made to interfere with passenger traffic or the U.S. mail trains; that a full crew of men would be furnished, free of charge, to move all city freight then in the yards that was intended for Pittsburgh firms, but that, under no circumstances, would through freight be allowed to be moved "until we are allowed sufficient wages for our labor to keep our families from actual want." The final resolution expressed appreciation for "the sympathy so fully tendered us by the public at large."[18]

At about one o'clock in the afternoon of July 21, a passenger train arrived at the Pittsburgh Union Depot. From six cars, uniformed Philadelphians emerged, armed and equipped with blankets. An hour later, another train arrived with several hundred more Philadelphians. The six hundred soldiers were furnished with refreshments at the depot; and when news came that the railroad officials wanted to send out a freight train immediately, the order was given for the Philadelphia troops to occupy those positions at which the most resistance was likely to come from the strikers and their sympathizers.

The news of the troop's arrival brought a vast assemblage of men, women, and children to the Outer Depot, where the freight trains lay idle. The crowd was quiet and orderly. At five o'clock in the afternoon, cries of "There they come!" arose. All eyes were turned toward the Union Depot. In the distance was seen a solid column of soldiers, marching steadily toward the Outer Depot, their bayonets glistening in the sun. At the head of the soldiers were Superintendent Pitcairn of the Pennsylvania Railroad, Sheriff Fife, and a posse of constables and police officers. The sheriff, the constables, and the police were accompanying the troops to arrest the strike leaders on a warrant issued by Judge Ewing at the request of solicitors for the Pennsylvania Railroad. The unnamed ringleaders were charged with riot.

As the troops approached the Outer Depot, the silence was broken by a storm of hisses, hoots, and yells. The women led the hissing and urged the men to outdo them in jeering at the Philadelphians. As the soldiers began pushing the crowd back so as to clear the tracks, the cries and yells grew louder and fiercer. Regiments of the local militia mingled with the crowd, and a number of its members urged the Philadelphians to "take it easy." Several strikers joined the refrain, and one shouted, "You sympathize with our cause, and you wouldn't shoot a working-man!"

At that very moment, an order was issued to the Philadelphia "Dark Blues" to charge with fixed bayonets. The soldiers responded, and several people were stabbed. When the crowd saw the blood trickling from these men, an angry roar arose. At this point, several boys let loose a volley of stones at the soldiers.

The command "Fire!" rang out, and immediately the troops began firing directly into the crowd. The panic-stricken men, women, and children, trapped and unarmed, surged in all directions, and several fell. The reporter for the *Pittsburgh Post* wrote:

Women and children rushed frantically about, some seeking safety, others calling for friends and relatives. Strong men halted with fear, and trembling with excitement, rushed madly to and fro, tramping upon the killed and wounded as well as upon those who had dropped to mother earth to escape injury and death.

Bodies dripping with blood and writhing in agony were lifted off the ground and carried to undertakers' establishments, to physicians' offices, and to private residences. The members of the local militia, who had watched the shooting into the crowd with horror, had to be restrained from firing on the soldiers from Philadelphia. But in their fury, they tore off their uniforms and left them on the ground.[19]

Within a few minutes, at least twenty were dead (including one member of Pittsburgh's Sixth Division) and twenty-nine maimed or wounded by the Philadelphia citizen-soldiers. The dead included a woman and three small children. A grand jury investigation termed the action of the troops "an unauthorized, willful and wanton killing . . . which the inquest can call by no other name than murder."[20]

Even before the full casualty list was known, the headlines in the *Pittsburgh Sunday Globe Extra* screamed:

FIRST BLOOD

Seventeen Citizens Shot in Cold Blood by the Roughs of Philadelphia.

The Lexington of the Labor Conflict At Hand.

The Slaughter of the Innocents.[21]

As the word of the massacre spread through the city, thousands of workers from the rolling mills, coal mines, and factories hurried to the scene of the killings. The angry crowds forced the Philadelphians to retreat to the roundhouse, where a siege began. Within fifteen minutes, the crowd had broken every window in the building. Only a last-minute decision prevented the soldiers from responding with the Gatling guns. A wagon bringing food for the soldiers was seized by the crowd.

With the Sixth Division practically disbanded, the police nowhere to be found, and the Philadelphia militiamen besieged in the roundhouse, the crowd had full control of the city. The aroused citizenry, determined to avenge the murders, put the railroad's property to the torch. The fire alarms were cut, but an alarm was somehow sent in. The first department responded, but upon arriving within a block of the fire, the engines were stopped by the crowd. Meanwhile, the striking of the alarms was a signal for thousands of additional people from all parts of the city to proceed to the scene of the blaze.[22]

The fire continued to spread until "it looked as if half the city would be burned."[23] Every car on the track between the roundhouse and Twenty-third Street was destroyed. Before this, however, men, women, and children broke into the cars and carried off everything they could get their hands on. An onlooker wrote later:

> People were hurrying up the hill [overlooking the railroad tracks] with all kinds of shipping cases, webs of cloth, silk, brooms, hams, bacon, umbrellas, liquor of every kind, in fact every conceivable kind of portable merchandise. . . .
>
> Many women were carrying flour in their aprons and anything else they could get hold of that might be useful or that they thought had a value.[24]

In its report, the state legislative committee stressed the role of the women in urging "the mob to resistance," and pointed out that "during Saturday night and Sunday, they [the women] brought tea and coffee to the men engaged in the destruction of property and were the most active in carrying away goods taken from the cars." What the report failed to mention was that in the testimony it took, the fact was emphasized that if the goods had not been taken, they would have been destroyed by fire.[25]

On Sunday afternoon, as the fires were raging, a mass meeting of citizens was hastily called, and a committee of five appointed to confer with the state, county, and city authorities, the strikers and other workingmen, and the Pennsylvania Railroad officials "to secure the protection of property from wanton destruction, and an arrangement of the difficulties betweeen the company and the striking employees." In taking this action, however, the meeting pledged the citizens' "faith to the working men that we have no purpose to facilitate the introduction of an armed force, but look solely to the protection of the rights of all by amicable means."

Immediately after the meeting adjourned, Bishop Tuigg, a member of the committee of five, hurried to the scene of destruction. Standing on a steaming locomotive, with his face blackened with the smoke and soot of the fire, he pleaded with all in the crowd, and especially those who were Catholics, to return to their homes. There had been faults on both sides, he maintained, and it was not his intention or that of the committee he represented "to condemn this party and uphold that." A voice interrupted: "What did the Philadelphia soldiers begin shooting for, and why did they kill innocent women and children?" Bishop Tuigg had no answer, but he assured the crowd that "on the authority of the citizens whom I represent, your wages will be raised to the old standard. I know that the citizens will do everything in their power to get back your wages." This brought applause and shouts of "That's all we want!" "Give us a chance to live!" But when Bishop Tuigg asked the crowd to disperse and give his committee twenty-four hours to consult with the railroad company, the crowd lost patience and resumed its destruction of railroad property.[26]

The fire extended through the freight cars for three miles to the city's limits. It enveloped 39 buildings of the Pennsylvania Railroad Company, 104 engines, 46 passenger cars, and over 1,200 freight cars. All of the buildings extending from Union Depot to Twenty-eighth Street that lay between Liberty Street and Penn Avenue were burned, as were all of the buildings in the vicinity of the Union Depot. The depot was ignited at about three o'clock, and the fire crackled for an hour and a half before the building was entirely consumed. At around five o'clock, the flames began lapping at a great grain elevator which stood beside Union Depot. It was 150 feet high and 80 feet square and took three hours to burn. The fire department was not permitted to throw a drop of water on it, although it was permitted to save the private property across the street.

With nothing left to burn, the rioters started to trickle home.

Subsequently, the Pennsylvania filed claims against Allegheny County for destruction totalling $4.1 million, and was awarded almost $3 million.[27]

The Philadelphia soldiers spent Saturday night in the roundhouse and the adjoining depot, supperless. But food was the least of the soldiers' worries. At midnight, cars with burning coal and petroleum were run down the track and against the sand house, a large building near the roundhouse, which was soon in flames. However, the roundhouse was saved when the soldiers used a hose belonging to the railroad company.

At about six o'clock the next morning, the smoke from the burning railroad cars seeped into the roundhouse and began to choke the men inside. An hour and a half later, the soldiers left the roundhouse, marching in a column of fours down Penn Avenue. As they marched along, they were followed by an infuriated crowd. Arms and ammunition shops were raided, and the soldiers were fired upon from street corners, alleyways, windows, and housetops. The Philadelphians returned the fire, and in the ensuing skirmish some twenty more Pittsburghers were killed, along with two or three of the soldiers, while an uncounted number of citizens and several soldiers were wounded.

When the Philadelphians reached the United States Arsenal, they were refused admission by its commandant, Major Buffington, on the ground that to do so would bring the wrath of the crowd down upon him. From there, and after leaving their wounded in the arsenal, the soldiers marched over the bridge and finally reached Claremont, where the command bivouacked and remained until they were ordered by Adjutant General Latta to return to Philadelphia.[28]

The events in Pittsburgh plunged the country into a frenzy of hysteria. "Madness rules the hour," screamed the *Missouri Republican*. "Nothing in the history of this country shows so extensive and continuous a reign of anarchy." "We are now in the presence of a great danger," warned the *Washington* (D.C.) *National Republican*, "which threatens to overthrow all law and social order, and, if not checked, to destroy our civilization itself, and plunge the country into Barbarism." The *Chicago Inter-Ocean* called the events in Pittsburgh "America's First Great Revolution"; the most the *New York Times* could bring itself to say was: "God help us, if these are the rewards of freedom."[29]

Sobered by the carnage, Pittsburgh itself settled down. Order was restored by organized patrols of strikers and citizen volunteers. On Monday morning, July 23, the Fóurteenth and Nineteenth regiments were recalled to duty.

Meanwhile, the strike not only continued but spread to other industries. The employees of the National Tube Works joined the railroad workers, and, in a marching brigade, closed down all the mills in the area, including the huge Edgar Thomson Steel Works. Thousands of iron and steel workers and coal miners, as well as railroad workers, were now out in a giant strike.[30]

On Monday evening, July 23, the railroad strikers issued a statement placing "responsibility" for the destruction of the previous two days squarely on the shoulders of Thomas A. Scott for having refused to negotiate with the men and thereby avoid the terrible tragedy:

> For the disorder, the outrages, the murders, the incendiarism, the awful responsibility rests alone upon the officials of the Pennsylvania Company. . . .
> We wish the public to distinctly understand that before and since the destruction of property and loss of life, we have done our part seeking a conference to settle the differences between us and the company, but we have not been deemed worthy of an answer from the officers of the P.R.R. Company.[31]

The strikers' request for a meeting with company officials to settle the dispute received wide support in Pittsburgh. James P. Barr, the editor of the *Pittsburgh Post*, not only published a lead editorial entitled "Why Not Arbitration?" pleading with the Pennsylvania's management to submit the issues to "arbitration *at once*," but appealed personally to Colonel Scott in Philadelphia

> . . . to agree to a board of arbitration to present a compromise, which will relieve you and labor without disturbing the rights or grievances of either. . . . You have it in your power to restore peace and preserve society. . . . I implore you not to assume the ground that the military can settle anything but defiance of law. Have this compromise effected at once, and the country will owe you a debt of gratitude.

But Scott was convinced that the "military" would "settle" the strike in the interest of the corporation, and he rejected the plea.[32]

Small wonder, then, that with all the destruction and increasing shortages, community sympathy still remained with the strikers. "I don't think they [the citizens of Pittsburgh] cared much for the Pennsylvania Railroad Company, even if it was burned up," Robert Ammon explained later.[33]

For three days, young Ammon was in complete control of Allegheny City—the important railway center on the Pennsylvania line, just across the river from Pittsburgh—which was the terminus of the Pittsburgh, Fort Wayne & Chicago, the Allegheny Valley, the Pan Handle, and the Connelsville division of the Baltimore & Ohio. The strikers at Allegheny City, all members of the Trainmen's Union, accepted Ammon's leadership and agreed to follow his advice to use no violence to prevent trains from running, and to let the freight trains go through if the company could get scabs to run them. Since the Pennsylvania Railroad was unable to find such men, the strikers' willingness to let the freight trains through was never tested.

Ammon told Mayor O. Phillips that the strikers would try to protect company property, and in return the mayor promised that as long as the situation remained peaceful, no troops would be summoned. The strikers stopped over ten miles of freight trains, organized regular shifts to guard them, requested that all saloons be closed, and worked in close cooperation with city authorities. When a rumor spread that a Pittsburgh mob was coming to destroy the railroad property, engineers took the engines out of the roundhouse, and the ten miles of cars were hauled out from the city and stowed away on side tracks until the strikes were over.

Then the strikers heard that the Seventh Division of the Pennsylvania Guard had been summoned to Allegheny City. Considering this a violation of the agreement with the mayor, Ammon and the strikers' committee prepared an appropriate reception. The ten miles of freight cars were moved further away, so as to be out of the line of fire; citizens were warned to stay home; the strikers equipped themselves with guns and brickbats, dug trenches, and threw up barriers a mile in front of the city, planted two guns at either side of the road, and settled down to wait. Every passenger train was stopped; a number of strikers went on board, and after being satisfied that there were no military among the passengers, allowed it to proceed.

Late Saturday night, July 21, Ammon received news that the statewide traffic tie-up had prevented the soldiers from coming. He thereupon instructed his men to abandon their positions and go back to guarding the freight trains.

On Sunday afternoon, July 22, Ammon took control of the dispatcher's office of the Fort Wayne and personally conducted the company's passenger traffic until the following Tuesday. On Monday, he worked in close cooperation with the company's officials, particularly its general manager, J. D. Layng, and also with Mayor Phillips, who sent him twenty-five constables to help guard the freight cars. When he heard that Governor Hartranft was coming to Allegheny City on his return from his western tour, he wired ahead to welcome him and to assure him of safe passage. Upon the governor's arrival on Tuesday, July 24, Ammon told the strikers to bring the freight cars back and turn the railroad over to its officers. Later that night, he urged the strikers to return to work and leave it to the railroad to settle their grievances.

It was at this point that "Boss" Ammon met his first opposition. Several strikers objected to his proposal to call off the strike, and when he persisted in his stand, he was hissed and shouted down. Infuriated, Ammon resigned his leadership and went home. But he had succeeded in antagonizing Chief of Police W. D. Ross, who was jealous of his managerial ability; he was arrested on July 30, but never brought to trial. As the Pennsylvania legislative committee commented: "Thus fell from his position of boss the man who, with only eleven months' experience as a brakeman, for four or five days successfully ran one division of a great railroad."[34]

After Ammon's withdrawal, the strike continued in full force in Allegheny City and was even extended to the workers in the machine and carpentry shops. The strikers remained cool and firm, maintaining excellent order and continuing to protect the company's property. Some remained on guard for forty-eight hours at a stretch to prevent looting. While no freight trains left the city, mail and passenger trains were dispatched.[35]

Meanwhile, the strike had spread through Pennsylvania into every major laboring town in the state. On July 22, brakemen and firemen in Philadelphia, the headquarters of the Pennsylvania Railroad, left their posts and asked the officers of the company to halt all freight traffic. Tom Scott, aware that he could not continue operations (the engineers left their trains and went home), prudently agreed. In the city itself, business came almost to a standstill, since no one could hope to ship or receive any supplies by rail. Soon the main line of the Pennsylvania Railroad, which ran from Philadelphia to Pittsburgh, was completely paralyzed, and elsewhere, too, company officials were unable to move any trains. In Altoona, the classic railroad town and the first stop on the Pennsylvania's main line going east from Pittsburgh, workers and sympathizers ranged throughout the city. When two militia trains attempted to pass through to Pittsburgh, they were attacked by the crowds. One detachment of troops surrendered and, after being fed by their captors, agreed to return home to Philadelphia. On their way home from Altoona, some of the militia were "recaptured" in Harrisburg, wined, dined, and sent on their way.[26]

In the nervous capital city of Harrisburg itself, Sheriff W. W. Jennings demonstrated restraint and intelligence in dealing with the inevitable large crowds that surrounded railroad property, and bloodshed was avoided.[37] In Erie, Pennsylvania, a large group of passengers, marooned by the strike, signed a statement denouncing the railroad company and praising its employees for their courtesy and kindness. (The strikers had even paid the hotel expenses for some of the travelers.) It was from Erie, too, that a "Committee of Firemen, Brakemen & Citizens" wired President Hayes on July 24 that the Lake Shore Railroad had refused to allow mail to move. "We would be pleased," they informed the president, "if you would in some way direct them to proceed with mails and also passengers."[38]

In practically every town and city of Pennsylvania where the presence of the railroad was felt (except in Philadelphia, where the mayor banned all meetings), there were public gatherings in support of the strikers. Most ended without any violence. But in some communities across the state, the repressive force of the railroad companies and their allies in government was brought into play. In Johnstown, where troops were stoned, several workers were shot. It was in Reading, however, that the next great tragedy in Pennsylvania took place.

That city's income was derived principally from the Philadelphia & Reading Iron & Coal Company, which, in turn, depended upon the Philadelphia & Reading Railroad. Both of these enterprises were under the leadership of Franklin B. Gowen, who had become their president in 1868. As we have seen, Gowen had just recently made even more bitter enemies of the city's workers by forcing his men to choose between the Brotherhood of Locomotive Engineers and his company, and by personally securing the hanging of ten "Molly Maguires" in nearby Mauch Chunk. A month after the executions, many of his three hundred former engineers, who had chosen to remain with their union, still lingered around Reading, blacklisted and embittered. The Irish Catholic miners of Reading nursed a deep resentment against the man who had crushed their union and railroaded their comrades to their death.

Their feeling was shared by many Reading workers, and was expressed in the words of a song which spread through the city:

> There's an army of strikers,
> Determined you'll see,
> Who will fight corporations
> Till the country is free.[39]

On July 22, 1877, the *Daily Eagle,* Reading's leading paper, noted that "popular sympathy" in the city was with the strikers in every railroad center, who had had their wages repeatedly reduced until their pay merely covered the bare necessities of life:

The last turn of the screw cut into the live flesh, and they rebelled against the extortions and tyranny of the corporations which used their enormous capital for their own ends, regardless of the rights and suffering of the working people.

It was the railroad corporations, the paper pointed out, that had struck the first blow, and the strikers were fighting back against tremendous odds:

The corporations have got a terrible advantage over their laborers in times like these. Labor is the underdog. The corporations can dictate their own terms, adopt what rules they please, pay just such wages as they see fit to allow, and the poor laborer can either accept what is graciously given or suffer the consequences which is virtually starvation. The corporations have the law on their side. They own the Legislatures. They retain the ablest lawyers. They control most of the newspapers and manufacture public opinion. And if the laborers protest in the only way that is left to them to assert their manhood, and contend for the rights of human nature and American citizenship, they are branded as rioters, met by force of arms, provoked to violence, and then shot dead.

Little did the *Eagle* realize that it was predicting precisely what would soon happen in Reading. When the news from Pittsburgh reached them, the workers of the city, long restive under the grip of Gowen's Philadelphia & Reading Railroad, spontaneously seized the railroad property. The company immediately moved to deal with the situation by calling for the militia. Just as promptly, the Reading Rifles made it clear that, while they would report for duty, "if ordered to fire, they will lay down their arms; that they are workingmen and do not desire to kill other workingmen."[40]

The company then called on Major General William J. Boston, who commanded the Second Division of Pennsylvania's National Guard. Boston at once sent one of his trusted aides, Brigadier General Frank Reeder, to Reading with the Fourth and Sixteenth regiments. The result was reported by the grief-stricken editor of the *Reading Daily Eagle:*

> The EAGLE has never been called upon to chronicle a more horrible slaughter of its peaceful and law-abiding citizens as it is its duty to-day. In the very heart of the city shortly after eight o'clock last night, took place one of the most terrible butcheries that has ever disgraced the pages of Reading's local history. The pavements, sidewalks and streets in the vicinity of 7th and Penn Streets, were literally baptized in blood; neighboring drug stores were for the time transformed into hospitals and operating rooms, and the dead and dying were carried home to their families they had left in health and strength but a short time before. It was the old story of military interference and military blunder over again, blunder whose absolute law is and has been for all time that the innocent are shot and the guilty escape.[41]

Night had settled upon the city when the militiamen marched in from the depot and proceeded to Seventh and Penn streets, where thousands of men, women, and children had gathered to witness the blockading of the tracks by the strikers. A few young men threw bricks and stones as the soldiers marched along. Suddenly, and without any warning whatsoever, the troops fired volley after volley in quick succession into the assemblage of men, women, and children. At first, it was thought that the volleys were blank cartridges fired in the air, but when several fell seriously wounded, panic ensued. Men, women, and children ran for their lives. All along Seventh Street, people were sitting at their doors and windows enjoying the cool air of the evening. They leaped up and disappeared, closing doors and windows after them. At Seventh and Penn streets, a large force of policemen was on duty and had succeeded in keeping the pavements and sidewalks clear. Before they could grasp what was happening, five of their number were shot and seriously wounded.

The military fired up and down Seventh Street and up and

down Penn Street. Men dropped like flies. Rifle balls penetrated the large plate glass windows of business houses, and some of the store fronts were riddled. In all, ten Reading citizens were killed and forty wounded![42]

"The shooting down of quiet, inoffensive citizens at Seventh and Penn Streets, and the wounding of good citizens who were standing in the doors of their residences by the militia is little better than cold-blooded murder," the *Daily Eagle* cried out in fury. The entire city agreed, and was even more enraged by the testimony of Sheriff R. Yorgey that he had never been called upon by any officer, "either civil or military . . . in reference to quelling the disturbance"; that he had had "no notice whatever that any troops were coming that night; . . . had no information of the troops being in the city, and knew nothing of their presence until I heard the firing": "I was never consulted in reference to the military at all."[43] In short, Franklin P. Gowen and other officials of the Philadelphia & Reading had simply ignored the civil authorities and moved to deal with the situation themselves. Clearly, the company considered itself to be the real authority in Reading.

On July 28, Gowen informed Sheriff Yorgey that Major General Hancock was sending United States troops to Reading and that if the sheriff cooperated, he was certain they would "be able to keep the peace."[44] It was true, for only federal troops were able to restore order to the troubled city. The fires that had been started as an answer to the shooting of innocent citizens were extinguished, and the uprising in Reading began to subside.[45]

The same pattern was unfolding elsewhere in the state. Railroad officials stubbornly refused to arbitrate and placed all their dependence on the federal and state authorities to break the strike. Federal officials were keeping in touch with local and state officials throughout the nation through the U.S. Signal Service. In Washington, at the Soldiers' Home (once the favorite summer retreat of Abraham Lincoln), President Hayes was receiving regular reports, including those from Governor Hartranft urging him to use U.S. troops to restore order in Pennsylvania.

Pennsylvania's first call for federal help came on July 22 in a wire from Harrisburg sent in Hartranft's name by Adjutant General James N. Latta and Matthew S. Quay, secretary of the commonwealth. (The governor, it will be recalled, was vacationing in Wyoming Territory and had delegated to Latta the power to act in his name to quell any disturbance.) The wire read:

Domestic violence existing in the state of Penn[sylvani]a—in the city of Pittsb[ur]g and along the line Penn[sylvani]a Railroad and other railroads in said state which the authorities are unable to suppress and the legislature of Pennsylvania cannot be convened in time to meet the emergency. I have therefore to request in conformity to the Constitution the Government of the United States shall furnish me with military force sufficient to suppress disorder.[46]

This wire brought no response, and at seven o'clock that evening, Hartranft personally wired the president from Creston in Wyoming Territory: "I call upon you for troops to assist in quelling mobs within the borders of the state Penn[sylvani]a. . . ." Hayes still refused to act, and Hartranft, now on the way home, wired the next day from North Bend, Nebraska: "I amend my requisition from the general government by adding the words domestic insurrection exists in Pennsylvania which the state authorities are unable to suppress and the Legislature is not in session and cannot be convened in time." Finally, the governor, having arrived back in his state, wired the president that in his opinion the disturbances had "assumed the character of a general insurrection" which could not be suppressed by the "organized forces" of either the state or federal governments, and he urged Hayes to consider calling for volunteers. At the same time, Scott and other railroad officials in Pennsylvania proposed to President Hayes that the strikers be considered as waging war against the United States.[47]

Late Wednesday, July 26, it was decided at a cabinet meeting that state and federal troops in Pennsylvania would begin on the following day to "open the road to Pittsburgh." After consulting with military and railroad authorities, Hartranft proposed to gather a large force and to proceed along the Pennsylvania Railroad's main line, opening up traffic along the way. On Thursday, therefore, using a special train furnished by the railroad as a mobile command post, the governor loaded three thousand U.S. regulars and twice that number of militia on special troop trains, picked up several Gatling guns and some ammunition in Harrisburg, and arrived at Altoona by Friday morning. There he issued orders to General Brinton at Blairsville to break camp and return to Pittsburgh. On Saturday morning, Brinton and Hartranft entered Pittsburgh with an overwhelming display of force. The strikers tried to confer with the governor, but he told them brusquely that he was not a mediator and was there only to restore order.[48]

One by one—at Philadelphia, Harrisburg, Altoona, and Pittsburgh—the critical points were forced open for traffic. Before the week was over, Reading was opened by four batteries of U.S. regulars.

On Monday, July 30, both the Pennsylvania and Reading companies announced that they would resume normal operations on the following day. General Hancock informed the War Department:

> The quiet occupation of Pittsburgh and opening of the Pennsylvania Railroad, I think, settles the question of order in this division, and the only trouble that seems to remain is that connected with the miners in certain points in the coal districts, such as Scranton. Possibly that may require similar treatment as that of the railroads.[49]

Governor Hartranft was the right man to dispense such "similar treatment." He left Pittsburgh with federal and state troops for the mining districts around Kingston, Plymouth, Natioke, Wilkes-Barre, and Scranton, and used the same tactics to break the miners' strikes as he had those of the railroad workers.

Scranton was the last city in Pennsylvania to be "conquered." On July 24, fifteen hundred workers of the Lackawanna Iron & Coal Company struck at noon "with a cheer," and at six that night they were followed by the firemen and brakemen of the Delaware, Lackawanna & Western and Delaware & Hudson railroad companies. The stopping of the railroads forced the city's miners into idleness, and on Sunday, July 29, all of Scranton's thirty-five thousand workers were on strike.[50]

Wages in Scranton had been depressed to the starvation level. One worker reported that he had made $28.40 in June, and out of this had had to pay $9.40 for his tools, leaving $19.00 to support himself and his five dependents. His meals consisted of corn meal mush and a few potatoes from his little garden patch. His family had not eaten beef for half a year. Another worker said that he had averaged $14.00 per month over the past year, and that his employer still owed him for fifty-nine cars of coal. Thousands of families lived on such wages, and yet the companies kept reducing them. From September 1876 to July 1, 1877, employees of the Delaware, Lackawanna & Western Company saw their wages drop 35 percent. Little wonder that the men told a reporter that "death would be better than this battle for life in which they are constantly worsted." Yet, he commented, death was "too expensive, a funeral too costly a heritage for the living, and so they struggle on to keep body and soul together as a matter of economy."[51]

Because of the town's sympathies for the strikers, Mayor Robert H. McKune failed in his effort to form a citizens' corps and enroll special police. But W. W. Scranton, general manager of the Lackawanna Iron & Coal Company, organized a private force of 116 citizens into the "Scranton Citizens' Corps," and turned over the company's general store to be used for its general headquarters. The group secured arms and drilled. However, the railroad official was not fully confident that the corps could handle the situation. He wrote to a friend in York:

I trust when the troops come—if they ever get here—that we may have a conflict in which the mob shall be completely worsted. In no other way will the thing end with any security for property here in the future.[52]

Before the troops came, the "Scranton Citizens' Corps" killed six striking miners. On August 2, Brinton arrived with the First Division and completed the process of smashing the strike. On August 15, Governor Hartranft wrote to the secretary of war:

The emergency for which the federal troops were brought into this State is over, but the situation in the mining regions is still very critical and for prudential reasons I request the retention for the present of such forces as are not needed elsewhere.[53]

So the army settled down to what amounted to an occupation of the coal region of eastern Pennsylvania. By mid-August, General Hancock had concentrated large numbers of troops in Scranton, Wilkes-Barre, and Mauch Chunk, with a smaller detachment in Reading.[54] Living conditions among the strikers and their families began to deteriorate rapidly. General Hancock reported that almost 100,000 men were idle and that they and their families were living on potatoes, wild berries, and whortleberries. The miners had little influence with the federal officers, but they made some efforts to win the sympathies of the enlisted men. General Hancock, worried, ordered that

. . . localities for summer camps of our troops in the disturbed regions should be somewhat removed from the influence of the strikers and persons in sympathy with them in recent disorders, whose influence might be brought to bear on their fellow foreign countrymen who may happen to be in our service. . . .[55]

The strike in Scranton and other mining regions lasted until mid-October, by which time the miners, although well organized and determined to stay out until they had achieved victory, were defeated by the federal troops.[56] On October 19, Governor Hartranft informed the president that the troops could be withdrawn. By October 30, the last of the troops had left Scranton with the blessings of the business community. The viewpoint of these citizens was expressed by the *Scranton Republican* as it bade the soldiers farewell:

Their brief residence among us has revolutionized our views and opinions of army men in general, and henceforth, we shall always feel that we have friends among the national defenders. . . .[57]

Thus, the Great Strike came to an end in Pennsylvania, crushed by local police, militias, citizens' vigilante groups, United States marshals, and federal troops.

The wall of fire in Pittsburgh engulfs Pennsylvania Railroad freight trains and the Union Depot.

IV

The Strike on the Erie and New York Central Railroads

In 1877, the Erie Railroad was in receivership. It is not necessary for us to deal here with either the notorious manipulations of Jay Gould, Daniel Drew, and James Fisk, or their struggle with Commodore Vanderbilt and his New York Central system over control of the Erie.[1] Suffice it to say that by the time of the panic of 1873, it would have taken a financial genius to have kept the Erie in a sound financial condition. That year it was disclosed that Gould, as its president, had embezzled some ten million dollars of the Erie's money, and public confidence in the road was virtually nonexistent. On July 15, 1874, Hugh J. Jewett took over the reins of the bankrupt Erie as receiver and proceeded to make the workers of the road the chief victims of its long mismanagement. Jewett shared the typical outlook of railroad management of his day that his sole duty was to gain a profit for the stockholders of the line, and he did not hesitate to cut wages in order to achieve it.[2]

Early in June 1877, Jewett sent a memorandum to all employees that a 10 percent wage reduction would take effect on July 1. The announcement stirred the workers all along the line, and meetings were held in the several cities to decide on a plan to get the order revoked. Finally, a committee consisting of fifty men from different points along the road was elected to go to New York City to talk with the receiver. An interview took place during the last week in June, in the course of which Jewett was told that the wage cut would mean earnings inadequate for the men to support themselves and their families, and he was asked to rescind the order.

Jewett replied that he was both surprised and hurt by the workers' action in organizing the committee, and that the order could not be revoked. However, he promised that if there was a change in conditions, wages would be restored to their previous level. He then reminded the committee that in ordering the reduction in pay, he had acted as an officer of the court, and

79

warned them that the order would be supported by every court in every state through which the line passed. And since the road was in receivership, anyone interfering with train service could be charged with contempt.[3]

After caucusing, the committee informed the Erie management that it could make no final determination until it obtained the views of the workers who had elected it. It was clear that the key answer would have to come from the men at Hornellsville, New York. That town was the western terminus of the Susquehanna Division, the eastern terminus of the Allegheny Division, and the southern terminus of the Buffalo Division—in short, it was the most important junction for freight transfer on the Erie line. (The railroad switching yards in Hornellsville occupied about thirty acres.) In addition, the locomotive shops at Hornellsville—covering over ten acres—constituted the chief service center for the road. In 1877, they accommodated up to forty engines and employed over two hundred men. Added to these workers were nearly five hundred firemen and engineers who were stationed in the town, making it the place with the greatest concentration of Erie workers. Moreover, these workers made up the majority of the town's population, and the businessmen were totally dependent on them for their income.[4]

A day before the meeting was held in Hornellsville to discuss the Erie's answer to the Committee of Fifty, the *Utica Observer* urged the men to be "sensible," and that "the best thing they can do is accept the situation and wait for better times."[5] The workers took this advice and, after a lengthy debate, voted against walking out.[6]

The Erie's management was much relieved by the decision, for Jewett knew that about 90 percent of the line's total business could be halted if the trains were not allowed to pass through Hornellsville. Moreover, there was no other point on the system at which the Erie's locomotives could be adequately serviced. Finally, Hornellsville was far from the large cities where there were great numbers of unemployed, making it much more difficult to get replacements for the strikers if the men voted to walk out.[7]

Indeed, Jewett was now so confident that the men would do nothing that when they reported to work on July 1, he ordered the members of the Committee of Fifty fired. He felt that, having voted against striking, the railroaders would not now reverse their stand. After all, in its report of the meeting at which the vote was taken, the *Hornell Times* pointed out: "Not even a large minority were in favor of a strike, much less any questionable means to make their strike effective."[8]

For the next two weeks, the company's confidence appeared to be justified. The men continued to report for work, and there was no word of any new talk of a strike. It therefore came as quite a surprise when, on July 20, the *Elmira Daily Advertiser* reported on its front page: "The great railroad strike which has been threatened for so long is fully inaugurated today. The strike began this morning. Hornellsville and Buffalo appear to have been the starting points."

What had happened was that the Erie workers, after hearing of the strikes in other sections of the nation, had presented an ultimatum to the company to the effect that unless their demands were met, they would strike at midnight on July 19. The demands were embodied in an eight-point proposal.

The first and most important was that all those who had been discharged for taking part in any meeting or for serving on the Committee of Fifty must be reinstated. The next four points were concerned with wages. Brakemen and switchmen were to receive $2.00 a day; head switchmen, $2.25 a day; trackmen in the yards were to get $1.50 a day, while those on the sections were to receive $1.40 a day. Firemen were to be given the same wages they had received before July 1, 1877.

The next demand dealt with ground rents. The company had forced many of its employees to live in houses owned by the Erie, and the rents for these shacks were exorbitant. (One worker later described the "homes" as "one-room shanties with a yard no larger than twenty feet square in which the occupants tried to raise a part of their food. As many as eight persons lived in each of these houses.") Although the railroad had cut the workers' wages 10 percent, it still maintained the same high rents.

The last two of the workers' demands were concerned with passes. The company had taken passes away from everyone, requiring the workers to pay for their transportation back to their homes from points where their work ended. The men asked that the monthly passes be reissued, and that pass rights be extended to brakemen and switchmen.[9]

The demands were quickly rejected. The company maintained, first, that the members of the Committee of Fifty had not been discharged because of that fact, but rather because they had absented themselves from work without leave, and for other "flagrant violations of discipline." It refused to take them back. As for the wage issue, the management insisted that the Erie was paying the highest wages of any eastern line before the reduction, and that the cut would merely serve to level off rates of pay. (It said nothing of the fact that the company's charges for ground rents ate up whatever difference may have existed between the wages of the Erie workers and those on other lines.) As for the demand that rents be lowered, management would not even consider the idea.[10]

When P. P. Wright, the company's transportation master, informed the workers that all their demands had been rejected, they were true to their pledge, and at one o'clock on the morning of July 20, the men went on strike on the three divisions of the road centering around Hornellsville. Later that same day, a committee representing the strikers served notice on the saloons in town that they were not to sell liquor to any of the railroad men until the emergency was ended. The strikers themselves took a "solemn obligation to drink no liquor" until their struggle was over.[11] All the newspapers reported this fact, and the *New York Times* commented that "a very creditable feature of the strike at Hornellsville is the entire absence of drunkenness on the streets."[12] However, the *Times*'s memory was short, for on July 26 it referred to the strikers as:

. . . disaffected elements, roughs, hoodlums, rioters, mob, suspicious-looking individuals, bad characters, thieves, blacklegs, looters, communists, rabble, labor-reform agitators, dangerous class of people, gangs, tramps, drunken section-men, law-breakers, threatening crowd, bummers, ruffians, loafers, bullies, vagabonds, cowardly mob, bands of worthless fellows, incendiaries, enemies of society, reckless crowd, malcontents, wretched people, loud-mouthed orators, rapscallions, brigands, robbers, mob, riffraff, terrible fellows, felons, idiots.[13]

The last train to leave Hornellsville departed just after midnight on July 20, and by the following afternoon at least ten trains were stranded in the yards of the town. For the moment, too, no trains could reach Hornellsville; the Erie superintendent, on being informed of the strike, had wired all trains scheduled to enter the town either to stop or to proceed to their destinations by other routes. This order was designed to both keep passenger and freight trains out of the hands of the strikers, and prevent other Erie workers from joining the men on strike at Hornellsville. In general, both objectives were achieved, but a reporter for the *New*

York Times noted that "in some instances train men thus disappointed in reaching their friends seized handcars and reached Hornellsville that way."[14]

From Hornellsville, the strike spread rapidly along the line of the Erie. Port Jervis, Corning, Painted Post, Buffalo, and other points were affected as the Erie brakemen, firemen, and other trainmen at these places joined the strike and stopped the trains.[15] But Hornellsville remained the key to the struggle of the Erie workers.

Governor Lucius Robinson of New York had been advised by the Erie receiver of the strike in Hornellsville, and although not a single act of violence had been reported, he immediately ordered the militia units from Rochester and Elmira to the town. However, the same drama unfolded at Hornellsville as had occurred in a number of other struck communities. As soon as the militiamen descended from the train, the strikers "commenced shaking hands and greeting their many acquaintances among the soldiers."[16] The soldiers stationed a guard around the yards and expelled all people from the railroad property except employees on duty, but they turned their eyes away when the strikers crossed the line and prevented engines from leaving the roundhouse.

While the strikers were willing to let mail cars leave, the company was determined to run all trains, and on the morning of July 22, a section composed of an engine, mail car, baggage car, and two passenger coaches started out of the yards for Tiptop Mountain, the only way for westbound trains to get out of Hornellsville. Thirty soldiers were detailed to guard the train; five were stationed on the engine, two on the bumper, and the rest scattered throughout the cars. On the long flat stretch before the ascent of Tiptop Mountain—one of the steepest grades on the road—engineer Dave Cary threw open his throttle to build up speed and momentum. The train reached twenty, then twenty-five miles an hour. At the base of the mountain, Cary opened his sand pipe a little for traction, and fireman Matt Dewey energetically shoveled coal into the furnace, as the train raced up the side of the hill. Then suddenly, its wheels began to slip. The strikers' wives had prepared buckets of soft soap, and the men had liberally slathered it all over the rails for a quarter of a mile up the hill.

As the train slipped backward, the strikers on the hillside cheered wildly and threw on more soap for good measure. The engineer, by making liberal use of the sand pipe, was able to conquer the grade, but the train could move only in spurts. As it slowed down from twenty to fifteen, to ten, to eight miles an hour, worried passengers began shouting. When it had almost come to a stop and was about to slide down again, the strikers rushed on board, shoved their way past the half-hearted militiamen, disabled the brakes, and forced all the passengers to get out. Superintendent John Biggs was speechless with anger. With everybody out, the strikers detached the passenger cars and sent them thundering down the hill toward the Erie freight yards. Engineer Cary was dispatched with the mail, and the troops and passengers were left to make their way through thickets and briars down the hillside to the Erie depot.

Half an hour later, persistent Erie officials started another train bound for Buffalo. The strikers jammed a switch, boarded it, bent its sand pipe, threw the engineer off, and expelled its passengers. Later in the morning, a third effort was made to start a train, but this, too, was foiled, and the Erie gave up its attempt to run a train out of Hornellsville that day.[17]

Not a single shot had been fired during any of the three episodes. The soldiers had been ordered to use only the butts of their guns. It was a wise order, for the familiarity between the militiamen and the Erie strikers was so great that if the soldiers had been ordered to shoot, they would probably have laid down their guns and gone home. In any event, the actions of the militia that day averted the kind of bloody massacre that had occurred in Baltimore, Pittsburgh, and Reading.[18]

But the *New York Times* was unhappy, and insisted that the soldiers be replaced by men who would act like the Philadelphians who had come to Pittsburgh. "We sincerely hope," it editorialized, "that when the next movement is made at Hornellsville, it will be with sufficient force and managed with sufficient energy and judgment to save our state from such disgraceful scenes as have taken place in Pittsburgh." What had "disgraced" Pittsburgh, in the eyes of the *Times,* was not the bloody massacre of men, women, and children, but the fact that the soldiers from Philadelphia had been forced to remain in retreat in the roundhouse, and that railroad property had been burned.[19]

Responding to the demand for sterner measures, Governor Robinson declared martial law in Hornellsville and called upon "all authorities, civil and military," to keep the strikers from preventing those who wished to do so from working. "It is no longer a question of wages," the governor's declaration concluded, "but the supremacy of the law. . . . To the maintenance of that supremacy the whole power of the State will be evoked if necessary."[20]

As soon as the governor's proclamation was issued, the Twenty-third Regiment was ordered to leave Brooklyn, New York, for Hornellsville. These soldiers, having no personal ties with the strikers, could be relied upon to enforce the proclamation. At the same time, General Brinker issued an order prohibiting anyone not working for the Erie from going onto the road's property without military permission. In fact, anyone who even stated his intention of entering the yards without this permission could be arrested.[21]

After praising Governor Robinson and General Brinker, Jewett reaffirmed the policy of no concessions to the strikers. Nevertheless, the company attempted to run only one train on July 23—the one bringing the Twenty-third Regiment from Brooklyn to Hornellsville. The train met little resistance until it reached Corning, about forty miles east of Hornellsville. From that point on, it had to fight its way. The strikers had torn up the tracks in front of the advancing train, and the soldiers spent much of their time repairing the damage. Five miles before Hornellsville, the spikes had been pulled and the plates joining the rails removed. As the engine passed over this point, the rails spread and the train settled to the ground. This caused a delay of about two hours. Finally, at six in the evening, the regiment arrived in Hornellsville.[22]

The Brooklynites were immediately dispersed to guard the Erie shops and grounds. The *Elmira Daily Advertiser* warned the strikers that now things would be different: "The troops look and act as soldiers and when called upon for duty, will obey orders, no matter what the consequences."[23] It did not take long for the strikers to see the difference. As soon as the troops were stationed around the company's grounds, some of the strikers tried to cross the guard lines as they had been doing since the beginning of their walkout. When challenged, the men made no answer, and a sentry fired a bullet over their heads—the only shot fired during the entire strike at Hornellsville.[24] The men left the area, and from that time on the military was in complete charge as the strikers remained off the railroad's property.

Still no trains left Hornellsville, and on July 23 the company invited Barney J. Donahue, a former Erie employee who had assumed leadership of the strike, and the strikers' lawyers, Miles Hawley and Matthew Bemis, to a meeting to try to reconcile the differences between the men and management. The spokesmen for the strikers indicated a willingness to accept the wage reduction, but demanded that ground rentals be removed; that promotions be based on length of service; that a ten-hour day be instituted; that the men be paid for the time they had to spend while delayed on the road, or when trips ended a great distance from their homes; and that the passes be issued to all workers as before. The three representatives also let it be known that even if all of these demands were granted, the strike would continue until those who had been dismissed for their membership on the Committee of Fifty were reinstated, since this had been the chief cause of the walkout.

In return for being granted an audience with company officials, the strikers' spokesmen stated that while all trains other than mail cars would continue to be stopped, no company property would be damaged. They stated that they wished "to meet the company in a spirit of candor and firmness."[25]

Bowen, speaking for the Erie, said he was glad the men were ready to talk reconciliation, but that the receiver would not allow the railroad to be run on any terms other than his own. While the dismissed men would not be returned to work, if the strikers went back to work they could rely on the receiver to overlook much of the damage caused during the strike and to retain those who had quit work. Before the interview ended, the counsel for the receiver told the delegation that they should remind the strikers that they "were in contempt of the highest court of the state, and were violating [its] . . . strictest penal codes."[26]

Although the meeting left the issues as far from settlement as they had been before, the fact that the company had made the first move toward meeting with the strikers, and had even discussed the terms of settlement, caused the distinct impression that eventually this strike, unlike most of the others occurring on the railroads, could be settled by mutual agreement. For a time, however, this seemed to be only wishful thinking. No sooner had Donahue returned to Hornellsville than he was arrested by the sheriff and a posse of several railroad detectives on a warrant sworn out by receiver Jewett, who charged him with contempt of court. He was ordered to report before Judge Donahue (no relation) in New York City on July 27. Meanwhile, Barney

Donahue went to the village lockup, where he was joined by four more strikers.[27]

The news of the jailings enraged the strikers and ended all talk of compromise for the time being. When concern was expressed that attempts might be made to rescue Donahue, he was removed to the depot under military guard and put on a train for New York. Even this did not still the fears, and an extra detail of soldiers was put on the train: "Men were placed on a handcar ahead of the train and as fast as any obstruction was found the train was flagged until it could move again."[28] The attempted rescue never took place, and the train eventually reached New York, thereby becoming the first to go the entire distance from Hornellsville to the eastern terminus since the strike had begun.[29]

The following day, however, turned out to be the last day of the strike. No trains other than the one that carried Donahue were running, and, despite the arrival of another regiment from Brooklyn, it appeared that no other trains would run until the strike was settled. Therefore, early in the afternoon, company officials met again with a committee of strikers and their attorneys. At this meeting, only slight concessions were made. The company agreed that Donahue's case would be left completely in the hands of the court, without any attempt on the part of the Erie officials to influence the decision. For their part, the strikers' spokesmen deferred the right of the men to passes to the receiver's judgment.

Later in the afternoon, another meeting was held in the company's offices, and it was at this meeting that a tentative agreement for settling the strike was drawn up. The firemen and brakemen were to accept the 10 percent wage cut, but the trackmen were to receive the same pay they had been getting before July 1. No man was to be discharged for his part in the walkout, except those who had destroyed railroad property. But the reinstatement of the Committee of Fifty was to be left to the discretion of the receiver and his aides.

This last point proved to be the major stumbling block. The men representing the strikers insisted that it gave too much authority to the receiver, but they finally agreed to take up the issue with the strikers and to abide by their verdict.

At six-thirty that evening, the strikers met secretly in Hornellsville and, after a heated debate, voted to reject the proposed settlement because it left unresolved the issue of reinstating the Committee of Fifty. At this point, the doors to the building were opened, and a public meeting took place. There, several businessmen, a few members of the strikers' committee, and their two attorneys joined in pleading for acceptance of the company's offer as the best that the men could hope for. They argued that the company could be expected to reinstate the Committee of Fifty if the man who had dismissed them agreed, and that discussions with this official had indicated that he would have no objection to returning them to their jobs once the strike was ended.

But several strikers spoke out against accepting this type of promise, since past experience had proved that company officials were perfectly willing to make promises during emergencies, but broke them with equal readiness as soon as the crisis was over. Since the company had already been forced to make concessions, these men maintained, why not hold out until the workers' demands were fully realized?

When it appeared that the vote would be overwhelmingly for continuation of the strike, a group of leading citizens guaranteed to provide financial support for the members of the Committee of Fifty until they could find work again. While this proposal did not lead to an immediate vote to end the strike, it did prevent the company's offer from being rejected. It was finally agreed that another conference should be held with the company in an effort to reach a satisfactory agreement.

Again, the strikers' committee visited the company's office, and was told that the Erie was willing to sign an agreement immediately on the terms set forth that afternoon, but would not go beyond those concessions. The committee returned to report to the strikers; the workers accepted the proposals, and at a quarter after twelve in the morning of July 26 the strike was declared over. The "Great Strike on the Erie" was at an end.

In addition to obtaining a promise that free passes would be restored, and an agreement that the company would not press for Donahue's prosecution, the strikers obtained a concession not listed in the written settlement. During the discussions, their representatives had informed the Erie officials that the track bosses had taken an additional 3 percent from the men's wages, making the total reduction 13 percent. Claiming that they had never heard of this vicious practice, the railroad officials promised to remedy the situation immediately, and orders to that effect went out to the track bosses right after the strikers went back to work.[30]

The compromise agreement ending the strike at Hornellsville was extended to other Erie workers. It was the first of its kind on any of the nation's major roads during the Great Strike, and it spared at least one other line—the Union Pacific—from a crippling strike. Following the Erie agreement, that company made similar concessions that kept the men from walking out.

Editorial comment on the Erie settlement stressed that it was a poor precedent for management to have compromised at all in such a confrontation. The reaction of the *Elmira Daily Advertiser* was typical.

> The terms may be all right, and they may be wise. But it looks to us like a surrender. True, the trains are again put in motion, but not through the supremacy of the law asserting itself against the will of a mob. It is because the mob, for a consideration, has given its consent that business may be resumed. It is a recognition of the idea that the mob is co-ordinate in authority over the railroad with the officers and directors. It is a premium on strikes, and invites another whenever the men imagine themselves afflicted with a grievance.
>
> This is the precise position of the Erie road today. The road is running, but it runs at the mercy of its employees, and not at the command of its officers.

As an example of how the Erie management should have dealt with the strikers, the *Elmira Daily Advertiser* pointed to William H. Vanderbilt, president of the New York Central & Hudson, and majority stockholder in its subsidiary, the Lake Shore & Michigan Southern.[31]

The strike on the Erie had spilled over in Buffalo to the New York Central and the Lake Shore, whose workers had also suffered a 10 percent wage cut and were persuaded to strike by the Erie men. The railroad workers were quickly joined by factory workers, who quit work in sympathy. The New York Central strikers placed an embargo on all freight, but announced their willingness to let passenger and mail trains proceed as usual. The Central management then proceeded to mingle passengers, mail, and freight, hoping to force the strikers to stop the entire train and thereby become liable to punishment by the federal courts for hindering passage of the mails. But the railroaders stopped the train, unhooked the engine and mail car, and sent them on.

The New York Central countered by refusing to run any trains at all. The strikers then wired the postmaster-general in

Washington, indicating their desire to let the mails go through and pointing out that they were being held up only by order of the New York Central officials. The postmaster-general asked the railroad for an explanation, and received the reply from the general superintendent of the road that not a single passenger or mail train would be run until the strikers were dispersed, order restored, and the freight blockade broken.[32]

Apparently this satisfied the postmaster-general, for not another complaint was voiced by him against the railroad. Instead, the full force of the "law and order" machinery was directed against the strikers. To break the blockade, Governor Robinson at first dispatched the entire Sixty-fifth Regiment, and Mayor Philip Becker of Buffalo swore in sixty special police. When the strikers fought back against attempts to smash their strike, Mayor Becker issued a proclamation that anyone found in the streets after ten o'clock at night would be arrested. One hundred and forty more special police were sworn in; the city council applied to Governor Robinson for more military support; the Grand Army of the Republic veterans volunteered their services; and Sheriff Joseph G. Haberstrom swore in 300 deputies. Even then, it was necessary to bring in additional military forces before the blockade could be lifted; the Forty-ninth Regiment was sent in from Auburn, the Eighth Regiment from New York, and the Seventy-fourth Regiment from Hornellsville. Governor Robinson issued a proclamation informing the strikers that on May 10, 1877, the New York legislature had passed an act stating that any person who destroyed railroad property or obstructed trains was liable to ten years' imprisonment and/or a $1,000 fine. Then, to add weight to the law, Robinson offered a $500 reward for the arrest and conviction of anyone caught violating it.

With the combined force of 1,600 militiamen, the regular and special police force, several hundred sheriff's deputies, 1,800 veterans of the Grand Army of the Republic, and three hundred citizen volunteers, the freight blockade at Buffalo began to be lifted. But before the strike on the New York Central and Lake Shore was broken, eight strikers were killed by militiamen.[33]

Meanwhile, the strike on the New York Central had moved southward to Rochester, Syracuse, and Albany (but not as far south as New York City). Up to this point, William H. Vanderbilt, of "the-public-be-damned" fame, had remained aloof from the events in Buffalo. He told the Lake Shore men, after they struck, that the 10 percent reduction would not be rescinded, "as the owners of the railroad cannot afford to let the employees manage it." "There is a great principle involved in this matter," he continued, "and we cannot afford to yield, and the country cannot afford to have us yield." Vanderbilt concluded by expressing "every confidence in the good sense and stability of a large majority of our employees," meaning, of course, the men on the New York Central line, and said that he felt that the Lake Shore men were "not equal as a class" to his own men.[34]

Despite Vanderbilt's professed faith in them, at the time he was making this little speech the New York Central workers were joining the Lake Shore men on strike in Buffalo. Ignoring this flouting of his judgment about the Central workers, Vanderbilt decided to say nothing further and leave it to the local officials to crush the strike. But he was soon compelled to break his silence. New York Central shopmen, switchmen, trackmen, and laborers in Albany met and drew up demands calling not only for the rescinding of the 10 percent cut in wages, but for an increase of 25 percent. It was impossible, they pointed out, to live on the 80 cents to $1 a day that switchmen, trackmen, and laborers earned on the New York Central, or the $1.20 a day earned by the best mechanics in the railroad's shops. The demands were forwarded to Vanderbilt at his summer home in Saratoga, New York, along with the information that if they were not met, the men would strike.

Reporters surrounded the Vanderbilt home and asked the Central president for his reaction. He released the following statement:

There is a perfect understanding between the heads of departments and the employes, and they appreciate, I think, so thoroughly the identity of interest between themselves and us that I cannot for a moment believe that they will have any part of this business. I am proud of the men of the Central Road, and my great trust in them is founded on their intelligent appreciation of the business situation at the present time. If they shall stand firm in the present crisis it will be a triumph of good sense over blind fury and fanaticism.[35]

Even as this was being published, "the identity of interest" between the New York Central and its employees in Buffalo was being demonstrated by the murder of strikers by militiamen brought in at the company's request.

When the Albany men struck as they had vowed, Vanderbilt sent them the following telegram from Saratoga: "The public interests should not suffer from any differences between the road and its employes. Keep at work until the excitement is over, and a fair conference can be held."[36]

Thereafter, Vanderbilt pursued a policy of ignoring the strike. He insisted publicly that his men were "too intelligent and grateful to strike, but that they were violently prevented from working by outsiders." He told a reporter that he was "not informed of any strike on the part of the Central employes. They had been driven out of the shops by a crowd of rioters, and had been forced to stop work." The interview continued:

Reporter—What about the demand for an increase of 25 per cent in wages?

Mr. Vanderbilt—I have received no such demand from the men of the Central. A dispatch was received last night embracing something of that sort, but I would not insult the men of the Central by attributing it to them. No such demand has been recognized. It was not signed by anybody, and I have not paid any attention to it. The shops have been visited by a mob, and my men have been forced to quit work. The desperate men who have done this are not the Central men, but probably men out of employment who would like the situations of those who are at work. They belong to the "rough" element, and have coerced the Central employes to leave the shops.[37]

To all demands for an increase in pay, Vanderbilt replied that the company was losing money and that as a result, everyone associated with it had to suffer—a "fact of life" that he was sure the intelligent New York Central workers understood. The recent heir to a ninety-million-dollar fortune declared blandly:

Our men feel that, although I may own the majority of the stock in the Central, my interests are as much affected in degree as theirs, and although I may have my millions and they the rewards of their daily toil, still we are about equal in the end. If they suffer I suffer, and if I suffer they cannot escape.[38]

Notwithstanding his refusal to recognize that there was a strike, Vanderbilt stopped all traffic until the strikers gave up (thereby ruling out the possibility of sustaining large financial losses), and also asked for troops to break the blockade. Governor Robinson called out the entire Third Division of the New York National Guard, located in Albany. Then, for good measure, he summoned the Ninth Regiment from New York City and accepted the services of a volunteer citizens' corps from Troy. By July 24, Albany had 2,248 men under arms. As in Buffalo, Governor Robinson warned the strikers of the consequences of violating the law of May 10, 1877, and here, too, he offered a reward of $500 for information about offenders.[39]

At a meeting in Capital Park, West Albany, on July 24, the strikers were addressed by John Van Hoesen, a young brakeman. Denouncing Vanderbilt for hypocrisy, he pointed out that when the workers in Buffalo had asked the Central president for bread, he had given them bullets. If that was to be his answer to the workers of Albany, he went on, then they would give bullets in return.

The very next day, Van Hoesen and other strike leaders who had shared the platform with him were arrested and jailed.[40]

On July 26, a committee of two was sent to Saratoga by the strikers for a conference with Vanderbilt. He agreed to interrupt his summer vacation to meet with the committee, but declined to discuss the wage issue, declaring that it would set a bad precedent to succumb to the men before they returned to work and perfect order was restored.[41] The committee brought this discouraging report back to Albany, and the strikers met to discuss what to do next. The outlook for a successful strike looked dim indeed. General D. P. Woods, commander of the New York Eighth Regiment, had smashed the blockade in Syracuse and Rochester, and the strike in Buffalo was being drowned in blood. Albany was surrounded by troops, and their commanding officer had vowed to open the blockade, "blood or no blood." With their leaders arrested, and with the engineers refusing to join the walkout, it did not appear that the men could hold out much longer.

A strikers' committee approached Mayor Banks and other prominent citizens for advice, and received their promise that they would send a petition to Vanderbilt for a restoration of the former wage scale. The strikers then voted to hold out until there was a response to the petition.[42]

But the petition was never sent. Instead, the following notice appeared in the New York Central's shops and depots in Albany:

The employes of this department will report for duty Monday morning, July 30, 1877, at 8 o'clock A.M. Those that do not report for duty at the time above specified will be considered as having left the service of the company, unless a good excuse or reason be given why they do not.[43]

Faced with this ultimatum, and with their resources at an end, the strikers at Albany voted to return to work and rely on Vanderbilt's magnanimity.

Similar notices appeared elsewhere along the line of the New York Central, warning the strikers to return on July 30 or face dismissal, and everywhere from Albany to Buffalo, the strikers voted to return in the hope that Vanderbilt would see the justice of their demand for the restoration of the former wage scale. By July 30, the strike on the New York Central was over. The Lake Shore men vowed never to yield, but they also ran out of money and gave up on the thirtieth.[44]

On August 1, Vanderbilt issued a lengthy bulletin from Saratoga "to the employes" of the New York Central. "We have passed through a period of unparalleled excitement, occasioned on all sides by a common enemy," he began. He was proud, however, that few of the company's workers were part of that "common enemy": "Of this company's 12,000 employes less than 500 have shown any disposition to embarrass it," the vast majority having continued at work everywhere, "except when overcome by outside violence." (It would have been more accurate to have said that the vast majority quit work and were forced back by the "outside violence" of the military.) As a reward for their "loyalty and faithfulness," Vanderbilt ordered that $100,000 be divided among the men.

But what about the 10 percent wage reduction? On this issue, he would say only that it had been "fair and equitable," since it had been applied to all who worked for the company and earned thirty dollars or more a month—including even the president of the road. He concluded: "Your pay will be increased the moment the business of the country will justify it."[45]

When the strikers in Albany had voted to return to work on July 30, they had done so with the assurance—posted in the bulletin of the New York Central—that all would be reinstated. However, on the same day that Vanderbilt issued his bulletin publicizing his gratitude to the employees of the road, newspapers carried the following dispatch:

Albany July 31. A hundred workmen were discharged from the West Albany shops of the New York Central for participating in the late disturbances there.[46]

V

The Strike on the Vandalia of Terre Haute: The Fruits of Class Harmony

Although William H. Vanderbilt preached class harmony and the identity of his interests with those of the New York Central workers, and had told the press that they shared his view, few of his workers went along with his ideas. Only at the very end, when their resources were exhausted and their chances of victory were all but nonexistent, did the New York Central strikers place themselves at the mercy of the man who preached identity of interests. However, in the case of one walkout during the Great Strike—that on the Vandalia Railroad in Indiana—it was the strikers who stressed class harmony and identity of interests, and who upheld that principle almost until the end. But, as we shall see, they suffered the same consequences as the strikers who rejected the doctrine.[1]

When Tom Scott announced the 10 percent wage reduction on the Pennsylvania in June 1877, the members of the Brotherhood of Locomotive Firemen's Vico Lodge in Terre Haute, Indiana, whose wages had been cut 23 percent between 1873 and 1876, and then another 10 percent between August 1876 and May 1877, knew that the smaller lines, including the Vandalia, for which they worked, would hasten to imitate Scott's action.[2] On June 22, a week after the strike began in the East, the firemen and brakemen in Terre Haute met in the Engineers' Hall to discuss the national and local situations. Robert Ebbage, the master of the Vico Lodge, was elected president, and, after some discussion, the men passed three resolutions to present to Riley McKeen, the Vandalia's founder and president. The first was to "respectfully request" a 15 percent increase to all employees, with a threat to strike the following morning if management failed to respond affirmatively. Second, they vowed to allow no freight cars to move until their wages were sufficient "to keep our families from actual want." Finally, the men informed McKeen that they would not use "in any shape or form intoxicating liquor in case we quit work." Eleven men, mainly firemen, signed the petition.[3]

When McKeen failed to respond the following morning, the strike began in Terre Haute at noon. In addition to the engineers and firemen, the six hundred machinists in the Vandalia repair shops also joined the strike. On Tuesday, July 24, with his employees in control of the depot and refusing to allow trains to enter or leave, McKeen informed the strike committee that he had not yet made up his mind as to what to do about their wages. He told them that since so much had occurred in the East during the past few days, he preferred to await an eastern settlement before committing himself to any set figure for his workers. On his own, either to prevent violence or to defuse the strike, McKeen himself stopped all trains, except mail cars, that originated in Terre Haute.[4]

After reading and discussing McKeen's letter, the strikers responded in a surprising way to his refusal to grant them a wage increase. They expressed "full faith" in McKeen's "honor and integrity," and in the belief that "he will do all he can to comply with our wishes." The strikers further resolved that they wanted no interference from "irresponsible parties such as tramps and roughs," that they would guard all railroad property, and asked support from "fellow citizens from all classes" to aid in "our resistance to the encroachments of capital upon unprotected labor." Arguing that the basic problem in Terre Haute, as well as nationally, was the lower freight rates, resulting from corporate "kickbacks," and that the proper response was not to lower wages but rather to raise the rates, the strikers' resolution assured the people of Terre Haute that they did not intend to instigate any permanent conflict, for "as soon as our object is attained, then this organized movement is to be abandoned."[5]

This approach brought the strikers wide community support. Daniel W. Vorhees, Indiana's Democratic senator, and Mayor H. Fairbanks of Terre Haute both endorsed the strikers' demands and urged them to remain nonviolent. A Protestant minister, the Reverend Ewell, assured them that they had the support of the entire community. A local grocer was summoned to appear before the strikers' committee to answer charges that he was opposed to the strike. He defended himself with the statement that this was a ridiculous charge, since he himself made his money through sales to the workers and it was in his interest that they receive higher wages.[6]

Asked by the *Terre Haute Express* to explain the reasons for the strike, the strike leaders replied that the problem was the monopolistic practices of the major railroad corporations, especially Tom Scott's Pennsylvania line. As Mark Miller, chairman of the strike executive committee, explained, their fight was only with the railroad corporations, and therefore they did not favor any other strikes in the city, and certainly saw no reason for a general strike.[7] Robert Nesbit, another strike leader, argued at a meeting on July 26 that the strikers should allow passenger trains already in transit to pass through Terre Haute, for

We . . . are not making war upon women and children. We are warring to break down the gigantic eastern monopoly, the Pennsylvania Road, in two words, we can put it—Tom Scott. It is not particularly upon Riley McKeen or Mr. Peddle [his superintendent] that we are warring. They, like us, are under the thumb of that road, and when they take up their thumb, they say jump.[8]

But this proposal went too far in the direction of class harmony. After communicating with other strikers in St. Louis and Effingham, Illinois, the Terre Haute workers decided not to allow any but mail trains through.[9]

The general approach of the strikers becomes understandable when it is realized that Riley McKeen's Vandalia system was one of the few important lines in the Midwest that was not owned by a large corporation. When he bought the Terre Haute & Richmond Railroad from Chauncey Rose in 1869, McKeen simultaneously obtained a charter from the Illinois Assembly to build a connecting line across the state to St. Louis. While he did not receive any financial aid from the Pennsylvania in constructing the new addition, McKeen did receive from that system a ninety-nine-year lease for the right-of-way over their part of the roadbed. As one local historian noted in commenting on McKeen's control, "The P.R.R. was napping," for such a lease was unheard of at a time when the major railroads were consolidating. McKeen retained the lease until 1893, when he sold the road to the Pennsylvania line.[10]

The railroad workers of Terre Haute believed that Riley McKeen was as much under Tom Scott's domination as they were. They accepted his argument that he could not raise wages until an eastern settlement had been reached. While some of them may have viewed this as a stalling device, the majority of the strikers believed that McKeen really wanted to help them and was thwarted only by Scott's giant monopoly.[11]

It soon became clear, however, that Riley McKeen's view of class harmony differed from that of the strikers. On Saturday, July 28, a detachment of the Third U.S. Infantry, under the command of General Benjamin Spooner, arrived at Terre Haute under orders to open the depot. Spooner was acting under the authority of Federal Judge Walter Q. Gresham.

The Great Strike had spread to Indiana on Saturday, July 21, when the men on the Pittsburgh, Fort Wayne & Chicago line stopped work in Fort Wayne. On Wednesday, Fort Wayne's factory workers also quit. A week later, the strikers gave up when the sheriff told them that the United States Army was coming. The same scene was enacted in other Indiana towns, but not in Indianapolis.

On Saturday, July 21, a large crowd collected in the State House courtyard in Indianapolis, and handbills were distributed calling for a meeting of the city's workers on Monday evening "for the purpose of sympathizing and taking action with our starving brothers in the East who are now being trampled under the feet of the railroad bondholders."[13] When Monday came, the strike had spread to the Pittsburgh, Cincinnati & St. Louis line, and then to the Cleveland, Columbus, Cincinnati & Indianapolis line, both of which ran through Indianapolis. In the afternoon, apprehensive officials moved all arms out of the United States Arsenal in Indianapolis, and fifty United States regulars who had been summoned from St. Louis moved in.[14]

Walter Quintin Gresham, then a circuit judge for the Circuit Court of the Seventh District of the United States—and therefore responsible for all the lines in his district that were in receivership—frantically wired the federal government for help. This plea was sent even before the workingmen's meeting that Monday night, which turned out to be completely peaceful.[15] But that same night, a small crowd stopped a train on the Indianapolis, Bloomington & Western line—a road in receivership. The following morning, before court convened, Gresham swore in his friends (including Benjamin Harrison, future president of the United States) as U.S. marshals, and announced that an emergency meeting would be held at noon. At that meeting, Gresham noted that the city was in the hands of a "mob," and that the sheriff, mayor, and governor were doing nothing about it. He recommended that a "Committee of Public Safety" be formed "for the preservation of peace." Thereupon, two companies were organized, comprising one hundred men each, were supplied with guns from the United States Arsenal and were placed under the command of General Daniel Macaulay.[16]

Despite Gresham's apprehensions, the strikers remained quiet on Tuesday. Fifty of them guarded their companies' property, and a strikers' committee prohibited all participants from drinking. But the trains did not move.

That evening, Gresham received word that no federal troops could be spared to help his marshals start the trains. On Wednesday, therefore, he sent an urgent appeal to President Hayes in which he announced that the situation in Indianapolis was "most critical and dangerous." "The mob is the only supreme authority," he warned, "[and] there may be an outbreak any moment."[17] No sooner was this sent off than General Spooner visited the strikers at the railroad yards and explained to them the legal issues involved in stopping trains on lines in receivership. The strikers immediately relinquished control, and thirty minutes later all such trains were on their way, manned by men who were later left unpaid for their services.[18] Meanwhile, the U.S. Signal Service in Indianapolis was sending Hayes another view of the situation: "Not the least sign of violence," reported the sergeant in charge. But Gresham carried more weight, and Hayes casually ordered in two hundred U.S. troops from the South.[19]

On Friday morning, Gresham had the leaders of the strike in Indianapolis arrested, and that evening the federal soldiers arrived from Louisville. The following morning, General Spooner departed for Vincennes via Terre Haute, with fifty regulars, to open up the lines in receivership there and to arrest the chief troublemakers. After he had passed through Terre Haute and was in Vincennes, Gresham ordered him back again to open up the Vandalia line.[20]

The Vandalia, of course, was not in receivership, but Gresham had agreed to open the line anyway, as a courtesy to Riley McKeen. On the morning the troops were scheduled to pass through Terre Haute on their way to Vincennes, McKeen announced that he would reopen his yards in the afternoon. As the troops approached Terre Haute, the strikers relinquished the depot even before they arrived. After a short stop, the troops continued on to Vincennes. The strikers met, reaffirmed their demand for a 15 percent wage increase, and told McKeen that his action that morning had "insulted" them. After the meeting, many of the men reassembled at the depot.[21]

McKeen did not respond to the latest message from his workers. Rather, with the support of many of Terre Haute's "best people," he wired Judge Gresham at Indianapolis the following request: "Engineers refuse to run our trains. I trust you will let the United States soldiers remain here for a few days. Please answer." Gresham immediately telegraphed Spooner at Vincennes, ordering him to return to Terre Haute. He suggested that the troops in Terre Haute would "have a good moral effect, and would be conveniently placed for duty at either Vincennes or Evansville." In conclusion, Gresham absolved Spooner in advance of any responsibility for violence in Terre Haute, although there had not even been a threat of violence up to that point: "If the Vandalia strikers think the troops are to operate against them, you will not be responsible for their mistake."[22]

When Spooner's troops arrived back in Terre Haute on Sunday, July 29, they found the depot again in the hands of the strikers. The general took command of a mail train staffed by master mechanics rather than by the regular engineers and, with his troops and without any violence, ran the train to Indianapolis. That same day, McKeen promised he would not discriminate against any striker. The strikers capitulated without obtaining any of their demands. At a meeting that night, the men voted to return to work the following day.

Secretary of the Navy Richard W. Thompson, a machine politician from Indiana and former chief counsel for the Terre Haute & Indianapolis Railroad (who viewed the Great Strike as "nothing more or less than French communism . . . so entirely at war with the spirit of our institutions that it must be overcome"), wrote of the outcome in Terre Haute: "McKeen stood up firmly and manfully and I regretted I was not at home to help him—or that I could not send him at least a company of my marines."[24]

McKeen's pledge of no recrimination against strikers proved as fragile as the doctrine of identity of interests. No sooner had the men returned than they were informed that some of the strikers would be suspended pending an investigation of charges against them.[25] On August 1, Mark Miller and three other strikers were arrested by order of Judge Gresham on federal charges of contempt of court. At their Indianapolis trial, Riley McKeen was the chief prosecution witness. They were sentenced to periods of from thirty days to six months.[26]

On this note, the Great Strike ended in Terre Haute. The strikers' vision of class harmony had not been able to survive the presence of federal troops!

PROCLAMATION.

St. Louis, Mo., July 25th, 1877.

FELLOW-CITIZENS : The daily press of the city—both English and German—persisting in misrepresentation of our movement in the present great struggle of our fellow-workingmen against the overbearing oppression of capitalists and monopolists,—we are compelled to issue the following in order to clear ourselves of the charges and abuses, which the daily press of St. Louis sees fit to throw upon us. Liberal thinking men may then judge, who is right and who is wrong.

As you all well know, work is very scarce now in all branches, and the compensation for work done is so little, to make it almost impossible for any man to make his bare living, and it is utterly impossible for married men to support their families. Where shall this end ? If now, during the summer season, such is the case, what shall we do next winter ? Has our government done anything for us workingmen ? We say No ! emphatically No ! Therefore, fellow-workingmen, me MUST act ourselves, unless we want starvation to stare to our faces the coming winter. There is only one way—**Help yourself!**

To this purpose a meeting was held last night at the Lucas Market, where the following resolutions were passed !

Resolved, that we, the authorized executive committee of the Workingmen's party of the United States, do not hold ourselves responsible for any act of violence which may be perpetrated during the present excitement ; but that we will do all that lies in our power to aid the authorities in keeping order and preventing acts of violence, and will do our utmost to detect and bring to punishment all guilty parties. We make an issue for our constitutional rights as American citizens—that is, the right of life, liberty and the pursuit of happiness. Our motto is, "Death to thieves, incendiaries and murderers."

Resolved, that, as every man willing to perform a use to society is entitled to a living, therefore, if our present system of production and distribution fails to provide for our wants, it then becomes the duty of the government to enact such laws as will insure equal justice to all the people of the nation.

Resolved, that, as the condition of an immense number of people now in forced idleness, and the great suffering for the necessaries of life caused by the monopoly in the hands of capitalists, appeals strongly to all industrial classes for prompt action, therefore, to avoid bloodshed or violence, we recommend a general strike of all branches of industry for eight hours as a day's work, and we call on the legislature for the immediate enactment of an eight hour law, and the enforcement of a severe penalty for its violation, and that the employment of all children under fourteen years of age be prohibited.

Resolved, that it is our purpose never to give up the strike till these propositions are enforced. **The Executive Committee.**

Mitbürger !

Da ein Theil der deutschen Presse — die „**Westliche Post**"—sich in gröbster Lüge und Gemeinheit über uns ergeht, sehen wir uns genöthigt, Euch Nachstehendes bekannt zu geben, und dann mögt Ihr als billig denkende Menschen urtheilen.

Wie Euch Allen bekannt ist, trotzdem daß wir jetzt Sommerzeit haben, die Arbeitslosigkeit allgemein, der Lohn der noch Arbeitenden aber so niedrig, daß es einem ledigen Arbeiter kaum möglich ist, sein Leben anständig zu fristen, noch viel weniger aber einem Familienvater. Wo soll das Alles noch hinaus ? Wie muß es da erst im **Winter** werden? Hat unsere Regierung schon irgend welche Schritte gethan um die herrschende Noth zu beseitigen ? — **Nein !** — Darum, Mitarbeiter, müssen wir uns selbst helfen; sonst können wir nächsten Winter in den Suppenanstalten oder als „Tramps" unseren Unterhalt suchen, während unsere Kinder in Lumpen gehen und verhungern müssen. Darum sei unsere Loosung : **Selbsthülfe!**

Um nun dieses auszuführen hat die gestern Abend am Lucas-Market stattgefundene, von mehr den Zehntausend besuchte Massenversammlung nachstehende Beschlüsse gefaßt :

„In Erwägung, daß die heutigen gesellschaftlichen Einrichtungen einer großen Masse unserer Mitmenschen nicht das Recht auf Leben erlauben, indem alle Producte und Productionsmittel von den Monopolisten mit Beschlag belegt sind, verlangen wir, daß die Regierung dahin gehende Gesetze erläßt, welche jedem Menschen das Recht auf Arbeit und mithin auf Leben garantiren.

Um daher Blutvergießen und sonstigen drohenden Vorkommnissen in unserem Lande vorzubeugen, fordern wir die Arbeiter in allen Zweigen der Industrie auf, die Arbeit einzustellen und sie nicht früher aufzunehmen, bis wir

1. einen durch das Gesetz garantirten achtstündigen Arbeitstag, und
2. das Verbot der Arbeit der Kinder unter 14 Jahren in den Fabriken—errungen.

Es sei ferner beschlossen, daß wir, als autorisirtes Executiv-Committee aller St. Louiser Sectionen der Arbeiter-Partei der Ver. Staaten, nicht verantwortlich sind für irgend welche individuelle Gewaltthätigkeiten, welche während der gegenwärtigen Aufregung verübt werden mögen, sondern daß wir nach Kräften darauf bedacht sein werden, Diebstähle, Brandstiftungen u. s. w. zu verhindern und die Verbrecher den respectiven Autoritäten zu überliefern. Wir machen dies als anerkannte Bürger zu unserer Hauptpflicht. Unser Motto ist: Tod allen Dieben, Brandstiftern und Mördern!"

Das Executiv-Committee.

VI

The Workingmen's Party of the United States

The Great Strike of 1877 occurred six years after the Paris Commune—the working class–led revolution which took power in that city on March 18, 1871, and, for the seventy-two days of its existence, established a new type of state. The news of the "Revolution of March 18" produced a wave of fear throughout the established circles in both Europe and the United States. It soon became the practice to blame the social tensions in the United States on foreign influence, and this technique was employed with increasing frequency during the economic crisis of the 1870s. During the troubles on the railroads in 1873-74, there were some references to the fact that the strikers were determined to establish a Commune in the United States. But it was in the Great Strike of 1877 that a large portion of the press came to view the outbreaks as the "long-matured concerted assertion of Communism throughout the United States."[1]

This theme did not emerge immediately. Indeed, at first even those newspapers that denounced the strike still found it possible to express sympathy for the strikers. They insisted that it was impossible to equate the situation of workers, whose entire livelihood had been threatened by the wage cuts, with that of the railroad stockholders, whose dividends may have been reduced. And they ridiculed management's defense that its salaries, too, had been cut 10 percent, along with the wages of the workingmen. As one newspaper replied:

> The officials can build palaces, the laborer can rent a hovel. The one can roll along in the bustling splendor of a four-in-hand, the other cannot hide the burnt and frost-bitten foot. These railroad authorities can afford salaries that will secure the costliest luxuries but cannot grant enough to the beggared, starving, crushed laborer and his family to meet the commonest necessities of life.[2]

Even though these newspapers urged the strikers not to resort to violence in the justifiable redress of their grievances, several added the observation that in the face of management's "arrogant impudence," violent, and even revolutionary measures might be in order. "Certainly, rebellion against lawful authority is never lawful," one paper put it, "but the principle that freed our nation from tyranny will free labor from domestic aggression."[3] The *Missouri Republican,* published in St. Louis, declared that "if the laboring men of this country must choose between revolution and abject submission to the heartless demand of capital, they will certainly not be condemned by this journal if they prefer war to starvation."[4]

But once the strike got under way, such expressions were no longer heard, and even before the great upheaval at Pittsburgh, the note of "Communism" was being injected into news and editorial columns alike. From the very outset of the strike in Martinsburg, the fear was voiced that if the "great mobs" succeeded in imposing their terms on the railroads by violence, "communism would be established in America." Thus, as early as July 19, the *Brooklyn Daily Eagle* warned that the strike was endangering American society, and that it had to be dealt with as if it were an "insurrection," and not just a "labor dispute":

It is not pleasant to think of men being mowed down by soldiers, but it will be a much worse spectacle for the country to have a mob triumphant in a state like West Virginia than to have the life blown out of men who refuse to recognize the right of every American to control his own labor and his own property. This is the nearest approach we have yet had to communism in America, and if we are to be saved from the darker horrors of that system, our authorities must act with unmistakable vigor in the present emergency.[5]

The Pittsburgh massacres were viewed by the labor press as a prime example of corporate and military brutality.[6] But the commercial press unleashed a veritable barrage of editorials blaming the events of July 22 and 23 entirely on the communists. Some newspapers bluntly accused the Pittsburgh strikers of being communists (a fact which, according to the *New York Tribune,* "does not need demonstration"[7]), and reprinted the editorial in the *Pittsburgh Leader* which concluded that "the workingman in Pittsburgh is really a communist, and there is no doubt that communistic ideas have widely spread."[8] Most papers, however, insisted that it was not the strikers themselves who were responsible for the violence in Pittsburgh and other railroad centers, but rather a group of men who were neither railroad strikers nor their sympathizers. They were the "destructionists," who had been unleashed by a powerful, secret, oath-bound central organization headed by men who saw in the Great Strike a "golden opportunity to establish the Commune in the United States":

> Secret meetings of the Communists were held at which committees and sub-committees were appointed. . . . Each committee was instructed to gather from the byways and dens and the hovels these miserables to follow the direction of these blind leaders of the blind.

The labor upheaval of 1877, therefore, was "a concentrated scheme on the part of these non-working agitators" to precipitate in the United States "a reign of disorder and pillage under cover of the railroad strike," which would "end in a Communist America."[9]

The "arch-conspirators" were sometimes referred to as the Brotherhood of Locomotive Engineers, the Knights of Labor ("probably an amalgamation of the Molly Maguires and the Commune," said one observer[10]), and more often as the "Internationalists" (the former members of the American sections of the International Workingmen's Association, the First International). But most often, the responsibility for the spread of the strike and the violence that accompanied it was placed at the doorstep of the Workingmen's Party of the United States (WPUS). According to newspaper accounts, there were party sections everywhere, and when the workers walked out, they turned to these sections for leadership: "It was said that this organization had not only money, but men with which to help the cause along." Through its sixty thousand members (the figure most commonly used), the "Communist leaders" of the Workingmen's Party took control of the uprisings, albeit behind the scenes:

> They do not appear at mass-meetings to roll out their frenzied rhetoric. . . . From the seclusion of the Star Chamber they issue their orders. . . . Like Robespierre and his brace of Fellow Conspirators, they sit in darkness and plot against the life of the nation. . . .
>
> This body, the Workingmen's Party of the United States, has manipulated this labor revolution throughout the country since its inception. Every trades-union and labor organization is infected with members of the American Commune.[11]

This characterization of the force behind the Great Strike continued to appear in the books published soon after the labor uprising. Allan Pinkerton, basing his conclusion on reports that he said had come from agents of his detective agency throughout the country, maintained that the Great Strike was the "direct result" of the activities of the Workingmen's Party of the United States. "On every railroad that was held by lawless men, in every city where violence reigned, . . . this accursed thing came to the surface," Pinkerton wrote in 1878. "If its members did not actually inaugurate the strikes, the strikes were the direct result of the communistic spirit spread through the ranks of railroad employes by communistic leaders and their teachings."[12] James A. Dacus, another contemporary historian of the Great Strike, subscribed to the same idea:

Taking advantage of the strikes of the railroad men, the "Working-men's Party of the United States" suddenly revealed itself in almost every city in the Union, not only as an element in the general disturbance, but as the prompting power in all the movements made subsequent to the transfer of the seat of the trouble from Martinsburg to the larger centers of population.[13]

This tendency to view the Great Strike as the handiwork of the Workingmen's Party of the United States persisted until at least 1937, when Ellis Paxton Oberholtzer, in the fourth volume of his *History of the United States Since the Civil War,* attributed the labor uprising to the "various agents" of the party. "Never before," he wrote, "had its hand been so clearly seen."[14]

Apart from their sinister implications, these comments about a party that was just celebrating its first birthday certainly gave it credit for an enormous amount of power and influence. But one must separate fact from fantasy in dealing with the actual role of the Workingmen's Party in the Great Strike.

The Workingmen's Party of the United States was born at a congress held in Philadelphia from July 19 to 23, 1876. It was the second Marxist party established in any country, the first having been set up in Germany in 1875. Like the Social Democratic Party of Germany, the Workingmen's Party of the United States was the result of a merger of two socialist groups—the disciples of Karl Marx and the followers of Ferdinand Lassalle.

For over a decade before the formation of the Workingmen's Party of the United States, the Marxists, led by Friedrich A.

Sorge, had made their influence felt through the American sections of the International Workingmen's Association. Through the International, they had sought to build a trade union movement that would provide the foundation for a socialist political movement and, at the same time, unite the German and other foreign-born workers with American workers in a joint struggle to improve the conditions of the working class and pave the way for a new social system.[15]

Between 1869, when Section 1 was founded in New York City, and 1871, a number of sections were organized with a total membership of five thousand. Most of them were German, but there were also Irish, Bohemian, French (exiled victims of the recently crushed Paris Commune), and American sections. The International, however, was seriously weakened by internal dissension. For one thing, middle class reformers took over Section 12 in New York City, and a struggle broke out between these elements and the Marxists. For another, the Lassallean influence began to make itself felt in the various sections, and they also came into conflict with the Marxists.

In keeping with Lassalle's ideas, his followers in the United States argued that it was impossible for workers, under capitalism, to raise their wages above the bare minimum necessary to sustain life, and that the only way for them to escape from poverty and bondage was by establishing their own cooperative enterprises and using the ballot to obtain state aid for these cooperatives. The Lassalleans entered the trade unions and sought to convert them from organizations devoted to the struggle for higher wages, shorter hours, and other improvements in the lives of workers into associations concentrating on cooperatives and on state aid to labor through the issuance of greenbacks.

The Marxists fought both the middle class reformers and the Lassalleans in the American sections of the International. In 1872, Section 12 and other American sections that were dominated by middle class reformers were expelled by the General Council in London. That same year, the headquarters of the International was moved from London to New York as Marx sought to prevent the Anarchists from taking it over. Sorge was entrusted with the responsibility for maintaining the organization until such time as it could be returned to its place of origin.[16]

Under Sorge's leadership, the Marxists in the International combatted the Lassallean effort to convert the trade unions into purely political bodies. In this, they were guided by Marx through his correspondence with their leaders. The "final object" of the workers' movement, Marx emphasized in letters to his American disciples,[17] was the "conquest of political power," but such an accomplishment required "a previous organization of the working class developed up to a certain point, which itself arises from its economic struggles." For this reason, both the "purely economic movement" of the workers (trade union efforts to force concessions directly from particular employers through strikes) and the "political movement" (such as efforts to achieve an eight-hour law) merited support, because both were "a means of developing this organization."[18]

The economic crisis of 1873 served to intensify the internal dissension within the International. While it gained prestige as the organizing center for the struggles of the unemployed, it is also true that the crisis tended to strengthen the position of the Lassalleans. Events seemed to reinforce their argument that trade unions, strikes, and unemployed demonstrations were useless, and that the only instrument for "lifting the yoke of capital" from labor was the ballot.[19]

The Marxists did not reject political action; in fact, they believed that every class struggle was a political struggle. But they held that the time was not yet ripe for the formation of a workers' party that would be strong enough to influence the elections. The trade unions, they contended, were the cradle of the labor movement, and it was the duty of the American sections of the International to both revive existing trade unions and to help in the organization of new ones. Unemployed demonstrations, far from being useless, helped secure relief for homeless and hungry families, stimulated workers to think along socialist lines, and presented opportunities to bring home to workers the message that only under socialism would exploitation of the masses cease.[20]

But the Lassalleans were confident that the situation was propitious for them to carry their policies into effect. In 1874, they left the International and established the Workingmen's Party of Illinois in the West, and the Social-Democratic Workingmen's Party of North America in the East. By February 1874, the Workingmen's Party of Illinois was publishing a weekly organ in German, *Vorbote,* edited by the Lassallean, Karl Klinge. *Vorbote* placed great stress on the fundamental Lassallean demand— state aid to cooperative societies. In keeping with Lassallean principles, it announced that the Workingmen's Party would have nothing to do with trade unionism, since "it never led to any lasting betterment for the workingmen in the several trades."[21]

The Social-Democratic Workingmen's Party of North America likewise emphasized that its object was to take "possession of political power as a prerequisite for the solution of the labor question." But within it were a number of Marxists, who constantly stressed the importance of combining trade union and political activities. As a result of their influence, the party gradually approached the ideas of the International.[22]

Events themselves also operated to heal the split between the Lassalleans and the Marxists. The Workingmen's Party of Illinois met with complete failure at the ballot-box in the 1874 elections, thereby vindicating the Marxist contention that premature political action was futile if the workers were not organized into trade unions. Applying the lessons of this experience, the advocates of trade union action in the Social-Democratic Workingmen's Party were able to increase their influence. At a party convention in 1875, a resolution was adopted asserting that "under the present conditions the organization of working people into trade unions is indispensable, and that each party member is obliged to become a member of the union of his trade, or to aid in establishing a trade union where none exists." The *Socialist,* English organ of the Social-Democratic Workingmen's Party, published in New York City, hailed the resolution and called for "the defense of the trade unions and their principles upon every occasion, in order that the reorganization of society may be speedily accomplished."[23]

In Germany, meanwhile, a reconciliation had been achieved by the Lassalleans and Marxists. At the famous Gotha Congress of 1875, they finally worked out a program acceptable to both groups. While Marx, in his *Critique of the Gotha Programme,* criticized the concessions made to the Lassalleans, the Social Democratic Party that emerged from the unity congress was primarily Marxist in orientation. The German example influenced socialists in the United States, and by the fall of 1875 socialist unity was the predominant issue in both Marxist and Lassallean circles.[24]

On April 16, 1876, at a convention held in Pittsburgh, the first real steps were taken to achieve that goal. Although it was sponsored by the Social-Democratic Workingmen's Party, it was attended by socialists of all tendencies, and out of the gathering emerged a "Declaration of Unity" which proposed a unified movement to be called the "Socialist Labor Party of the United States of North America."

The "Declaration of Unity" issued a call for a unity congress to be held in Philadelphia toward the end of July 1876, to which the Social Democratic Workingmen's Party, the International Workingmen's Association, the Workingmen's Party of Illinois, and the Social Political Laborers' Union of Cincinnati would each send one delegate for every five hundred paying members in good standing. "Immediately after the completion of the labors of said congress," the call went on, "all the societies therein represented shall enter the newly organized party."[25]

First to arrive in Philadelphia were ten delegates representing the American sections of the International Workingmen's Association. They came on July 15, 1876, and in less than a day the delegates had dissolved the once-powerful International and entrusted its archives and documents to Sorge and Karl Speyer.[26]

On July 19, the unity congress opened in Philadelphia. Seven societies sent delegates, but only four of them were considered in good standing and entitled to representation. Seven delegates were accepted: Sorge and Otto Weydemeyer from the International; Conrad A. Conzett from the Workingmen's Party of Illinois; Charles Braun from the Social Political Workingmen's Society of Cincinnati; and Adolph Strasser, Adolph Gabriel, and Peter J. McGuire from the Social Democratic Workingmen's Party of North America. These seven delegates represented approximately three thousand organized socialists in the United States—635 in the International, 593 in the Workingmen's Party of Illinois, 250 in the Social Political Workingmen's Society of Cincinnati, and 1,500 in the Social Democratic Workingmen's Party of North America.

The unity congress lasted four days and established a united socialist party, called the Workingmen's Party of the United States. (The word *socialist* in the name had been objected to in preconvention discussion on the ground that it would frighten English-speaking workers, but one commentator observed shrewdly: "In any case, we will be called communists regardless of what name we adopt,"[27] which proved to be an accurate prediction.) The platform was the result of a compromise. It adopted the trade union policies of the International, but conceded to the Lassallean request that a national instead of an international organization be established. On the key issues of political action and trade unionism, the platform said:

The political action of the party is confined generally to obtaining legislative acts in the interest of the working class proper. It will not enter into a political campaign before being strong enough to exercise a perceptible influence, and then in the first place locally in the towns or cities, when demands of purely local character may be presented, providing they are not in conflict with the platform and principles of the party.

We work for the organization of trades unions upon a national and international basis to ameliorate the condition of the working people and seek to spread therein the above principles.

The National Executive Committee, which was based in Chicago, was dominated by the Lassalleans. A further concession was made to the Lassalleans in a resolution put forward by McGuire and opposed by Sorge, Strasser, Weydemeyer, and Conzett. It empowered the executive committee to allow local sections to enter political campaigns when circumstances were considered favorable. Again over the objection of the Marxists, the platform endorsed the Lassallean principle of governmental transfer of industrial enterprises to producers' cooperatives.

The *Vorbote* in Chicago and the *Sozial-Demokrat* in New York were designated as official organs, with the latter's name being changed to *Arbeiter-Stimme.* The English-language organ of the Social Democratic Workingmen's Party of North America was also declared an official organ. Its name was changed to *Labor Standard,* and J. P. McDonnell, a Marxist, was selected as editor.

Neither the united party's Declaration of Principles nor any of the eleven specific measures proposed "as a means to improve the condition of the working class" dealt with Black Americans,[28] but a resolution was adopted dealing with women's rights. It acknowledged the "perfect equality of rights of both sexes," but said nothing about women's political rights. Instead, it emphasized that "the emancipation of women will be accomplished with the emancipation of men, and the so-called women's rights question will be solved with the labor question."[29]

By the time the unity congress closed on July 22, 1876, a unified socialist party, Marxist in orientation, had come into existence in the United States for the first time. In order not to endanger this unity, the congress made no provision for a referendum vote on the actions taken there, and the Workingmen's Party of the United States began functioning immediately. Its existence was noted in the *New York Times* of August 11, 1876, which began the process of exaggerating its strength by stating that the new party "now numbers over fifty thousand members."

It is likely that the organization had less than three thousand members at the time of its founding. But whatever its size, by the first week in August the Workingmen's Party of the United States was a functioning organization, and the *Labor Standard* expressed optimism that as its principles became known, more and more workingmen would be "falling into the ranks of the Workingmen's Party."[30]

For several months after the unity congress, the Marxists seemed confident that the opposition to trade unionism in socialist ranks had been more or less laid to rest, and that the time was ripe for a drive to bring the workers into the trade unions. The disastrous decline in membership that the unions had suffered since 1873 made the need for organizing drives more urgent than ever, and the Marxists were convinced that the Workingmen's Party of the United States had to spearhead these campaigns.[31] At a meeting of the New York American section of the party in October 1876, the Marxists, lead by J. P. McDonnell, joined forces with Adolph Strasser and several other former members of the Social Democratic Workingmen's Party of North America to adopt a resolution which read:

> Whereas trade unions are organized for the protection of the working classes against the rapacity of the employing class.
>
> Be it resolved—That we recognize the Trade Unions as a great lever by which the working class will be economically emancipated, and we consider it the duty of all the members of the W.P.U.S. to support and promote their Trade Unions.
>
> Be it further resolved that the organization of Trade Unions on a national as well as international basis is highly desirable.[32]

The former Internationalists and their supporters saw trade unionism as a necessary prelude to working class politics and expected the new party to pursue this course in accordance with the platform and principles adopted at the founding congress. But the Lassalleans, who preached political action first and foremost, were determined to ignore and eventually revise the mandate of the unity congress that political campaigns be organized only when the party was "strong enough to exercise a perceptible influence." As early as September 1876, they won an important victory when the Lassallean-dominated National Executive Committee granted the New Haven section the right to engage in electoral campaigns. With the encouragement of the executive committee, New Haven nominated a ticket in the fall election of 1876, and was speedily followed by sections in Milwaukee, Cincinnati, and Chicago—all in defiance of the official platform. When the electoral results showed that the socialist candidates in New Haven, Chicago, and Cincinnati had gained large votes, and that six socialists had been elected in Milwaukee, the Lassalleans were more determined than ever to ignore the official regulations.[33] Indeed, Peter J. McGuire, their leader, insisted that as long as the depression continued, it was pointless to try to organize the workers into trade unions or for any other type of economic activity: "As long as the times are such that the majority of the people can just barely live they will suffer on."[34]

Thus, on the eve of the great social explosion that was to disprove McGuire's thesis, the Workingmen's Party of the United States was being torn apart by the conflict between the "trade union" and "political action" socialists. In an article published in the early 1890s in *Die Neue Zeit,* the theoretical journal of the Social Democratic Party of Germany, Sorge noted that while the unity congress united the socialist movement, "no real unity reigned among the disparate elements, that is no unity which was based on conformity of principles and tactics, and thus disagreements soon broke out again."[35]

Preoccupied with internal issues, the socialists in the Workingmen's Party of the United States played no part in instigating the Great Strike. After studying the manuscript minutes of the Hoboken and Philadelphia sections, Robert V. Bruce concludes that "the members . . . showed not the slightest advance knowledge of the great labor uprising."[36] The same can be said for every other section. Certainly, the newly organized party had had little contact with railroad workers during its first year of existence. In the summer of 1876, the Cincinnati section had adopted resolutions condemning the labor policies of the Ohio & Mississippi Railroad, whose workers were on strike, and had urged the revocation of its charter. The section had forwarded the resolutions to the strikers, but after the Lassalleans took control, it became so involved in political campaigning that it failed to follow up these contacts. When the great upheaval of 1877 started, only one member of the Workingmen's Party appears to have had any close contacts with the railroad workers—Harry Eastman, a machinist in East St. Louis.[37]

Nevertheless, as we shall now see, once the strikes got under way, the Workingmen's Party of the United States did become deeply involved in the titanic struggle, and in at least one key center, took over its leadership.[38]

VII

The WPUS and the Great Strike, I: New York City, Louisville, and Cincinnati

On Saturday, July 22, the Chicago-based National Executive Committee of the Workingmen's Party of the United States met, and decided to issue an appeal calling upon all workingmen to assist the strikers "in the warfare which they are now waging in defense of justice and equal rights." A subcommittee was appointed to draft the appeal. Meanwhile, a telegram was sent to President P. M. Arthur, head of the Brotherhood of Locomotive Engineers, pledging the assistance of the WPUS to his union.[1] That same afternoon, the NEC issued a communiqué to all sections, supporting the strikers and advancing demands for the eight-hour workday and for the nationalization of the railroads and telegraph lines. In view of the fantasies surrounding the party's activities before and during the Great Strike, it is worth reprinting this document in its entirety:

A CIRCULAR.

To all sections of the Workingmen's Party of the United States: COMRADES—In the desperate struggle for existence now being maintained by the workingmen of the great railroads through the land we expect that every member will render all possible moral and substantial assistance to our brethren in misfortune, and support all reasonable measures which may be found necessary by them.

(Signed)
THE EXECUTIVE COMMITTEE
PHILIP VAN PATTEN, Corresponding Secretary

To all labor organizations and working men in general:

Comrades, we call your attention to the following questions, believing that the measures suggested will, if adopted, soon solve the difficulty now pending on all the great railroad lines of the land:

1. Proper steps should be taken by the National Government to enable it to take possession of and operate all the railroads and telegraph lines in the country, as is now done in all of the most advanced countries of

Europe, thus destroying the greatest and most powerful monopolies of modern times.

2. The establishment in every State and by the National Government of an eight-hour work day, thus absorbing all the idle workmen whose ever-increasing number constantly added to by the rigid introduction of labor-saving machinery, is a constant menace to all those fortunate enough to have employment, and must inevitably reduce wages to a rate consistent with the standard of living of the most ignorant and uneducated workers, whose labor can be utilized.

> (Signed)
> EXECUTIVE COMMITTEE
> Workingmen's Party of the United States.
> VAN PATTEN, Corresponding Secretary[2]

Thus, a week after the strike got under way, the National Executive Committee was plainly seeking to provide organizational leadership and a program for the developing strike movement. But after issuing the first communiqué, it was unable to give cohesion to the strikes in a score of local communities. Members of the NEC became preoccupied with events in Chicago. Consequently, the party section in each city was left on its own, and its role in the Great Strike varied from city to city. One thing, however, was constant: in no city did the Workingmen's Party of the United States advocate armed insurrection, and everywhere its influence on the 1877 strikes was a moderating one.

In some cities, the party exercised no influence at all. With less than 4,500 members, many of whom could hardly speak English,[3] and with sections in only certain urban centers, the party played no role whatsoever in the strikes in Martinsburg and other parts of West Virginia; in Baltimore and other areas of Maryland; in Hornellsville and Buffalo, New York, or in Terre Haute and Indianapolis, Indiana. Even in Pittsburgh, where editorials and articles charged that the events of July 22 and 23 were the result of the party's work, the WPUS appears to have exercised no influence. Not a single Pittsburgh paper mentioned the presence of one member of the party among the strikers or "the mob" in general. A study of the more than one thousand pages of the *Report of the Committee Appointed to Investigate the Railroad Riots in July, 1877,* the Pennsylvania legislature's inquiry into the Great Strike in the commonwealth, does not reveal a single reference to the influence of the Workingmen's Party in the strikes in Pittsburgh, Reading, Harrisburg, Allegheny City, Allentown, Scranton, or the other Pennsylvania centers. It is also significant that in his survey of the origins and development of the Great Strike, J. P. McDonnell, editor of the party's leading English-language organ, *Labor Standard,* not only denied that the labor uprising in any railroad center was organized by its members, but did not list a single party meeting in support of the strikers in West Virginia, Maryland, Indiana, Hornellsville, Buffalo, Rochester, Syracuse, Albany, Pittsburgh, Reading, or Scranton.[4]

In some cities, the WPUS confined itself to a single meeting expressing sympathy with the strikers. In San Francisco, the leaders of the party were able to hold a meeting on July 23 on the sandlots in front of the city hall "To Sympathize With the Strikers in the East," but only after they had promised that there would be neither threats of violence nor incendiary language. The meeting was addressed by party organizer James d'Arcy, D. J. H. Swain, Mrs. Laura Hendricks, and others. They denounced the railroads and voiced support for the eastern railway strikers. Resolutions were adopted expressing sympathy for the strikers, attacking the evils of "watered stock," opposing the granting of franchises, land, and money subsidies to private parties, deprecating the encroachment of capital on the rights and privileges of the people, and demanding immediate action by the state and federal governments to provide public works for the unemployed.

When the huge sandlot meeting, which was attended by at least eight thousand people, erupted into anti-Chinese violence which led to several days of attacks on the Chinese sections of the city, the two local sections of the WPUS canceled all future meetings and issued a circular that read: "Citizens and comrades: Our cause lives only through law, order and good government." The party applauded the Committee of Safety that was formed by businessmen to combat the anti-Chinese rioters.[5]

In Boston, Paterson, and Newark, the WPUS sections held one rally of sympathy with the strikers, expressed their opposition to lawlessness, and condemned the use of "military power." Before adjourning, the Boston meeting also endorsed the program outlined in Van Patten's communiqué, calling for the eight-hour day and the nationalization of the railroads.[6] The sections in Philadelphia called several meetings, but Mayor William S. Stokley, overlooking the fact that the act of the Pennsylvania legislature of May 13, 1850 (on which he based his action), did not authorize either the banning or dispersal of peaceful assemblies, invoked the act to ban public gatherings altogether. He also acted without legal authority to double the police force by adding 1,200 men. (The mayor's sole authority for this action came from a Committee of Safety, made up of 200 citizens, mainly businessmen, which he had appointed.) Thus, when large groups of workers attempted to meet under the auspices of the Workingmen's Party, the police charged the gathering and broke it up. Police arrested Workingmen's Party leader Joseph Steiner on a charge of inciting to riot when he persisted in an attempt to address the peaceful assembly. They then confiscated all copies of the *Labor Standard,* which listed meetings scheduled by the Workingmen's Party in Philadelphia by specific dates and times.

When the party again attempted to hold a meeting, the police once more moved in and broke it up. This time, William McBride, a young worker, was killed by a police bullet in the back of his head. After this tragedy, the Workingmen's Party again tried to hold a meeting, and this time they took the precaution of presenting the resolutions to be presented at a meeting to the mayor. These upheld the strikers, but objected strenuously to the "wanton destruction of property" and promised to use only "honorable and lawful means" in support of the strike. However, once again the meeting was banned. A committee was dispatched to Mayor Stokley to demand that he uphold the right of peaceable assembly. The mayor responded that there would be no meetings permitted "for the present." With that, the Philadelphia sections of the Workingmen's Party gave up and announced that they would concentrate instead on organizing workers into trade unions.[7]

Only one Philadelphia paper, the *Record,* condemned Mayor Stokley's autocratic conduct, and asked if the mayor had decided to make himself "king of the city." A Philadelphia worker was more vehement in his criticism. Writing in the *Labor Standard,* he complained: "We—the *free* men of the great Republic, who habitually boasted of the freedom of our land are here at once brought to the condition of the European." None of the critics pointed out that Philadelphia was the largest stockholder of the Pennsylvania Railroad Company; that Mayor Stokley regularly served as chairman of the annual meetings of stockholders, and that he and the other leading city officials had "strong *financial* reasons" for wanting the strike speedily crushed and all strike sympathizers silenced.[8]

In New York City, on Wednesday, July 25, red flags were flying on the Bowery; and that night, in the glare of hundreds of torches, a crowd of some twenty thousand listened to socialist orators at a meeting sponsored by the Workingmen's Party. Only at the last minute did the party get permission to hold its assemblage at Tompkins Square, scene of the brutal 1874 police attack on men, women, and children gathered at an unemployed demonstration. When Justus Schwab (himself a victim of the 1874 attack) applied to the park commissioner on July 23 for permission to hold the meeting, the commissioner indicated his clear displeasure. "You mustn't make such a disturbance as you made there in 1874," said the commissioner. "Mr. Commissioner," Schwab shot back, "[that] *you* made in 1874." After conferring with municipal authorities, the commissioner and Mayor Ely granted the party's request, and the meeting was scheduled for Wednesday evening, July 25.[9]

City authorities immediately took measures to prevent "another Pittsburgh."[10] All police leaves were canceled, and the First and Second divisions of the New York National Guard were called out. Tompkins Square was connected to the armories by telegraph wires; the New York Central's roundhouse and depot were garrisoned; two Gatling guns were placed at the heads of Wall and Pine streets, and seventy-five volunteers were mustered to protect the United States Subtreasury building. Finally, on Wednesday afternoon, two hundred policemen were assigned to the meeting, six hundred were put on reserve nearby, and over a thousand sailors and marines were held ready. It was estimated that 8,000 rifles and 1,200 clubs stood ready to put down a "Communist riot."[11] All day long, telegrams had been pouring into the city from mayors and governors who were worried that a large riot in New York would start more difficulties in their own areas, and who pleaded with Mayor Ely to call off the meeting. But Ely stuck doggedly to his decision. "The Dreaded Assemblage" took place, but not the expected riot.[12]

Not that the crowd was not angry. The previous Sunday, Reverend Henry Ward Beecher, speaking before his wealthy Brooklyn congregation, had infuriated the workingmen of New York City when he asked, "Is the working class oppressed?" and replied, "Yes, undoubtedly it is." Nevertheless, he went on:

God has intended the great to be great and the little to be little. . . . The trade union, originated under the European system, destroys liberty. . . . I do not say that a dollar a day is enough to support a man and five children if he insists on smoking and drinking beer. . . . But the man who cannot live on bread and water is not fit to live.[13]

John Swinton, editorial writer for the *New York Sun* and labor champion, who had led the protests against the 1874 Tompkins Square outrage,[14] opened the meeting with a biting attack on the Brooklyn preacher:

It gives me great pleasure in gazing upon this immense multitude to be able to say you don't look like a mob of rioters; that, on the contrary, it seems to me that you are quite as good-looking, in my opinion, as Henry Ward Beecher's church, for instance.

It was more than a little presumptuous, Swinton continued, for a man like Beecher, who earned at least $30,000 a year, to advise workingmen to be satisfied with a dollar a day and a diet of "bread and water." Of course, it was not a diet Beecher recommended to everyone: "The rich should have bread and meat and wine, but the workingmen should have bread and water."[15]

Turning to the issue that had brought the vast audience together, Swinton praised the Pennsylvania Sixteenth Regiment for refusing to fire on the strikers at Reading:

Glory, gentlemen! Glory to the militiamen who refused to fire on these men! (*Cheers.*) Glory, glory to that brave regiment. (*Cheers.*) Glory to the 16th Pennsylvania! (*Cheers.*) Let us send the echo of these cheers to Pennsylvania, and to that 16th Regiment, and let them know that a hundred thousand stalwart voices in New York were raised in acclaim of glory on such patriotism, and honor, and courage.[16]

After this, Leander Thompson, secretary of the New York section, read the resolutions submitted by the Workingmen's Party with regard to the Great Strike (which the *New York Times* somewhat disappointedly described as "only half as inflammatory as it was anticipated they would be").[17] They expressed the "heartfelt sympathy" of the workingmen of New York with the "railroad men on strike in different localities of the country," denounced all corporations as "the most despotic enemies of the working classes," urged the working class of the country to unite in their own political party as soon as possible in order to emancipate themselves, and concluded with the assertion that while the Workingmen's Party of the United States stood for law and order, once in power, it would confiscate the wealth of the corporations for the benefit of the workers.[18]

Then an address to President Hayes was read, pointing out that three million of the "bone and sinew of the country" were "wandering vagabonds," while "a large portion" of those employed were "on the verge of starvation." Yet all the government had thus far been able to offer these unfortunate Americans was "the hangman's rope and the soldier's bullet." The calling out of troops in the struggle between the railroad workers and miners and the corporations, it declared, was a foolhardy blunder, since it showed the working classes that their government served only the interests of the corporations. The address went on to note that although the government was supposedly committed to a *laissez faire* policy, it had consistently legislated in behalf of capital and ignored labor. This was the primary cause of the Great Strike, and the only way to prevent future outbreaks like it was to seize control of the nation's transportation and communication system and its banks. Unless the trend in favor of capital was halted, the nation would face a revolution of the "white wage slaves of the North" which would cost the Republic "more blood and treasure than ever the emancipation of the black chattel slaves of the South did. . . ." It was up to President Hayes, the address concluded, to prevent this awful calamity by proving that the government understood that "the prosperity and perpetuity of this nation rests upon the principle of justice to labor."[19]

After the resolutions and the address to the president had been approved, Thompson launched into a long attack on corruption in government circles. He charged that such corruption was inherent in the political structure of the United States government and referred sarcastically to Hayes's current civil service reform as a mere change of officers that would not end the "boodling." He recommended that the United States transform itself into a socialist state and thereby eliminate class inequalities.[20]

After a series of speeches in German at a separate stand, in which the substance of the proceedings was repeated, the meeting broke up quietly. On their way home, many members of the audience were repeatedly attacked by the police, who had apparently been spoiling for a fight.[21]

The fact that there had been no mention in any of the speeches at the meeting or in the resolutions and address to President Hayes of either trade unionism or the need for workers to organize more effectively on the economic front stirred the Marxists in the New York section of the Workingmen's Party to call another mass meeting the following night to voice the sympathy of the trade unions for the strikers. Present on the platform when the Cooper Union meeting got under way were delegates representing the custom tailors, ladies' shoemakers, bootmakers, cabinetmakers, carvers, cigarmakers, fresco painters, and the typographical unions. The chief speaker of the evening was J. P. McDonnell, Marxist editor of the *Labor Standard.* He pointed out that since the onset of the panic in 1873, American workers had been engaged "in a sort of guerrilla warfare for their rights" in order to survive, and yet had been unable to avoid being reduced to "the verge of starvation." Still, he contended, these struggles were not in vain, for they had "culminated in the present revolt against oppression," and no matter how quickly the Great Strike would end, and regardless of the final outcome, it would "leave marks behind that will never be forgotten." It revealed, for example, the identity of interests of workers throughout the nation. Workers in every city, town, and village now saw that "they could not live in decency"; and, without prearrangement, they had "resolved to make a determined stand against their oppressions." The Workingmen's Party of the United States had had nothing to do with initiating or spreading the labor uprising: "There was no concert of action at the start. It spread because the workmen of Pittsburgh felt the same oppression that was felt by the workmen of West Virginia and so with the workmen of Chicago and St. Louis." It was, in short, a spontaneous uprising against oppression, without careful premeditation or organization.

Then again, McDonnell went on, the Great Strike had revealed in one fell swoop that all obstacles to working class unity could vanish in the crucible of the class struggle:

It was a grand sight to see in West Virginia, white and colored men standing together, men of all nationalities in one supreme contest for the common rights of workingmen. (*Loud cheers.*) The barriers of ignorance and prejudice were fast falling before the growing intelligence of the masses. Hereafter there shall be no north, no south, no east, no west, only one land of labor and the workingmen must own and possess it. (*Tremendous applause.*)

But, he insisted, unity and militancy were not enough: "We must organize. Unorganized we are a mob and rabble; organized in one compact body we are a power to be respected. (*Cheers.*)" And if the workers permitted themselves to be fleeced by the employers, it was their own fault:

You have neglected your unions and allowed yourselves to be led by the nose by every swindling politician. (*Applause.*) You are sheep without a shepherd. Union is your shepherd. Union thorough and complete—if you had that, do you think that one man could by nod of his head sentence you and your families to starvation? All this could be done without shedding a drop of blood or burning one depot. It is only the desperation of madness that prompts such acts, but it is justifiable because human nature cannot lie down to die. (*Applause and cheers.*) Do not be rash; you have no power because you have no organization. This you can do, you men of different trades—join under the banner of your trade unions and become one powerful national federation. Then you can do something; then you can become a power that no one can afford to despise.

Adolph Strasser, of both the Workingmen's Party and the Cigarmakers' Union, echoed McDonnell's advice in German. "Fellow workingmen," he pleaded to great applause, "organize yourself, organize your trade unions, form a state central committee and a national union of all trade unions, and we shall be able successfully to resist the tyrannical capitalists." The resolutions, unanimously adopted, stressed the same theme. After voicing a "strong protest against the manner in which the militia have been used against the people," and offering "fraternal greeting to the volunteer soldiers who fraternized with their fellow workmen," expressing "sincere sympathy with the railroad men and others who are now on strike," and pledging "to use every effort to render financial aid not only to the men on strike but to those work-people who have suffered by it," the resolutions concluded:

That it is the imperative duty of all workingmen to organize in trade unions and to aid in establishing a National Federation of all trades so that combined Capital can be successfully resisted and overcome.[22]

Thus, while both wings of the Workingmen's Party in New York had spoken out in support of the strikers, each offered a different solution for the problems facing American workers. The Lassalleans called for immediate political action of labor while the Marxists urged the rebuilding of the trade unions, organization of new unions, and the establishment of a powerful national federation of trade unions. Having expressed these views, the New York City sections of the Workingmen's Party ceased their activity with respect to the strike for its duration.

On July 1, the Louisville & Nashville Railroad began cutting wages 10 percent. When this was accepted without a strike, the Louisville, Cincinnati & Lexington Railroad, commonly known as the "Short Line," announced a similar 10 percent wage reduction to take effect on August 1. Even this did not disturb the *Louisville Courier-Journal*, which predicted that while disorders were the rule elsewhere, the working class of Louisville was too wise to wage war against their bread providers. But the paper soon had to swallow its words. On Sunday, July 22, informal groups of railroad workers began meeting to discuss their problems, and the next day a committee of Louisville Short Line employees was formed. Since John MacLeod, receiver for the line, was out of town and could not be contacted, the committee called on Chancellor H. W. Bruce at Chancery Court and requested that he rescind the wage cut order. Bruce acceded to their request.

That same evening, the railroad workers of the Louisville & Nashville line, except for the firemen and engineers, met at the Falls City Hall. They appointed a committee to meet the next day with Dr. E. D. Sandiford, president of the Louisville & Nashville, and to present three demands: (1) all laboring men should receive a minimum of $1.50 per day; (2) all brakemen and switchmen should receive $2.00 per day; and (3) all other employees should have their pre-July 1 wages restored to them. The committee was instructed to inform Dr. Sandiford that he would have until 5 p.m. that day to answer; if the demands were refused, the Louisville & Nashville workers would quit.[23]

On the morning of July 24, the committee visited Dr. Sandiford and were told that even though they did not represent the engineers and firemen, he would restore the wages in existence prior to July 1.[24] The news of this concession stirred other workers in Louisville, including, in the words of the *Courier-Journal* reporter, some "idle negroes," led by "a strange one from Cincinnati" called "Buffalo Bill." They made the rounds of sewer construction projects and "induced" the men working on the sewers to strike for $1.50 per day instead of the prevailing $1.00. The Black sewer workers joined the demonstrators. The *Courier-*

Journal stressed the fact that few whites were among the demonstrators, and described the sewer strikers as "half-dressed, dirty-looking persons, evidently belonging to the worst class of colored men, . . . armed with jacks, shovels, and some with pieces of wood and sticks."[25] Later, Allan Pinkerton also emphasized the predominance of Blacks among the demonstrators, adding the gratuitous slur that anyone understanding the "mercurial nature of that childish and ignorant race" should know that Blacks require "but the veriest trifle to stimulate them into making a show of themselves."[26]

At around noon, the striking sewer workers reached the waterworks project at Crescent Hill, where about 370 men were employed at wages ranging from $1.00 to $1.28 per day. There the strikers announced that the men would not be allowed to continue to work until their wages were raised to $1.50 per day. Workers stopped what they were doing, and a number joined the ranks of the marchers. From the waterworks, the group marched to the center of the city, dwindling in size to about fifty persons, and by 4:30 p.m. they dispersed.[27]

While the strikers were making the rounds of the sewer construction projects, Mayor Charles D. Jacob issued a proclamation to the Louisville workingmen, admonishing them to preserve order, not to listen to any "incendiary language," and "to heed not the talk of idle and worthless creatures who, unwilling to work themselves, would gladly get you in trouble, that they may feast upon your misfortune." He claimed that in other cities, it had been "vagrants and tramps" who had caused the trouble, while the "poor workingmen" had to bear the "burden of the outbreak."[28]

During the afternoon, a number of leading citizens met at the request of Mayor Jacob and Police Chief Colonel Isaac W. Edwards and organized themselves to defend the city from any attack. City Hall was converted into a virtual fortress, and a detachment of several hundred men was dispatched to pick up arms and ammunition from the Frankfort Arsenal.

That evening, following a meeting in front of the courthouse during which Mayor Jacob was shouted down when he tried to read his proclamation, a procession was formed, and an estimated six hundred persons, prominent among whom were the Black sewer workers, headed for the railroad depot. With stones that lay at hand near street excavations, the paraders shattered street lamps, one by one, broke windows in the homes of wealthy residents, and smashed the windows at the freight depot of the Louisville & Nashville Railroad. At the depot, a police contingent, with some difficulty, arrested two white men and one Black, who were accused of being the leaders. But the remaining paraders proceeded up Broadway, "yelling like fiends," and continued to break the windows of homes of the wealthy. When the crowd reached the Short Line depot, fifty armed police opened fire, and the crowd dispersed. By midnight, the streets were quiet. Seven hundred militiamen, many of them "influential and wealthy citizens," were on duty to assist the 175 policemen.[29]

The Workingmen's Party of the United States in Louisville had played no part whatsoever in the demonstration. While the crowds were parading through the streets, its English and German sections met jointly, appointed a committee to canvass every ward of the city to raise funds for the benefit of the strikers, and adopted resolutions expressing "deep regret of the recent vast destruction of property at Pittsburgh," but proclaiming the "necessity of workingmen all over this land taking a positive and emphatic stand for the rights of the laboring class of mankind." While fully supporting the striking railroad workers and urging a "restoration of the ten per cent, recently cut off their pay," the Workingmen's Party of Louisville expressed itself as "unfavorable to strikes," and as convinced that "the ballot-box is the medium between us and capital." It cordially invited "all workingmen to join in the Workingmen's Party of the United States":

Let us present one unbroken front, we with our ballots and the capitalists with their dollars, and if we are true to ourselves victory will perch upon our banners.

The *Louisville Courier-Journal* reported the proceedings with some surprise: "The meeting was very quiet and orderly, and the feeling, though earnest and decided, was not in the least violent or incendiary."[30]

In spite of this, Mayor Jacob failed to include the Workingmen's Party in a proclamation he issued at 2:20 a.m. on July 25, praising all who had not joined the "brutal, cowardly mob," and especially commending the veteran soldiers, men who had "adorned the Blue and honored the Gray," for subduing these "creatures" who were "brutes lower than those of the animal creation."[31] On the morning of the twenty-fifth, the mayor sent a telegram to Governor James B. McCreary, requesting additional men, ammunition, and guns, and the governor responded by sending several hundred rifles by special train. In addition, four hundred troops were ordered to proceed to Louisville to afford protection against further disorders.[32]

That Wednesday, the wildest excitement prevailed in Louisville. Striking laborers marched through the city, and business was completely suspended. With over a thousand men enrolled in the militia, the mayor anxiously awaited the arrival of United States troops. The police angrily denied the charge that they had fired only blank cartridges at the mob on the previous night, asserting that live ammunition had been used and that, in fact, several workers had been wounded. At the Short Line and the Louisville & Nashville Railroad, workers, with arms in hand, were guarding the railroad property.

At just about this time, young Louis Brandeis, recently graduated from Harvard Law School, returned from a party with his brother and found that the large front window of his family home had been smashed. The businessmen of Louisville held a long meeting to consider what should be done, and the Brandeis brothers joined the militia and patrolled the streets.[33]

"All's Well," the *Courier-Journal* reported, as it hailed the armed citizens who had patrolled the city, and wrote almost poetically:

The silver moon is shining with luminous serenity upon homes peaceful and secure, while the only sounds that break upon the midsummer night air are the steady tramp of the patrol and the occasional hoof-clatter of the mounted guard.[34]

The Workingmen's Party of Louisville was totally uninvolved in any of the exciting events of July 25 and 26. The English section actually condemned the "lawlessness" of the "mob" when it applied for permission from Mayor Jacob to hold a meeting in Phoenix Hall Park. It even cited as evidence of its noninvolvement in the "mob's activities," the fact that the windows of the home of M. J. Nolan, secretary of the section, had been smashed, along with those of the wealthy residents. The permission was granted, and the English section of the Louisville WPUS did hold a meeting on July 27, at which the speakers stressed that the party "deprecated the spirit of violence which had manifested itself all over the country," and which had "made itself felt even in our own city"; that it opposed "riots and mob violence," and counseled "moderation and peace in resistance to the oppression of capital." More than that, the party urged the workingmen to develop a "feeling of reciprocity with the capitalist, consistent with their interests and their dignity as men and citizens" (whatever that meant). It also announced that it rejected strikes, and instead "urged the necessity of finding a remedy for all evils at the ballot box."[36]

It was here that one of the instances of the fact and fantasy surrounding the Workingmen's Party manifested itself. Although the *Louisville Courier-Journal* published the remarks of the speakers quoted above, it nevertheless denounced them editorially as "the enemies of organized society," and blamed the riots in Louisville on the "spirit of communism" spread by the local members of the WPUS. The paper then called upon the authorities to ban the party:

It is utterly repugnant to the spirit of our institutions. It will, if allowed to grow, prove a menace to our city in the future. Hence the first development of its destructive tendencies cannot be too promptly and severely dealt with.[37]

Other voices, however, argued that it was best to allow the Workingmen's Party to lead the working class struggle at the ballot box, as it proposed to do, and predicted that it would get nowhere. However, as we shall see, these people were in for a rude political awakening in the August elections for the Kentucky legislature.[38]

The headline in the *Cincinnati Enquirer* of July 23, 1877, read: "THE RED FLAG. IT CASTS ITS UGLY SHADOW OVER OUR QUEENLY CITY."

On the day before, the *Enquirer* had carried the following notice inserted by the Workingmen's Party of Cincinnati:

GREAT MASS-MEETING
THIS AFTERNOON
At 2 o'clock at the Court Street Market Place.
All Good Citizens Are Invited to Appear.
Subject,
THE GREAT STRIKE OF THE RAILROAD MEN.

That morning, Cincinnati workers had read the news of the massacre in Pittsburgh and of the crowd's angry attacks on the

Philadelphia soldiers. They drifted out of their houses to talk about the subject on the streets. At two in the afternoon, many fell in behind members of the German, Bohemian, and English-speaking sections of the Workingmen's Party, led by the Eureka Brass Band—headed by a man carrying "the blood-red flag of the Commune."[39] An "immense crowd," estimated in the thousands, filled the market place and was divided into four sections—two for the German-speaking contingent and two for the English. On the English side, Charles Thompson, the Workingmen's Party candidate for mayor, led off by emphasizing that if the strike reached Cincinnati, as it was bound to, since the railroad workers there had also had their wages cut 10 percent, all labor would support it, "for it was a law that whenever a reduction was made in the wages of one class of laborers, it was speedily followed by a reduction in others, and so all workingmen are concerned in seeing that the strikers succeeded in obtaining their rights." Furthermore, if, when the strike did come to Cincinnati, the authorities took possession of the depots and roundhouses to prevent the trains from being moved, and promised not to call out the militia, the Workingmen's Party would pledge that "it would support them in efforts to protect property and preserve law and order." Naturally, mail trains would be allowed to go through, but no freight or passenger trains.

C. M. Sawyer, the next speaker, blamed the Great Strike on the "wages system under which we are compelled to beg for employment from those who own the instruments of production." He predicted that such strikes would continue "with increasing bitterness" until this "dependent relationship" was abolished, and a system of "government control" substituted. Finally, he wanted it understood that while extending sympathy to the strikers, the Workingmen's Party of Cincinnati was convinced "that no permanent relief came from strikes, but only through the ballot-box." W. C. Haynes followed, and endorsed this last statement, adding that there was only one party the laboring men could trust, and that was the Workingmen's Party: "It is for the workingmen now and forever."

Resolutions were then presented and adopted. They charged the Baltimore & Ohio Railroad Company "and similar monopolies" with having reduced the wages of their employees "to a starvation point, and thereby forced them to desperate measures in order to better their condition"; condemned the governors of West Virginia, Pennsylvania, and Maryland, and President

Hayes, for using the military powers "in favor of said monopolies, regardless of the will of the people, and against the people, slaughtering innocent men, women, and children," and concluded by pledging to "use all *lawful* means to support the downtrodden, outraged railroad employees now on strike."[40]

Then came the key speech of the afternoon, which was delivered by Peter H. Clark, Black member of the English-speaking section.[41] He condemned the railroad companies and their political allies, denounced the slaughter of workers by federal troops and state militia, and analyzed at some length the causes of the economic crisis and its impact on the working class. "I sympathize in this struggle with the strikers," he declared, "and I feel sure that in this I have the cooperation of nine-tenths of my fellow citizens." But sympathy, he said, was not enough. It was necessary to create a society in which the widespread suffering that provoked the strike would be eliminated. "Every railroad in the land should be owned or controlled by the government. The title of private owners should be extinguished, and the ownership vested in the people." And this was only the beginning. Machinery—indeed all the means of production—had to be appropriated and used for the benefit of the people and not for private gain. There was only one "remedy for the evils of society"—socialism. "Choose ye this day which course ye shall pursue," Clark concluded to thunderous applause.[42]

The *Cincinnati Commercial,* which published Clark's speech in full under the heading, "Socialism: The Remedy for the Evils of Society," reported that he was "well received." *The Emancipator,* official organ of the Workingmen's Party of Cincinnati, said that his speech was "characterized by that deep pathos of feeling that is to be expected of one who can look back at the time when the wrong and injustice of capital abused his race, which by its labors and sorrows helped to build the greatness of this nation."[43] Clark's speech to the railroad strikers was probably the first widely publicized proposal for socialism by a Black American.

Although the *Cincinnati Commerical* had published Clark's speech, it made it clear that it did not agree with him. "Mr. Peter H. Clark," it noted editorially, "can not understand why it is that the military are always against the strikers. It ought not to be a great mystery to a man of his analytic powers." According to the newspaper, a worker had the right to leave his employment if he was not satisfied with his wages, but he had no right to take possession of his employer's property and dictate to him what he should or should not do. The employer had a perfect right to appeal for protection, and, if the sheriff could not provide it, the governor of the state was thoroughly justified in calling out the militia. The worker, having "done an unlawful thing," had "put himself outside the law, defied the civil authority, and has made himself penally liable." That was all there was to it. "It seems to us," it concluded, "if Mr. Clark would give his mind to the subject for a few hours he would be able to discover why it is that the military are in such crisis as the present on the side of law and order."[44]

Clark, however, was not persuaded. In "A Plea for the Strikers," he reminded the newspaper that he had experienced enough of what it meant to be poor to understand the meaning of the words in Ecclesiastes: "I beheld the tears of such as were oppressed and they had no comforter." "With this fact imprinted on my memory by many years' sympathy with and service in unpopular causes, I do not marvel when I see the oppression of the poor, and violent perverting of judgment and justice." As for himself, he was "in every fiber and nerve a law-abiding citizen," one, indeed, who deprecated "violent words and violent deeds as much as any one can. I am, sir, emphatically a law-and-order man." But not all the violent deeds and words "are on the part of the strikers and their friends." The advocates of "law and order" boasted openly that they were prepared to "wipe out the strikers and their sympathizers. Thumbs have been drawn significantly across the throats, and law-and-order men have pulled at imaginary ropes to give me an inkling of the throat-cuttings and hangings in reserve." The press, Clark pointed out, had no words of condemnation for such conduct. But the workers could hardly be blamed if they took such threats seriously and also took steps to defend themselves. Nor should the reaction of the workers to what they saw about them on the railroads be considered surprising. They were told that wages must be reduced because the railroads were losing money:

But when they see high railroad officials receiving the salaries of princes, when they hear of dividends on stock and interest on bonds, they cannot understand why there is no money for the man whose labors earn these vast sums. . . . When they complain, they are told that they are at liberty to quit and take their services elsewhere. This is equivalent to telling them that they are at liberty to go and starve. . . . Hence they make the effort to obtain an increase of wages and to retain their places at the same time. Understanding their motive, and the dire necessity by which they are driven, I pity, but I can not condemn them. . . .

Then too, the door of justice seemed shut in their faces. They have no representation on the Board of Directors. Every State has laws punishing conspiracy, punishing riot and unlawful assemblages, but no State has laws providing for the examination and redress of the grievances of which these men complain. The whole force of the State and National Governments may be invoked by the railroad managers, but the laborer has nothing.

Clark declared that every man possessed the right to resist injustice, and that no laws could take it away from him. "Hedged in and despairing, the railroad men have exercised this right," yet, as the newspapers could attest, "the strikers themselves, are neither destructive nor men of blood."

Clark concluded by defending the Workingmen's Party against the charge that it had stirred up the strikers to acts of violence. Actually, he maintained, there was probably "not a section of that party in any one of the centers of disturbance." Had there been there would have been less tendency to disturbance: "When workingmen understand that there are peaceful influences at work to relieve them of the thraldom of wages slavery, they will be more patient." Clark even proposed that the railroad managers "plant a section of the Workingmen's party at every station. They would guard their property more effectually than the whole United States army can do it."⁴⁵

The *Emancipator* applauded Clark's advice to the railway management and called it "correct every word of it." Clark, it observed, had put his finger on the real reason for "mob violence"—the refusal of the capitalists to permit the workers to organize and defend themselves against exploitation. "In endeavoring to weaken the power of the working people to protect their rights, by preventing organization, employers have increased the danger to their possessions an hundredfold. Gentlemen, the way to prevent another reign of terror is to help organize the laborers of the country."⁴⁶

Although both Clark and the *Emancipator* demonstrated genuine sympathy for and understanding of the problems of the strikers, the proposal they advanced as to how the Workingmen's Party of the United States could help eliminate the class struggle was naive indeed.

While the debate between Clark and the *Cincinnati Commer-*

cial was going on, the Great Strike came to Cincinnati. It broke out at ten in the morning of Monday, July 23, when the workers of the Ohio & Mississippi line quit work and promptly besieged the railroad's roundhouse. A large crowd assembled and later paraded up and down the tracks, blocking switches, pulling spikes, and preventing anyone from taking out the trains.[47]

On Tuesday morning, the Louisville Short Line announced that it would rescind its reduction and thereby avoided a strike. At nine o'clock, the crowd at the Ohio & Mississippi roundhouse adjourned to the Dayton Short Line freight depot, and the men there quit work. Then the crowd proceeded to the Cincinnati, Hamilton & Dayton yards, where it stopped a passenger train.[48]

At four thirty, Mayor R. H. Moore arrived and pleaded with the strikers not to turn "this fair city" into a "little Pittsburgh." He announced his sympathy with the strikers, said he wanted to see them get a fair wage, and promised that he would not call on Governor Young for military support. "Military!" he shouted. "Well, we don't want any of that."[49] The strikers cheered and went off to stop another passenger train. The *Cincinnati Daily Gazette* accused the mayor of doing the bidding of the local Workingmen's Party, and called his speech to the strikers "insipidly sweet, wishy-washy, old grannyish, silly, senile, canting, whining, truckling, toadying, crawling, groveling, fawning, flattering, and in effect, encouraging to rioters and humiliating to the city authorities."[50]

It is difficult to determine just how much influence the Workingmen's Party had on the mayor's decision to act rationally. Its members were reported to be "active among the men in the yards," and the conduct of the strikers and their sympathizers up to that point clearly showed the party's restraining hand.[51] But Mayor Moore soon revealed that his sense of reason had limits. On Tuesday evening, July 24, the crowd at the Cincinnati, Hamilton & Dayton depot was temporarily dispersed by a cloudburst, and the company managed to sneak out four passenger trains to Dayton. The news of these successes quickly brought the strikers and their sympathizers back, and all other trains were stopped. By noon on Wednesday, July 25, the crowd had swelled to a thousand, and the president of the line wired Mayor Moore for help.

Although the Workingmen's Party spokesmen appealed to the mayor not to surrender to corporate dictation, Moore decided that he really did not sympathize with the strikers. Shortly after one in the afternoon, he swept down on the crowd with 125 constables, drove the strikers out, and arrested their leaders, including several members of the Workingmen's Party who had still been cautioning against violence as the constables approached. Then the mayor closed all the saloons, swore in special police, organized a citizens' corps, and stationed an armed guard in the railroad yards with instructions to shoot anyone trying to stop trains.[52] The next day, the trains moved out under police protection, and the Great Strike was over in Cincinnati. By the end of the month, all of the companies were operating on their normal schedules.[53]

Militia shoots strikers at Frederick and Baltimore streets, Baltimore, Maryland (above). Strikers drag scabs from trains on the Baltimore & Ohio at Martinsburg, West Virginia (below).

INSURRECTION!

THE RAILROAD WAR.

A Day and Night of Blood and Horror at Pittsburg.

TROOPS OVERPOWERED AND DRIVEN OUT

The Great Railroad Strike Becomes a Savage War.

34 KILLED—110 WOUNDED.

Military Moving to the Point of Danger.

A HASTY ORDER TO FIRE

Exasperated at the Slaughter; the Mob Attack the Philadelphia Militia.

THE SIEGE OF THE ROUND HOUSE.

Oil Cars Fired by the Frantic Men and Rolled Against the Troops

A WALL OF FIRE

Desperate Sortie and Fight and Flight for Life.

THE WORK OF DESTRUCTION.

Armories, Gunshops and Pawnshops Sacked for Arms.

A WHOLESALE PILLAGE.

Two Pennsylvania Regiments Desert in the Crisis.

ACTION OF THE MUNICIPAL COMMANDER.

Oil Cars Burned and Bitter Feeling in Baltimore.

SPREAD OF THE STRIKE

Fort Wayne, Lake Shore and Wabash Freightmen Quit Work.

TROUBLE ON THE ERIE LINE.

Map Showing Area of Territory Covered by the Railroad Strike in New York, Pennsylvania, West Virginia, Ohio and Other States.

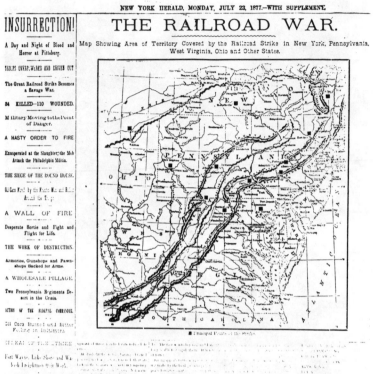

■ Principal Points of the Strike.

New York Herald maps spread of strike through July 23 and recounts the battle of Pittsburgh under the headline "INSURRECTION!"

THE GREAT RAILROAD · STRIKE.

Map Showing the Railroad Systems of the North and West Involved in the Present Disturbances, with the Lines on Which Traffic Is or Has Been Suspended and Those on Which Suspension is Threatened.

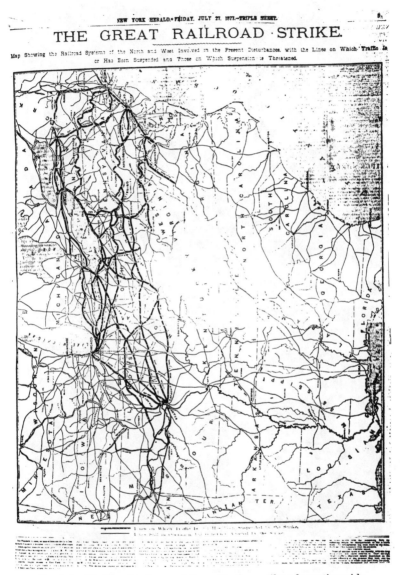

By July 27, *Herald* shows strike affecting railroads nationwide.

DRIVING THE RIOTERS FROM TURNER HALL.

FIGHT BETWEEN THE MILITARY AND THE RIOTERS AT THE HALSTED STREET VIADUCT.
THE GREAT STRIKE—SCENES OF RIOT IN CHICAGO.—From Sketches by C. and A. T. Sears.—[See Page 647.]

Scenes from Chicago: Troops drive strikers from Turner Hall (above).
The battle at Halsted Street viaduct.

VIII

The WPUS and the Great Strike, II: Chicago

In 1877, Chicago was the most important city in the Midwest. Its center was choked with railroads—the Lake Shore & Michigan Southern, the Baltimore & Ohio, the Chicago & Northwestern, the Chicago, Burlington & Quincy, the Rock Island, and the Pittsburgh, Fort Wayne & Chicago, to mention just a few—and on its fringes were a host of lumberyards and stockyards. On the ashes of the Great Fire of 1871, Chicago contractors had thrown up hundreds of factories, which drew thousands of workers and plunged them into the squalor and misery of tenement life. Discontent bubbled under the surface. As the depression continued, demonstrations of the unemployed grew more and more frequent, and in January 1875 it was seriously predicted that within the next decade, "a proletarian revolution" would occur in the Windy City.[1]

In the summer of 1877, well within the time set, it looked as if the prediction might come true, for as the strikes spread in the East, "a feverish feeling" began to take hold of Chicago. At first, the local newspapers dismissed the possibility of any strike in the city, but they soon acknowledged that Chicago's railroad workers, too, felt "hard" toward the railroads for cutting wages below family needs. All the major newspapers expressed sympathy with the "genuine grievances" of the eastern railroad strikers—"substantial, honorable and reasonably intelligent men"—and the press bitterly attacked the grasping railroad corporations for bringing on the strike.[2] The *Chicago Times,* published by Victor L. Lawson, was most outspoken and, after criticizing the Baltimore & Ohio for paying its workers "a contemptible sum" even before the most recent 10 percent cut, said boldly that if the road could operate profitably only "by robbing the workingman, then we say it ought to be fenced in, and marked in ten-foot capitals: 'Closed, because the workingmen won't starve to death.'"[3]

Even while they affirmed their sympathy for the plight of the strikers, the Chicago newspapers expressed the fear that any local walkout would trigger a larger upheaval. "The fact that there are 15,000 unemployed in this city," worried the *Times,* "many of whom are desperate, is a sermon in itself."[4] But even aside from these public statements, even greater fears of an approaching riot were being expressed privately. "It is estimated we have thirty thousand idle men in Chicago," wired a local railroad manager. "There is much excitement here over the riots, and the sympathy is with the strikers, it being talked of on street-cars and in streets as a bread riot."[5]

By the weekend, rumors already were circulating in Chicago of open strike discussions among the city's eleven thousand railroad workers. That weekend, at formal meetings, these workers discussed the events in the East, along with their own grievances and the possibilities for strike action in Chicago. What most alarmed the newspapers was the appearance of Workingmen's Party leaders at the railroad workers' meetings. Albert R. Parsons, the brilliant, handsome, twenty-nine-year-old "moving spirit" of the Chicago socialists, attended a meeting of the Pittsburgh, Fort Wayne & Chicago railroad workers, and was loudly cheered when he urged an immediate railroad strike in support of the eastern strikers.

By Saturday, July 21, the Chicago sections of the WPUS had already begun to mobilize the city's workers. Several thousand working people gathered that afternoon at a WPUS street corner meeting at Halsted and Twelfth streets, and that same afternoon the party's American section staged another large meeting in a packed Stack's Hall. ("The hall was crowded almost to suffocation," the *Tribune* report conceded.) John Schilling, the first speaker, endorsed the WPUS National Executive Committee's call to place the management of all railroads and telegraph lines in the hands of the government: "This would do away with railroad kings and monopolies generally, who draw princely salaries, and then plunder the people at their leisure." It would also, he predicted, do away with railroad strikes, and he cited as a precedent the fact that the post offices of the country had never known a strike: "This is because the Government knew what was necessary for the men to live upon." (It is doubtful if any post office employees in the audience would have agreed with this appraisal of the government's labor policies.)[6]

Albert Parsons then made a most forceful presentation of the socialist program. After being "uproariously cheered, showing his popularity," he launched into an attack on the country's newspapers, accusing them of being spokesmen for "monopolies and tyrants." He quoted scornfully from editorials in the *Chicago Tribune,* in which that paper upheld the principle that "the proprietor has a right to fix wages and say what labor is worth."[7] In that case, Parsons cried out angrily, "We are bound hand and foot—slaves, and we should be perfectly happy: content with a bowl of rice and a rat a week apiece."

Parsons insisted that Chicago's huge unemployment was the result of the indiscriminate introduction of new machinery by the capitalists. In seeking to maximize their profits, they were at the same time reducing the working people to vagrancy. Rather than oppose the new machinery, however, Parsons called for its responsible use. He maintained that workers deserved a large share of the benefits of new machinery, and argued that work could be shared and the unemployment problem solved by reducing the workday to eight hours.[8]

The "grave situation" in Chicago, particularly the enthusiastic response to the socialist speakers, and the news on Sunday that Pittsburgh crowds were burning the railroad yards, prompted Chicago's business leaders and city authorities to begin preparations for an impending conflict. Local railroad managers began moving their rolling stock out of Chicago. Retail employers, like Field, Leiter & Co., started arming their employees; large manufacturers, like Cyrus McCormick, strengthened their factory guard force; and grain dealers organized protection for their stock. The newspapers, completely forgetting their earlier editorials about the justified grievances of the strikers, urged immediate military preparation: "Chicago must not fall into the hands of a mob."[9]

The authorities needed little prompting. With Pittsburgh in flames, and with workers beginning to meet in Chicago, the city authorities braced themselves. Mayor Monroe Heath and members of the city council met over the weekend with officials of the police department, the sheriff's office, and the fire department. Mayor Heath also met secretly with National Guard commanders and ordered them to prepare the two Chicago regiments and to keep all the armories under guard. Upon Heath's request, Secretary of War McCrarry ordered six companies of the Twenty-second U.S. Infantry, on their way from Dakota to the East, to stop in Chicago.

By Monday, the newspapers were announcing the mobilization of Chicago's 450 policemen and 2,000 reservists in the two local regiments of the state militia. Arms were prepared and the armories were placed under guard. There was much speculation that the First Regiment—"the sons of capital"—would not be up to a conflict with workers, while the working class Second Regiment would be sympathetic to their brethren. Therefore, the announcement that the "Indian fighters" from the Dakota Territory were en route to Chicago produced some reassurance.[10]

After a weekend of rumors that the strike had already begun in Chicago, work resumed as usual on Monday morning. But a handbill was circulated calling for another Workingmen's Party mass meeting in the evening. The handbill began:

WORKINGMEN OF CHICAGO!
Have you no rights? No ambition?
No Manhood?
Will you remain disunited, while your masters rob you of all your rights as well as the fruits of your labor? . . .

The leaflet went on to claim that vagrancy laws made the workers criminals for being unemployed, while workers' combinations for wage increases were illegal, and that now the "money lords" were conspiring to rob workers of the ballot. It urged workingmen to defend their "rights" and "manhood," for throughout the "entire land," workers were calling upon their brothers and sisters in Chicago "to rise and protect our labor." The appeal closed:

For the sake of our wives and children, and our self-respect, LET US WAIT NO LONGER! ORGANIZE AT ONCE!
Mass-Meeting on Market Street, near Madison, to-night.
Let us act while there is yet time!

THE COMMITTEE
Workingmen's Party of the United States.[11]

That evening, as many as fifteen thousand members of the "Grand Army of Starvation," as they called themselves, gathered in response to the WPUS summons for a three-hour "monster affair" in the heart of Chicago's industrial district. Workers marched from various sections of the city, converging at the meeting place in torchlight processions. They carried placards in

English, German, and French, reading: "Life by labor or death by fight"; "We want work not charity"; "Why does over-production cause starvation?" and "United we stand, divided we fall."[12]

The *Chicago Tribune*'s account of the great meeting began on a note of puzzlement. It conceded that it was an orderly meeting, attended by "respectable workingmen who deprecated attacks upon property." It then expressed surprise that such an orderly meeting could be held under the auspices of the socialists, "who, contrary to general expectation, counseled (at least openly) moderation, and deprecated any resort to violence." However, forgetting these introductory remarks, the reporter went on to describe the speeches as "dangerous"—especially that of Albert Parsons, which, he said, "bordered upon the inflammatory."[13]

After saluting the "Grand Army of Starvation," Parsons hailed the strikers in the East. These men, he said, had "demanded of those who have possession of the means of production that they be permitted to live," and that they not be turned into "vagrants and tramps." While it was to be regretted that these men—"our distressed and suffering brothers" in the East—had had to "resort to such extreme measures," yet "we recognize the fact that they were driven to what they have done." Parsons denounced railroad magnates Scott, Gould, and Vanderbilt for forcing their employees to work for ninety cents a day and then expecting them to feed and clothe their wives and children and care for and educate their sons and daughters, "and to teach . . . [them] how to grow up to lead good and virtuous lives." After attacking the press for filling its columns with stories of sex and crime but never bothering "to go to the factories and workshops to see how the toiling millions give away their lives to the rich bosses of the country," he wound up:

Let us fight for our wives and children, for with us it is a question of bread and meat. Let the grand army of labor say who shall fill the legislative halls of this country. . . . Go to the ballot-box, and say that the government of the United States shall be the possessors of all the railway lines in this country. If the people . . . take possession of the railroads and telegraphs, we extract the sting from the mouths of Jay Gould and Tom Scott, and they can no longer sting us to death. (*Loud applause.*) We take out of their hand the means by which they now enslave us. Let us not forget the fact that all wealth and civilization comes from labor alone. . . . It rests with you to say whether we shall allow the capitalist to go on exploiting us, or whether we shall organize ourselves. Will you organize? (*Cries of "We will."*) Well, then enroll your names in the grand army of labor, and if the capitalist engages in warfare against our rights, then we shall resist him with all the means that God has given us. (*Loud and prolonged applause.*)[14]

The resolutions adopted by the great meeting denounced the railroads for having steadily cut wages "until human nature can no longer suffer in silence." They charged that wage reductions, which were bad at all times, were, "especially during the present prostration of business, a direct injury to society," since as the purchasing power of the people was reduced, the volume of business was "proportionately decreased"; they urged that a reformed national government be created which would take over and operate the railroads and telegraph lines, "just as in the case of the principal railroads and telegraph lines of Europe." They also called

. . . upon all comrades of toil to commence without further delay the organization of a great federation of labor, and assisting and encouraging the building up of strict and sensible trades unions upon a national and international basis, and aiming at political power to secure legislation in the direct interest of the working classes.

Resolved, That only by elevating and improving the condition of the people as a whole can the benefits of progress and civilization be enjoyed and maintained,

Resolved, That to this end the hours of labor must be reduced as new labor-saving machinery is developed, else the most terrible consequences will ensue, and the civilization of the nineteenth century become a farce.[15]

Speakers continued to address the audience from four wagons. All but one counseled militant but moderate action. The exception was John McAuliffe, who warned the militia not to fire at striking workers: "If they shoot us, we'll shoot them. As the crowd cheered wildly, Philip Van Patten got up and urged moderation. Finally, Parsons called for another rally on Tuesday evening, and the crowd retired peacefully.[16]

Later that night, the city authorities guaranteed reporters that Chicago's crisis had passed.[17] Actually, of course, it had only begun.

The Great Strike came to Chicago on Monday evening, just a few hours after the WPUS meeting, when forty switchmen on the Michigan Central Railroad struck for more pay. Early the next morning, they brought out the workers from the Central's shops and freight yards, and together the strikers continued along the river to, in the words of one striker, "clean out the other monopolies."[18] They called out workers at the freight yards of the Baltimore & Ohio and Illinois Central. Then they staged a brief meeting at which they announced: "We hope to gain our rights, bread for our families, and a decent living for ourselves." After affirming their determination to halt all railroad traffic without violence, they left in several groups, one to the downtown freight yards along the lake and the river, and another to the railroad yards south along the river.

As the railroad workers and their supporters moved through the streets, they were cheered by onlookers in the working class neighborhoods. A banner announcing the WPUS meeting that night, carried by two of the workers, also brought cheers. Upon reaching the railroad yards and machine shops, small delegations were sent in, and the men at work proceeded to discuss the need to spread the strike. In most cases, they joined the railroad strikers, who then moved on to other establishments, chanting "Down with the Thieving Monopolies." The Excelsior Iron Works, the National Boiler Works, Greenbaum's Iron and Nail Works, and the Chicago Die and Machine Works all received visits and were put out of operation.[19]

"The Chicago Strikers Moving Over the City and Stopping Work Everywhere," the *Chicago Daily News* headline screamed the next day. Lumber yards, planing mills, brickyards, and packinghouses were visited and closed down by crowds chanting "We want Labor and Justice" and "Down with the Wages of Slavery." Twelve packinghouses, including Armour & Co., were compelled to sign an agreement to pay two dollars a day for the next eighteen months.[20]

As for the railroad strikers who had initiated this wide upheaval, they were careful to allow passenger trains to continue running, and sought only to halt freight traffic. The railroad companies made no attempt to resist the crowds, and several closed down before the deputations arrived. By nightfall, all freight traffic was at a halt in Chicago.[21]

From the beginning, then, the Great Strike in Chicago was obviously more than just a railroad strike. The Chicago police historian, John Flynn, caught the spirit and sweep of the uprising, even though he could not fully understand the years of discontent that had triggered the "labor explosion":

All through the afternoon . . . strikes were in progress from the lake to

Western Avenue; from the North Side rolling mills to the town of Lake. The disposition or propensity to strike became a mania. Workingmen who had no earthly cause to complain, who could not call to mind a grievance, threw down their tools, tore off their "overalls," snatched up their coats and hats, shook their clenched fist at their employers, and joined the nearest mob. The railroad employees, the lumber shovers, the saw and planing mill men, the iron workers, the brass finishers, the carpenters, the bricklayers, the stonemasons, the furniture makers, the polishers, the shoemakers, the tailors, the painters, glaziers, butchers, bakers, candlestick makers—all went out without motive or reason, and helped to swell the crazy mobs that paraded endlessly through the streets.[22]

The crowds ranged in size from a few hundred to a few thousand, and they were reported to be composed of women and children as well as workingmen. There were a few reports of pillaging, and there were rumors of attempts to loot gun stores; but mostly the action of the crowds forced work stoppages. Although armed with sticks and stones, the crowds dispersed without resistance upon encountering small bands of police. "No Bloodshed in the City," the *Times* reported.[23]

By midafternoon, most work in Chicago had come to a halt. Dispatches from the city to the nation's press bore the headlines: "The Strike General in Chicago."[24]

During the entire day, individual members of the Workingmen's Party had been actively encouraging the strikers. In the morning, Thomas Morgan, a leading party member, was selected as spokesman and negotiator for the striking Illinois Central workers. Morgan urged the strikers to join the WPUS, and he successfully advanced strike demands for higher wages and shorter hours, although the strikers refused his plea to include the nationalization of the railroads as part of their strike demands. George Schilling, another party leader, was instrumental in organizing a strike among his co-workers, the coopers, while other socialists helped initiate strikes among the lumber shovers and cabinetmakers.[25] Late that Tuesday evening, over fifty trades delegates—American, German, Irish, and Scandinavian—gathered with WPUS leaders at Aurora Hall. They recommended the drawing up of citywide strike demands for the eight-hour workday and 20 percent wage increases. They then established a permanent executive committee to conduct the strike, and called for a Wednesday afternoon meeting of delegates from all shops, factories, and trade unions "to lay out a plan how to work and better our situation."[26]

In the meantime, it was essential that the strikes be led in an organized manner. "Fellow Workers," the WPUS appealed, "Under any circumstances keep quiet until we have given the present crisis a due consideration."[27] But this plea made little impression on the press or the authorities. Either despite or because of the socialists' attempt to channel the uprising into a disciplined citywide general strike, the newspapers accused them of fomenting crowd violence. "The different crowds moving about the city today closing factories were committees of the Commune," the *Daily News* charged.[28]

Next came the harassment. Charles A. Dana, the publisher of the *New York Sun*, had made no comment to John Swinton, the editor, when the latter came to work the day after speaking at the Tompkins Square meeting called by the New York Workingmen's Party.[29] But Albert R. Parsons, a printer on the *Chicago Times*, was not so lucky.

Parsons had been the subject of a brief editorial on the same day that the *Times* reported his speech at the Market Square meeting: "His name is Parsons. Until very recently he was a 'rat' printer. He joined the Typographical Union while running for Alderman in the last election. Now he is leading the commune. A model workingman truly!"[30] The meaning of the editorial became clear the very next morning, when Parsons reported to work as usual. He was immediately fired by the foreman of the composing room and blacklisted in his trade. That afternoon, he was taken by police to City Hall and ushered into the presence of the superintendent of police and several members of the board of trade. The superintendent insultingly asked Parsons questions about his life. He blamed him "for the great trouble" he had brought on the city of Chicago and charged him with inciting "the working people to insurrection." As Parsons noted later in his autobiography (written while he was in prison in 1887, awaiting execution in the Haymarket frame-up):[31]

I told him I had done nothing of the sort at least I had not intended to do so, that I was simply a speaker at the meeting that was all. I told him that the strike arose from causes over which I, as an individual, had no control. Those present in the room were much excited and when I was through explaining some spoke up and said "hang him," "lynch him," "lock him up," etc., to my great surprise holding me responsible for the strikes in the city. Others said it would never do to hang me or lock me up. That the working men were excited and that act might cause them to do violence. It was agreed to let me go.

After two hours, the superintendent of police let Parsons go, but as he pushed him to the door, he snapped:

Parsons, your life is in danger. I advise you to leave the city at once. Beware. Everything you say or do is made known to me. I have men on your track to shadow you. Do you know you are liable to be assassinated any moment on the street? . . . Why, those board of trade men would as leave hang you to a lamp post as not.[32]

That same afternoon, Mayor Heath issued a proclamation closing all saloons and ordered the fire bells rung, summoning the militia to their armories. Veterans' clubs and military companies of all nationalities were mobilized, and the mayor recruited several thousand "men of high standing" as special police, after a prominent citizen offered to pay for them. Citizens brought guns and ammunition to City Hall while businessmen loaned horses for new cavalry companies. Despite assurances that six companies of the Twenty-second U.S. Infantry were en route, and that six more companies of the Ninth Infantry were moving from Omaha to Rock Island, the mayor also urged the "better class of citizens" to begin organizing for self-defense in their wards and communities. The morning papers of July 25 reported a booming business at the gun stores, with sales restricted to the wealthy class, which was alarmed over the size, character, and implications of the work stoppages: "The whole town was aroused either for defensive or offensive purposes, and Chicago presented the appearance of a city in a state of siege."[33]

The morning papers reported another ominous development. The previous evening, the WPUS gathering of five thousand workers was broken up by a wedge of police firing blank cartridges and swinging clubs. "The Abortive Meeting: The Police Take a Hand," the *Tribune* reported gleefully, as it detailed the fact that "half a dozen heads were broken, most of them the heads of unoffending individuals."[34] It was obvious that the Chicago police were spoiling for a fight.

For its part, the Workingmen's Party was trying almost desperately to avoid violence. When Philip Van Patten was called to the central police station on the morning of July 25 to be given the "Parsons treatment," he disavowed any connection with crowd violence, and reaffirmed the socialists' desire for peace. That afternoon, the party issued the following proclamation:

WORKINGMEN OF CHICAGO!

The success of our honest effort to increase wages depends entirely upon your good conduct and peaceful though firm behavior. We hereby declare that any riotous action in our meetings will be immediately put down by us. The grand principles of Humanity and Popular Sovereignty need no violence to sustain them. For the sake of the Cause which we hold most dear, let every honest workingman help us to preserve order. Let us show the world that with all our grievances and misery we can still act like men and good citizens.[35]

In contrast to the WPUS, the city authorities and the wealthy classes armed for war. Meeting in special session, the Common Council announced that there existed in Chicago "a rebellion against lawful authority," and authorized Heath to make any expenditures he deemed necessary for the preservation of peace. It also called upon all good citizens to enroll as special police to aid "in suppressing the rebellion." That afternoon, at a large citizens' meeting in Moody and Sankey Tabernacle, Mayor Heath put out a call for five thousand "good and experienced citizens" as volunteers, and Reverend Robert Collyner endorsed the call with an appeal that they fight to the death "in defense of order and our homes." Immediately after the meeting, the police force was augmented by volunteers. Two hundred veterans were organized into companies, furnished with Springfield breech-loading rifles and forty rounds of ammunition each, and stationed at the armory on Harrison Street. The North Side Germans organized a cavalry squadron of one hundred mounts. Two companies of the Twenty-second U.S. Artillery arrived, and four hundred men of the First Regiment of the Illinois National Guard sweated impatiently in their armory. "They mean business," the *Chicago Inter-Ocean* assured the city's middle class.[36]

Meanwhile, a frantic Common Council, acknowledging that "thousands of workingmen are idle in the city of Chicago at the present time, whose families are suffering," enacted the legislation they had claimed was impossible for four years, which allowed the city to borrow half a million dollars for construction projects to provide more work.[37]

Early in the evening of Wednesday, July 25, the first serious clash occurred between the strikers and their sympathizers and the police. A crowd of several thousand working people, railroad strikers, and neighboring residents gathered at the Chicago, Burlington & Quincy switchyards on West Sixteenth Street, probably to check whether the work stoppage was being observed there and to make sure that the company was not sneaking out any trains. Once satisfied, the crowd began to trickle home. Just then, an omnibus rattled up, and eighteen policemen piled out with their revolvers drawn. The police charged the crowd with their revolvers blazing, and a slow retreat began, which turned into a rout. By this time, thousands of working people had spilled out into the streets around Halsted Street. Some joined the crowd, while others stoned railroad buildings, ditched locomotives and railroad cars, halted streetcars, and broke into a gun store and a local hardware store. The police were driven to the Halsted Street viaduct over the railroad tracks, and at one point they were surrounded, but they were reinforced by another carload of police, then another, and bullets started to fly into the crowd again. After it was all over, three persons were reported dead and eight wounded—all members of the crowd.[38]

An hour later, two miles to the north, the Workingmen's Party held another outdoor meeting, at Market and Madison streets, which was well attended and had an abundant supply of banners. Van Patten presided, but no sooner did he open his mouth than a squad of police attacked the audience from behind and clubbed it into a stampede. Van Patten and the speakers' stand were both bowled over. At this point, a regiment of one thousand torch-waving, drum-beating workers marched up, prepared to hear the WPUS speakers, but the police immediately fired a warning volley into the air and threatened to lower their aim unless the workers dispersed immediately. The crowd swiftly did so, but not without some open resistance from the assembled workers.[39] However, this was only a prelude to the major action, for on Thursday the police would meet a crowd that really offered resistance.

Meanwhile, Mayor Heath had decided to seek federal help; he appealed to Governor Shelby Cullom, who formally requested military assistance from President Hayes. On Thursday morning, the president authorized General R. C. Drum, of the Division of the Missouri, to use six companies of the Ninth Infantry, then stationed at nearby Rock Island, to help Heath in case of trouble.[40]

At the same time, local forces were being prepared. Albert Day, a prominent grain merchant, recalled the feeling of all "that the worst had not come," and their fears that "the mob" would attack "the best residence sections of the city." Day attended a citizens' meeting of the Eighteenth Ward where prominent bankers, merchants, and lawyers were sworn in as special police. They elected their own officers and were given U.S. Army muskets. These neighborhood citizen military defense organizations were formed in at least half of the city's wards, under the leadership of such "solid citizens" as Wirt Dexter and Marshall Field, as protection against "stray strikers and tramps." After sporadic efforts at standing guard, Day's company actually stood guard duty during Wednesday night, July 25; and early Thursday morning, they reported to police headquarters as citizen reinforcements.[41]

By that time, Chicago's forces of "law and order" were fully mobilized. Railroads like the Illinois Central and the Chicago & Northwestern, business houses, lumber yards, and manufacturers had organized their trusted employees into armed companies to protect their property. Private militia companies, veterans' organizations, newly formed citizens' cavalry companies, ward patrols, and special police—all were prepared to support the local police, the state militia, and the United States Army. Over twenty thousand men were under arms, with six companies of the Ninth Infantry now en route from Rock Island. They awaited the impending conflict in the spirit voiced by the *Inter-Ocean:* "Squelch them out, stamp them out, sweep them out with grapeshot."[42]

The crowds re-formed on Tuesday morning, continuing the citywide forced work stoppages of the previous day. But by now, a new mood was in evidence. Up to this point, as the *Tribune* noted, there had been a "holiday" spirit in "the mob," which expressed itself in a feeling of "jocularity."[43] But as the police became more aggressive, and the authorities, joined by the upper and middle classes, prepared for civil warfare, the mood of the crowds changed from a festive spirit to one of fury at the police tactics against the crowds. The use of guns by the police on Wednesday in the breaking up of a peaceful WPUS meeting enraged many workers. And the large number of "citizens" acting as special police, who were reported to be quick to club and shoot, only served to sharpen these tensions.

This new mood quickly manifested itself. Although dozens of crowds across the city continued to enforce the work stoppages on Thursday, the viaduct at Halsted and Sixteenth streets became a focal point for a massed conflict between the working people and the representatives of law and order. The location of the battle was not accidental, for the viaduct not only spanned the tracks and rolling stock of several railroad lines, but it was also adjacent to the lumber district. This was the neighborhood that had spawned a bloody lumber shovers' strike in 1876, and that had been at the center of the upheaval in the southwestern part of the city for the past two days, including the pitched battle of the previous evening.

The battle started early in the morning when a crowd began cutting telegraph wires and stopping streetcars near the viaduct. A police squad arrived, and the battle was on. The police broke up the crowd, but it soon re-formed. More police were sent, and soon the conflict was joined and fought with sticks and stones, clubs and guns. Using their clubs, the police drove the crowd over the Halsted Street viaduct and down the slope onto Sixteenth Street. There, another crowd, numbering about five thousand, came to the rescue of its advance guard. The police fled back to the viaduct and, having decided to make a stand, whipped out their revolvers and started firing into the crowd. Six men dropped in their tracks, but the crowd pushed nearer. With most of their ammunition gone, the police turned and fled. Then more police arrived, plus a company of mounted militia. The original squad fell in behind, and a fierce charge followed, with the police clubbing and shooting. This time, the crowd turned and fled south on Halsted, then on Archer Avenue. The police clattered after them in hot pursuit, clubbing and shooting as they went. Federal troops were called in and the Second Regiment also marched in, flying the American flag and a Fenian banner with "the harp of Ireland," and bringing along two ten-pound guns.[44]

No sooner did the riot near Halsted and Sixteenth streets end than another started at Halsted and Twelfth streets. A portion of the Sixteenth Street crowd ran down to Twelfth Street and tried to merge into a small crowd standing outside of Turner Hall, on the corner of Twelfth and Halsted streets. Inside the hall, several hundred German socialist cabinetmakers of the Harmonia Association of Joiners were gathered to discuss their strike and the eight-hour day. The meeting spilled out into the street just as a squad of regular and special police reinforcements arrived. The latter made no inquiries about the purpose of the assemblage; instead they unmercifully and viciously attacked the crowd outside and crashed through the doors. When the proprietor of the hall protested, a Sergeant Householder split his head open with a club and ordered his men to attack everyone in sight. The police opened fire and clubbed people at random, killing one and wounding several others, and driving the panic-stricken working-men into a heap on the floor, tumbling down the stairs, and jumping through the windows into the street. (They "ran hither and thither like rats in a pit," the *Chicago Tribune* reported.) One man was pinned to the top of a table, while two policemen took turns beating him. Outside, a Sergeant Brennan shot indiscriminately at passers-by and at men running out of the hall. When the police had finished, the Second Regiment arrived and, with bayonets drawn, drove everyone in the neighborhood, including women and children, into their houses.[45]

The battle raged on through the morning, especially along Halsted and Twelfth streets, near the viaduct at Sixteenth Street, and at the bridge near Archer Avenue. Thousands of working people milled and massed in the streets, with smaller groups among them taunting the troops and actually engaging them with guns, sticks, and stones. Despite gunfire and repeated charges, the crowds would not disperse, and the authorities continued to send reinforcements into the area. And from midmorning on, as news and rumors of the Halsted Street battle spread, working people from across the city began massing there.

One of the most remarkable and revealing—or, as the *Tribune* put it "one of the most terrible, audacious, and unreasonable"— events of the day was a march by several thousand Irish packinghouse workers down Archer Avenue toward Halsted Street and the conflict at the viaduct. The appearance of the Irish butchers had been rumored since Wednesday night, and now they marched along Archer Avenue, wielding butchers knives "to cut their way through any obstacle to their march," as well as the customary street weapons. They closed lumber yards and other businesses, and forced employers to raise wages. Preceded by two Irish butchers carrying a banner proclaiming "Workingmen's Rights," they made an awe-inspiring sight. ("They were men in every sense of the word . . . were brave and daring, and scattered terror in their way," the *Tribune* reporter wrote.) When they reached the bridge that crossed over the river branch to Halsted Street, they were met by the police, along with a large crowd of wildly cheering Czech workers, and other "demonstrations of sympathy." Although the Irish butchers were eventually routed by the police, the tumultuous greeting they received showed the effect of the Great Strike in eradicating ethnic differences among the workers. The tensions between Irish and Czech workers, as sharp as any in the city, suddenly became irrelevant in the common battle against the police, the authorities, and the "respectable citizens." The newspapers took note of this startling development among working people, "who ordinarily draw the line of nationality in making up their gangs."[46]

The papers also pointed out that sexual differences, too, were overcome in the heat of the struggle. "It is a noticeable fact," reported the *Times* the next day, "to all who have taken more than a casual view of the crowd of 'strikers' that at least one-fifth of the gathering were women." The *Tribune*, in fact, gave the women credit for most of the crowd activity, and charged that "the women had been exciting the men to action throughout the morning." "The women," the paper concluded, "are a great deal worse than the men."[47]

However, it was the *Chicago Inter-Ocean*'s account of the role of women in the crowd action that aroused nationwide attention, and was reprinted in newspapers the country over. Headed "Women's Warfare: Bohemian Amazons Rival The Men In Deeds of Violence," the account told of how, when groups of men in the crowd became "thoroughly demoralized," "hundreds of these Amazons" rushed to replace them. It continued:

Women with babes in arms joined the enraged female rioters. The streets were fluttering with calico of all shades and shapes. Hundreds were bareheaded, their disheveled locks streaming in the wind. Many were shoeless. Some were young, scarcely women in age, and not at all in appearances. Dresses were tucked up around the waist, revealing large underthings. Open busts were common as a barber's chair. Brawny, sunburnt arms brandished clubs. Knotty hands held rocks and sticks and wooden blocks. Female yells, shrill as a curfew's cry, filled the air. The swarthy features of the Bohemian women were more horrible to look at in that scene than their men in the Halsted Street riots. The unsexed mob of female incendiaries rushed to the fence and yards of Goss & Phillips' Manufacturing company. The consternation which this attack created extended to Twenty-second Street, at that hour very quiet. A crowd of men gathered on Fisk Street to witness this curious repetition of the scenes of the Paris commune. The fence surrounding the yard gave way, and was carried off by the petticoated plunderers in their unbridled rage.[48] There was fear for a while that the Amazonian army would continue their depradations. Word was dispatched to the Himmon Street Station, and a force of officers under Lieutenant Vesey pushed down to the corner of the contest. The women hissed as they saw the blue coats march along. Some of the less valorous took to their heels. . . . Others stood their ground.

A shower of missiles greeted the boys as they came smiling along left front into line. One woman pitched a couple of blocks at the heads of the officers, and then moved on to attend to her family duties. The men were weak in the strength and forcefulness of their language compared to these female wretches. Profanity the most foul rolled easily off their tongues with horrid glibness. Expressions were made use of that brought the blood mantling to the cheek of the worst-hardened men in the crowds of spectators. It was awful. . . .

The police finally drove the women off with their clubs and revolvers, but they remained in the area, threatening any man who said he was "not in sympathy with the mob," and joining women of other nationalities in caring for the wounded. As fast as any man was injured, he was taken into some house in the vicinity, "and the women being in strong sympathy with and doing all in their power to aid the rioters, they would not say whether they had any wounded in the house or not." The *Chicago Inter-Ocean* viewed the unprecedentedly large number of women involved in the crowd action, and their militancy, as "the most disgusting revelation that has yet deepened the already black record of riot and villainy which for nearly a week has disgraced the fair name of Chicago."[49]

Another feature of the events of Thursday was the guerrilla warfare that developed after large crowds were broken up by the charges and firepower of the police and troops. (As the *Tribune* put it, "when the mob was defeated, guerrilla war was established.") Smaller groups and crowds of working people continued the battle, skirmishing, fighting on the run, charging and retreating, coalescing into crowds and fragmenting into small groups, using the friendly neighborhoods and the homes of sympathetic women as protection for the ongoing struggle. The crowds fought on through the afternoon, using the alleys, streets, rooftops, fields, and narrow passageways of the area for safety. While the police and troops were refused water in these working class neighborhoods, the workers who darted into buildings and homes for refuge were welcomed. Finally, the exhausted police ordered all windows and doors shut and all rooftops cleared, as they slowly established control.[50]

The victory of the forces of law and order was insured by the arrival of the six companies of the Ninth U.S. Infantry, which President Hayes had ordered in from Rock Island, and of two more companies of the Twenty-second U.S. Artillery, from Dakota. To make certain, however, Mayor Heath swore in two thousand more special police, organized more citizens' companies, and had over four hundred demonstrators arrested.[51]

By Friday, July 28, the Battle of Chicago was over. There were still a few skirmishes around the city, especially in the "notorious neighborhood called Hamburg," at Halsted and Thirty-fifth streets, where "a fighting class" of butchers and railroad and rolling mill workers continued to occupy the streets. The end of the battle also left a residue of strikes by streetcar workers, stonecutters, lumber shovers, coopers, harness makers, iron moulders, cigarmakers, switchmen, and ship carpenters. Although the city's corporation counsel acknowledged a distinction between trade unionists and rioters, he insisted that "violent agitators" controlled any meetings that took place, and the police thereupon prohibited all meetings.[52]

That weekend, Chicago was quiet, but the fighting had cost the city eighteen lives. As funerals were held on Sunday for those workers killed during the riots, the resentment in working class neighborhoods was so much in evidence that police, citizens, and troops continued to patrol the streets.[53]

Although it was apparent to anyone who read the detailed accounts of the great battle of July 26 that the Workingmen's Party of the United States had had nothing to do with the events, all of the Chicago papers blamed the party for the rioting. "Red Rabble Routed," alliterated the *Inter-Ocean* the following day.[54] "The Fight with the Communists is at an End," the *Tribune* headlined on Saturday.[55] During the events, the *Times* reported all the details under the title of "Red War."[56]

In the thriller he wrote about the 1877 strikes, Allan Pinkerton blamed the Chicago rioting of July 26 on the "ranting of a young American communist named Parsons."[57] But the truth is that Parsons and other leaders of the Workingmen's Party had tried to *restrain* the crowds, but had lost complete control of the workers, who were enraged by the calculated brutality of the police. It was the police who deliberately inflamed the situation when they broke up a peaceful meeting of the Workingmen's Party and invaded a peaceful meeting of furniture workers, spreading death and destruction. An enraged *Daily News* reporter called such police "a uniformed mob."[58] The cabinetmakers later preferred charges against Sergeants Householder and Brennan for their brutal conduct. The judge found the sergeants guilty of provoking a "criminal riot," and fined them six cents each![59]

IX

The WPUS and the Great Strike, III: The St. Louis General Strike

Dramatic as Chicago's "Battle of Thursday, July 26," was, it still had to take second place to the developments just a few hundred miles to the south, in St. Louis. The *Chicago Tribune,* which attributed the violence in Chicago solely to the activities of the Communists, used the same standard in measuring the outbreak on the banks of the Mississippi when it editorialized: "The cool audacity and impudent effrontery of the Communists have nowhere shown so conspicuously as in St. Louis."[1] And that city's leading paper, the *Missouri Republican,* exclaimed: "It is wrong to call this a strike; it is a labor revolution."[2]

Actually, what occurred in St. Louis was unique in the history of the American labor movement and, indeed, in that of the entire world. Its uniqueness did not lie in the fact that it was a general strike. There were at least three other general strikes either called or planned during the upheaval of 1877. At Kansas City, a "monster meeting" of railroad workers on Monday, July 23, declared a general strike to begin at noon the next day as it demanded the restoration of wages to the level of January 1, 1874. It was on that same evening that thousands of workingmen assembled in a mass meeting in Chicago and that the movement for a general strike got under way there. Meanwhile, at the same time, a vote for a general strike was being taken in Toledo, Ohio.

Of the three, the Kansas City general strike never got under way, and the shutdown in Chicago was incomplete. But in Toledo the city authorities lent their full support to the strikers for a few days, and there all business operations were actually closed down. On the evening of the twenty-third, Police Commissioner Coyle told the strikers: "You are not slaves, gentlemen, and I am glad to see you assert your manhood."[3] And Major General James Steadman, the head of the local militia, gave his fiery encouragement to a strikers' rally held the following evening at Eversman's Hall. On Wednesday morning, the city's workers formed a "Committee of Ten" and drew up a list of resolutions calling for wages of $2.50 to $3.00 per day for skilled labor, and $1.50 for unskilled workers. Then a crowd of three hundred laborers formed ranks, four abreast, and started moving through the manufacturing district to enforce their program. They were quickly joined by stevedores and all other classes of workingmen, and the crowd of strikers notified all establishments that they would either sign agreements embodying the demands or they would be closed down. The business interests pleaded with Mayor W. W. Jones to end the demonstration, but Jones said that he was in full sympathy with the workers, and ordered his police force to make no arrests.[4]

By the end of the day, lumber yards, mills, factories, and other business establishments had been shut down. "Every large manufacturing establishment in the city is now closed," announced the *Toledo Blade* on Thursday. "The banks decline any advance on bills of lading, and the commercial as well as the manufacturing business of the city is at a standstill."[5]

That same day, in response to a call issued by the sheriff, five hundred citizens assembled at the Court House. They were organized into companies, given arms, and instructed to patrol the streets. Two days later, on Friday, July 27, Mayor Jones experienced a change of heart. He swore in four hundred police and had the leaders of the general strike arrested. Within a day, the Toledo uprising was over.[6]

While there was a general strike in Toledo, that city was small compared to St. Louis. As David T. Burbank points out:

The St. Louis general strike of 1877 was certainly one of the first strikes anywhere in the world to paralyze a major industrial city, and without doubt was the first general strike of the modern, industrial labor movement in the United States. . . . The St. Louis strike deserves to be recognized as the first exercise in America of labor's ultimate weapon.[7]

With its 300,000 inhabitants, St. Louis was somewhat smaller than Chicago in population, but its working class seethed with the same discontent. Since the completion of the great Eads Bridge in 1874, the city had come to be considered another gateway to the West. Its industries shot up almost overnight, led by the construction of breweries, and they drew thousands of workers into grimy tenements and left them penniless and starving during the terrible years of the great depression. As a result of the brewery construction, the predominant foreign-born element in St. Louis was German, which provided the German-language section of the WPUS with a steady stream of recruits. Local membership of the party's four sections (German, English, French, and Bohemian) numbered one thousand, or one-quarter of the party's total national membership. The German section, with about six hundred members, was by far the largest.[8]

Like Chicago, St. Louis was choked with railroads, and all of them funneled in through East St. Louis, Illinois, across the river. That city constituted a western railroad center second in importance only to Chicago. When the strike spread to Chicago, it was inevitable that it would reach East St. Louis. The latest wage cuts had caused a considerable amount of bitterness among the railroad workers, and the refusal of the railroad officials even to discuss the rescinding of the reduction intensified this feeling of anger. Still, there was no immediate interruption of rail traffic. On July 21, a large meeting of railroad employees was held in East St. Louis, but it merely adopted resolutions of support of the strike in the eastern states.[9] The news of the rioting in Pittsburgh excited no one in St. Louis except the *Missouri Republican* ("Pittsburgh in the Hands of the Commune," it headlined)[10] and James H. Wilson, the receiver of the St. Louis & Southeastern Railroad Company. On Sunday afternoon, July 22, before the Great Strike had spread to either East St. Louis or St. Louis, Wilson expressed a gloomy view of the situation in a personal letter to Carl Schurz, secretary of the interior in President Hayes's cabinet. He indicated his fear that serious trouble lay ahead, since "the strike seems to be traveling westward, and our men may be forced into it." He urged immediate and resolute action by the federal government, informing Schurz, "I am managing property now in the custody of the U.S. Courts, and I shall certainly not permit my employees to fix their own rate of wages, nor dictate to me in any manner what my policy shall be."[11]

Later, on the night of July 22, Wilson wired Schurz that his fears had been confirmed: "The railroad employees met at East St. Louis tonight and have resolved to stop all freight trains and switching engines after midnight."[12]

The meeting referred to by Wilson had taken place that afternoon in East St. Louis's Traubel's Hall and began with speeches by several railroad workers from the Vandalia, Rockford & Rock Island, and the Cairo & St. Louis (Narrow Gauge) roads. But the mood was still quiet. However, it changed a half hour after the meeting began when the Brotherhood of Firemen members filed into the hall "in a body amidst great cheering." The cheering was caused by the news that the Brotherhood had decided to strike.[13] The enthusiasm mounted in intensity when a messenger from across the river in St. Louis brought assurances from the Workingmen's Party of the United States of their sympathy with the strike, and the information that they were coming across the river to join the meeting. Three cheers were given for "the Internationalists," and it was suggested that the meeting adjourn to the open air. The proposal was immediately approved, and, with a roar, the crowd swarmed out of the hall and down to the Relay Depot. As they marched through the streets, their ranks were swelled by the addition of workingmen from St. Louis.

An open car was pressed into service as a rostrum. A president and secretary were chosen. The former, a machinist on the Narrow Gauge, opened the meeting by declaring that as a workingman he knew very well why the meeting was being held: "The capitalist was trying to starve the workingmen, and was educating his children to look down on them, despise and grind them under foot at every chance." Now, while their brothers were struggling nobly in the East, was the time to act. Taking note of the fact that representatives of the press were present, the machinist-chairman added that he could not say he was glad to see them, since the press was subsidized and was "playing into the hands of the capitalists."

The next speaker was a railroad worker who began by addressing the assembly as "brother slaves!" and went on to explain: "Yes, brother slaves, we are also serfs if we continue to work on the present reduction of wages, on which we can barely live, and certainly not save up anything for a rainy day."

It was at this point that a body of the members from the Workingmen's Party of St. Louis was seen marching to the meeting, singing "La Marseillaise." All speaking stopped until the procession, five hundred strong, reached the gathering and, amidst tremendous cheering, mingled with the crowd.[14]

On Saturday night, July 21, even before the strike movement of the railroad workers in East St. Louis had begun, the Workingmen's Party had met at Carondelet, a concentration point of heavy industry on the extreme south end of St. Louis. The meeting adopted resolutions of sympathy with the railroad strikers and collected money in order to forward telegrams to all railroad centers, conveying these resolutions.[15] The following afternoon, the party's English and German sections met in St. Louis's Turner Hall, on Tenth Street between Market and Walnut. The English section heard speeches by Harry Eastman, a railroad machinist from East St. Louis, and Peter A. Lofgreen.

Lofgreen was the assumed name of Laurence Andreas Gronlund, who was born in 1844 in Denmark and graduated in 1862 from the University of Copenhagen, matriculating as a *privat* (an individual student with no connection with any particular school) and specializing in literature. He emigrated to the United States in 1867 and became a teacher of German in Milwaukee schools. He was admitted to the bar in Chicago, although he does not appear to have practiced law. After 1873, when he settled in St. Louis, he became a clerk on the *Globe-Democrat* newspaper. With his knowledge of German and English, Lofgreen soon rose to a prominent place in the local socialist movement and was elected financial secretary of the Workingmen's Party of St. Louis.[16]

The English section adopted resolutions supporting the workingmen of the different railroads who were "rising up to demand their just rights," and denounced the federal government for having "allied itself on the side of capital and against labor." They expressed sympathy for the railroad workers, who were trying "to secure just and equitable reward for their labor," and assured them that "we will stand by them in this most righteous struggle of labor against robbery and oppression, through good and evil report, to the end of the struggle." The same resolutions were presented to the German section, where they were also adopted. Albert Curllin, a German emigrant and a baker by trade and, at the age of twenty-four, a full-time functionary in the German section, insisted that it was not enough to express sympathy for the strikers; the party had to provide "men to back them." At this, both sections decided to hold a public demonstration in support of the railroad workers in East St. Louis, to "assure the strikers that, not only by their words, but by their presence, they are with them." About five hundred strong, they marched through the streets of St. Louis, decided to boycott the bridge as a monopoly, and instead took the ferry across the Mississippi. As they crossed, they sang "La Marseillaise" with the aid of the French section, while the members of the German section made the streets of East St. Louis ring "with the strains of the inspiring hymn" in honor of the red flag. As the WPUS delegation approached the strikers, the railroad workers sent up a great cheer and dispatched a deputation to escort the socialists: "They marched up amid the enthusiasms of their friends, and soon mingled in the general throng."[17]

The open-air meeting at the Relay Depot now resumed with a speech by East St. Louis Judge William G. Kase (described as "a friend of the workingmen"), who declared that the wages received by the railroaders were "outrageously small," so small, in fact, that when all deductions had been made, there was "not enough to support a family." The audience cheered as he told them that that very morning, at church, he had rendered thanks "not only for property gained, but for property *destroyed at the hands of the people*"—a reference to events in Pittsburgh.

The judge was followed by Peter A. Lofgreen, who brought greetings from the Workingmen's Party. "All you have to do," he told the railroad workers, "for you have the numbers, is to unite on one idea—that the workingmen shall rule the country. What man makes, belongs to him, and the workingmen made this country." The trainmen roared their approval. He then read the text of a resolution adopted by the Workingmen's Party which denounced the United States government for "having taken the side of capital by sending troops into West Virginia," and which assured the workers that if they struck against the railroad monopolies, the party would give the strikers "hearty support in sympathy, money and muscle." This brought cries of "Hear, hear," which also greeted the reading of telegrams to the workers of Pittsburgh, congratulating them on having forced the Philadelphia militia into the roundhouse and driven them out of the city. Then followed a speech by a house painter, who insisted that the time had come for labor to avenge the many injustices heaped upon the working class by the capitalists and their political allies:

Look at the late action of the governor and railroad company against the poor Pennsylvania miners who toiled in the bowels of the earth, only making enough to keep body and soul together. They never received a cent of money, only orders for grocers and house rents, and when they banded together for the protection of their interests, the railroad company called them "Molly Maguires," hounded them, and hung eleven of them like so many dogs.

The crowd roared its approval as the speaker called the

hangings "one of the blackest stains upon the escutcheon of the United States." They cheered, too, when he pointed out that their "heroic brethren" in Pittsburgh were waiting for the workers in East St. Louis and St. Louis to act. Would they or would they not help both them and themselves by going out on strike? Cries of "Yes, yes" was the answer.

Another speaker reminded the railroaders that if they voted to strike, they would have friends across the river—"good, warm friends, and the fact is exhibited in the strong delegation from the St. Louis party of workingmen present at the meeting."[18]

At six o'clock, the meeting was adjourned, and the members of the Workingmen's Party took the ferry back to St. Louis. At eight o'clock, the trainmen met in Traubel's Hall. The chairman told them that the issue they faced was "a question of life and death, and for his part he was willing to stake his life for his family." "Gentlemen," he continued, "do you want to go out?" "Out, out, out," many responded. Representatives of nine roads present— the Ohio & Mississippi, the Indianapolis & St. Louis, the St. Louis & Southeastern, the Vandalia, Rockford & Rock Island, the Cairo Short Line, the Cairo & St. Louis (Narrow Gauge), the Toledo, Wabash & Western, the Illinois & St. Louis, and the O & A—were then polled as to where their workers stood on the question. The answers were the same from each line: the men were ready to hold out until they got their terms, and had vowed "not to send out a freight train until their companies gave in."

As each representative expressed the intention of the men on his road to join in the strike, he was greeted with loud cheers. After a brief debate, it was voted not to allow any but passenger, mail, and express trains to leave. The strike was then ordered to begin at midnight, July 23, and not to be ended until the railroad companies informed the workers, through committees to be appointed for the various roads, that they were ready to pay what was demanded. It was also voted that all workers be included in the strike: engineers, trackmen, platform men, brakemen, firemen, wipers, and all others employed on freight trains. Thus, the strike in the area would transform the principle of the Trainmen's Union into a reality.

At this point, the chairman asked the men whether their demand should be simply the recall of the 10 percent reduction, or the restoration of the wages in effect before the Panic began in 1873. He recommended that they "might as well do things right" while they were about it. This was greeted with cheers and cries that the demand should be for the old standard. A vote was then taken on the question, and it was decided that "the strike continue until the old wages were restored."

As a final step, the meeting elected an executive committee that would attend to all "necessary work" involved in conducting the walkout and reaching a settlement with the officers of the respective roads. The meeting then adjourned to allow the railroad workers to put the strike into effect. As one group of workers leaving Traubel's Hall told a reporter: "We are in for it now. It is the death struggle. If we fail this time, it is all up with us, and the companies can grind us down to the starvation wages, if they will."[19]

With this determination, and with "a speed, efficiency and discipline unequalled by any other strike center,"[20] the East St. Louis railroad workers began the blockade. It is necessary to describe in such minute detail the proceedings of the meetings, both indoor and outdoor, that led to the strike action because the very newspapers of St. Louis that covered them so thoroughly were later to charge that the decision to strike was put over on the railroad workers by the agents of the "secret Communist cabal": the Workingmen's Party of the United States.[21]

Shortly before twelve o'clock, Engine 53 of the Indianapolis & St. Louis Railroad came into the yard to take freight train No. 5. The executive committee, preceded by a fife and drum corps, approached the train and requested the crew to leave. The firemen and brakemen left the train at once, and the engineer took the engine back to the roundhouse. One after another, the freight trains were abandoned. At 2 a.m., a *Globe-Democrat* reporter visited the main crossing and wrote: "A hundred men kept watch. They were orderly and undemonstrative, but firm and determined that no trains should pass that way." None did. "General Order No. 1" stopped all freight traffic. When the superintendent of the Indianapolis & St. Louis pleaded with the strikers for permission to let nine freight cars pass through, he was told: "The buckwheat will be growing under your cars before they start again." As his horse and buggy left, the fife and drum corps followed, and the superintendent was "literally drummed out of town."[22]

In East St. Louis, the strikers took possession of the railway depot and made it their headquarters. With coolness and discipline, they then proceeded to take over the running of the town. They closed all saloons within six or seven blocks of the depot and made sure that no freight was stolen or railway cars destroyed. Meanwhile, the strike spread to other industries in East St. Louis, and men from the car works and the stockyards joined the railroad workers. With only about a dozen policemen at his disposal, Mayor John Bowman, who depended on the strikers' votes, proposed to them that they select men whom he would appoint as special police to guard the railroad property. The proposal was accepted and put into effect. The strikers were now in full control of East St. Louis.

Across the river in St. Louis, Mayor Henry Overstolz infuriated the press by refusing to take any precautions against a spillover of the strike. On the day after the East St. Louis railroad men went out on strike, he went for a drive and spent the rest of the day quietly at home. When a reporter tracked him down, he assured him that the St. Louis police force was one of the best equipped in the country, and that the armories were well stocked. If necessary, a force of nearly five hundred men could be placed under arms within an hour, but he doubted that the situation would become that serious.[23]

As we have seen, however, receiver James H. Wilson took a far more drastic view of the matter than did Mayor Overstolz. When he heard the news that the men had gone on strike, he wired Secretary of the Interior Schurz, and, after terming the situation "alarming," he asked if there were any United States troops at the U.S. Arsenal in St. Louis who could be used in an emergency. Schurz turned the request over to Secretary of War McCrary, who ordered General John Pope, commander of the United States Twenty-third Infantry, to take whatever men he could spare and proceed to St. Louis at once. The following morning, Pope left Fort Leavenworth, Kansas, with six companies of regulars.[24]

On Monday afternoon, July 23, the Missouri Pacific line—on which the workers had struck after the Traubel's Hall meeting—gave in and restored wages to the scale existing before January 1, 1877. On the basis of this settlement, the railroad was prepared to accept all freight. When Wilson heard the news, he told a reporter that as far as his own line was concerned, it was "out of the question to talk of making any concession to the strikers. If this were done, there would be no end to their demands, and the railroads would have to submit to being controlled by their employees." For its part, the strikers' executive committee rejected separate agreements with the various lines, insisting on the "all or none" principle. The group then issued "Order No. 2" declaring that no one was empowered to settle with any road except the executive committee. The Missouri Pacific's freight did not move.[25]

On Monday evening, the Workingmen's Party called a mass meeting in the very heart of St. Louis, at Lucas Market. "The crowd was a far better looking one than might be supposed," the *Globe-Democrat* commented. "They were all laboring men but evidently of the better class. . . . The speaking was in several languages, but was listened to respectfully by everybody, whether it was understood or not." As the meeting progressed, the crowd grew to such size that a second and a third speaker's stand had to be set up, so that three meetings were going on at once. Apart from the composition of the crowd, its size amazed the press. That a small group using "no flaming advertisements . . . no music, . . . no transparencies, . . . no banner and no torches," could pull off "so large, so enthusiastic a political meeting" was something to be pondered.[26]

After Lofgreen had been elected chairman, Albert Kordell was introduced as the first speaker. He took off his coat, rolled up his sleeves, and said:

I have taken off my coat just the same as I would when I go to my daily toil; and I do it honestly because I am doing it in a noble, honest cause. . . . We are the very bone and sinew of the country and why should we be kept down, as we are, in serfdom? We have now a worse time than the slaves had in 1850, and there is no man who dares question the fact. Monopoly has us by the throat, and it will crush us if we show it that we allow it to do it to us. . . . If we have any rights, now is the time to demand them, and if it is to result in bloodshed, let it be so, and it will be for the sake of our wives and children. No man can die a more heroic death than to die in the present cause. . . . I believe that our railroad monopolies today have no other object in view than to take the government in their possession and rule it for the next fifty years to come, to the injury of our free institutions, and while we have some knowledge of their scheme, we propose to prevent them. And how will we do it? Why, if it must be by arms, let it be by arms.

At several points during this speech, Kordell was interrupted by cries of "Give it to 'em," "Hear, hear," but it was the last statement that produced the loudest cheers and cries of "You bet!" Cheers also greeted his statement that he was not in favor of the Missouri Pacific's strikers accepting the terms offered by the company, even though it met their demands: "I say, stand by each other, even if it leads to the sacrifice of life. . . . If you must accept any compromise, let it be with the railways in the hands of the Government, and let every man have his fair share."

The next speaker was John E. Cope, who introduced himself as an "Old Englishman," which he was, having been a member of the Bootclosers' Society in London, of the Central Council of the International Workingmen's Association in 1864, and of the General Council of the First International from 1865-1867. He had come to the United States some time after 1869, and had settled in St. Louis. In 1877, at fifty-four, he was working at his trade as a shoe-fitter, and in his spare time as organizer of the "English" or "American" section of the Workingmen's Party in St. Louis.[27]

In his speech, Cope insisted that the workingmen were not going to destroy the railroads. Rather, the railroads were going to become national property for the benefit of the people, and the working class would not destroy its own property. If the railroad corporations starved their workers, he went on, it was as if they murdered them, and whoever murdered a man should be hung. Yet under the existing system, these "murderers" were honored: "A man who stole a single rail is called a thief, while he who stole a railway is a gentleman." Cope concluded by warning the workers to be prepared to meet the military once the authorities called them in to crush their strike.

Albert Currlin then followed with a speech in German, and he, too, insisted that if the government should send the military "to stop the laboring man from obtaining his rights," it would be necessary to fight back. The next speaker, Joseph N. Glenn, a shoe workers' organizer and a national officer of the Knights of Labor, reached back into history to make his point. He reminded the crowd that in France under Louis XIV, the people had "become desperate with hunger and feasted on blood," while in England, the people who called themselves "Chartists" "took possession of the streets, and proceeded to help themselves." By contrast, American workingmen tolerated a situation under which monopolies were "robbing the laborer of his products, and filling the land with paupers, vagrants and tramps. . . ." Although American workers had it in their power to change all this, he declared, they lacked "the intelligence or courage to emancipate themselves by the ballot. At the present moment, however, it was necessary to use any means to prevent the capitalists from "bringing down labor into serfdom." He concluded, to loud cheers and cries of "Give 'em Hell!":

Workingmen must either fight or die. The blood of the unfortunate miners of Pennsylvania, and of the workmen of Pittsburgh and Baltimore, cries aloud for Industrial Liberty, and we must have it. Labor must be free, even though every town and city in the country perishes.

Harry Allen, one of the party's most enthusiastic members, picked up the theme of resistance: "We must fight or die. Which shall we do?" The crowd yelled back: "We'll fight! We'll fight!" In that event, Allen predicted, the outcome was inevitable:

We workingmen can present such a force that even the government itself must and will comply with our demands. We will take such steps as that the old and the young, the sick and the healthy, will be provided for.

Other speakers addressed the meeting from three stands. The *Missouri Republican* reported:

All the speakers spoke in deep sympathy with the strikers, generally premising their remarks with an outline of the difficulties and privations in the way of making a living by honest toil. . . . It was the sight of the wives and children, hungry and unprovided for, which was driving them to assert what they believed to be their rights. . . .

The speakers also attacked the newspapers for speaking out in the interests of the capitalists who controlled them. Other targets were the military; President Hayes, for his orders sending federal troops against strikers; and Mayor Overstolz, for not providing public works so that idle men might obtain employment. "Notwithstanding that the cheering at times became deafening," the *Globe-Democrat* reported, "the utmost good order prevailed."[28]

One of the speakers was Reverend John Snyder, pastor of the Church of the Messiah. Although his speech was mild in comparison with the others, he was "severely criticized" by his parishioners. In a "card" published in the local press, Dr. Snyder explained that he had attended the meeting in order to learn, if possible, the grievances of the workingmen and the methods they proposed for their removal. While there, he had been recognized and invited to the platform to address the crowd. This he did, and he went on to explain that he did so eagerly, since he would have the opportunity thereby to dispel "several false notions" of the other speakers, such as the attacks upon the government as corrupt and as an agent of the corporations. He had informed the crowd, he wrote, that the government was just what they had made it, and had urged them, if they were dissatisfied with the existing government, "to form a new political party . . . and elect men to office who shall honestly and faithfully represent what they regarded as sound political principles." Since his speech had gone unrecorded in the press, he felt it necessary to reveal what he had actually said.

As for those critics who felt it was wrong for him to have even attended the mass meeting, he would remind them of "one whose chief title to the love and reverence of men was in the fact that the common people heard him gladly; and who shared the feeling, the sympathies, the privations—all the experiences of the poor man. . . ." Now, however, the workmen of both continents considered the church as nothing "but a rich man's club, and the clergy but the pious conservators of social selfishness in high places." While he sympathized with the strikers' grievances and condemned the fact that so many workers were "compelled to work for insufficient wages, gradually seeing their wives and children slip from comfort and respectability," he did not share their opinions as to how to redress these wrongs. Still, he insisted that it had truly been a workingmen's meeting, and not, as some newspaper reporters charged, made up of "Bummers," "Socialists," "Communists," "Red Republicans," and "Internationalists." Dr. Snyder concluded by warning that "respectable citizens" could not afford to remain ignorant of the grievances, real or imagined, of the genuine laboring class."[29]

Even though it was a rather feeble defense of the workers whom he had addressed, the fact is that, as David L. Burbank points out: "Dr. Snyder was about the only well-known citizen to say even that much for the strikers publicly during the strike."[30]

After calling upon the workers to join the Workingmen's Party and announcing that signatures for membership would be taken at Turner Hall the next day, the leaders adjourned the great Lucas Market meeting at about 11 p.m. A committee of five, including a Black man named Wilson, who had addressed the meeting briefly and had been well received, was elected to visit the mayor and request that he inform the governor of Pennsylvania of the meeting's sympathy "with the suffering laborers" and also that he urge President Hayes not to send federal troops to St. Louis. Aside from Wilson, all of the committee members were also members of the Workingmen's Party, an indication that the party had indeed taken over the leadership of the strike in St. Louis. Across the river in East St. Louis, however, the party's influence was minimal, and the railroad workers' executive committee continued to lead the struggle in that city.[31]

On Tuesday, July 24, the committee of five met with Mayor Overstolz, who received them politely and expressed his "sympathy" but made it clear that he could not, as the committee desired, urge the federal government not to send troops to St. Louis. That very evening, six companies of the Twenty-third Infantry arrived in the city. There were three hundred soldiers, commanded by General Jefferson C. Davis, along with two Gatling guns. The general announced that he had come "merely to protect government and public property," and not "to quell the strikers or run the trains."[32]

The workers cheered, but James H. Wilson, the receiver, was furious. He had persuaded Judge Drummond to send a U.S. marshal to East St. Louis to break up the strike, and he felt that this job should now be done by Davis's troops, especially since they had arrived at his request. He therefore wired Secretary of the Interior Schurz that the strikers in East St. Louis would allow "nothing to go out but the mails which we shall have also to suspend," and that the U.S. marshal "has come to my assistance but can do nothing without fifteen hundred or two thousand regulars" to crush "the mob still in possession at East St. Louis."[33] Schurz did not reply.

As the defenses of St. Louis began to take shape, so, too, did the general strike. Workers from the various shops and plants appeared at the Workingmen's Party headquarters at Turner Hall, requesting that committees be sent around to notify the men in different establishments "to stop work and join the other workingmen." One after another struck the note of militancy and defiance of the corporations and the authorities. The fact that the workers came to the party and reacted in this manner was clearly a result of the mass meeting of the previous evening, where the socialists took over the leadership of the strike in St. Louis.

The Workingmen's Party responded promptly to these requests and sent representatives to the different shops. The results were astounding. The coopers went on strike, marching from shop to shop with fife and drum, shouting, "Come out, come out! No barrels less than nine cents!" Newsboys went on strike against the *St. Louis Dispatch.* There were walkouts among the boatmen on the levee. Engineers of the packet *City of Helena* won an increase of ten dollars, bringing their wages up to forty dollars a month, and this was only one of several wage increases.[34]

There had been an announcement at the Lucas Market meeting that there would be a "grand procession" the following evening, ending up at another mass meeting in the same place. The parade of workers, many of them molders and mechanics, went four abreast through the streets to Lucas Market, headed by a single torch and a fife and drum. Some of the men carried lathes or clubs on their shoulders, which made the progression, in the eyes of the *St. Louis Times,* "an awfully suggestive spectacle."[35] At the Market, the paraders joined a crowd which, the *Times* said, could be estimated "by acres." The *Daily Journal* put the crowd at 10,000, while the *Globe-Democrat* reported that it was "a very large meeting, and larger, if anything, than the gathering of the previous night."[36] Since the previous night's meeting had been called the largest in St. Louis's history, it is clear that it was an immense assemblage.

A rough square platform had been erected for the speakers. Half a dozen torches were placed around the platform, in the center of which was an American flag. To the reporters' surprise, they were provided with tables and chairs, an indication, one paper observed, that "at least the Workingmen's Party saw the policy of recognizing reporters in a gentlemanly manner." More likely the party realized in advance that the mass meeting would mark the beginning of the general strike in St. Louis, and wanted to make sure that the speeches were reported accurately—at least to the extent that reporters for the capitalist press could do so.[37]

Peter A. Lofgreen called the meeting to order in the name of the party. The first speaker, J. P. Kadell, a cooper, who was described as "one of the ringleaders of the party," opened on a moderate note by stating: "What we want is fair compensation and no more than eight hours as a normal day's work in the future." But as he swept on, his speech became more "inflammatory." After vigorously condemning the shooting down of men, women, and children in Baltimore and Pittsburgh, and the officials responsible for having made such a catastrophe possible, he declared to the accompaniment of cheers:

There was a time in the history of France when the poor found themselves oppressed to such an extent that forbearance ceased to be a virtue, and hundreds of heads tumbled into the basket. That time may have arrived with us. As long as we can avoid the shedding of blood, we will do it. But if it must come, let it come.

Already, he went on, hundreds of federal soldiers were stationed in St. Louis, and they were itching to shoot down strikers, despite the disclaimer of their commanding general. He wanted it known that "we have 7,000 stands of arms in our possession tonight to fight with, if you want them." This was greeted with cheers and enthusiastic cries of "Let's have them!"

Since Kadell ended his speech on this fiery note, he neglected to specify precisely where the arms were. It is likely that what he (and other leaders) had in mind was that, if necessary, they could obtain arms "either by raiding an arsenal or by getting strikers' squads the status of militia units and so get them armed legally." Perhaps the fact that the strikers in East St. Louis had been designated as special police may have encouraged this view. At any rate, while it may have bolstered the strikers' determination to stand firm, it is hardly likely that Kadell's bold statement about arms meant that the party actually had access to the quantity he mentioned.

Before the next speaker, the chairman read a telegram from the Workingmen's Party of Chicago, describing the great labor demonstration in Market Square the previous night under its sponsorship, and closed: "Chicago struck today." The news was greeted with great cheering.

A. Barker, the next speaker and another member of the party, described the movement in which they were engaged as the greatest of the entire century—an uprising of the producers of the wealth of the nation, "the men who have made the United States what it is." He asked the crowd: "What is the object? What has made the people rise *en masse* from the Atlantic to the Pacific?" The crowd responded with cries of "Bread," and the speaker added: "They simply want their rights, and a share of that which they have produced. Shall they have it?" "Yes," thundered the crowd. The workers, he continued, were told that they must respect the majesty of the law, but what did such talk mean to workers "when their wives and daughters were starving and when they were branded as tramps and vagrants?" The present movement was aimed not only at getting back the 10 percent wage cut, but also at bringing about a thorough reform in the railroad system. The strikers intended to accomplish their objective "or die in the struggle." As for shooting, they did not intend to shoot; they were educated to work. "But if the authorities and monopolies shoot at us," Barker declared, "we will shoot at them in return. We are determined to have our rights even though the Heavens fall upon us."

"Negroes too?" someone asked. "Yes!" the crowd shouted back, and a Black steamboat man was called upon to speak. He described the plight of the Black roustabouts: "We work in the summer for $20 a month, and in the winter time can't find the man we work for." After telling his story, he asked the crowd: "Will you stand to us regardless of color?" "We will! We will! We will!" the crowd responded.

Harry Eastman, an East St. Louis striker and a member of the party (in fact, the only member among the railroad strikers of East St. Louis), spoke on behalf of the railroad men and urged that they be supported. The crowd shouted its assurance. James McCarthy, a member of the committee that had visited the mayor that day, then called upon the workingmen to organize into companies of ten, twenty, and a hundred to establish patrols in order to "protect property" and "organize force to meet force."

A theme that was hammered at throughout the evening was that the workers constituted the bone and sinew of the American nation; they were the producers of its wealth and were just as good as the men who claimed to have been chosen to rule and control the country. As one speaker cried out angrily:

> You are just as law-abiding as those who rob the public treasury. Just as decent as those lecherous bondholders who derive their revenue by cutting off coupons. Your wives are just as virtuous as the wives of the rich capitalists, who, decked in silks and satins, ride in their carriages, and your children are just as pure and upright as the bastard offspring of those bastards themselves.

J. J. McBride, a lawyer who had championed the eight-hour law in the state legislature, made the same point in denouncing the St. Louis press for characterizing the strikers as the "*canaille*," which, he pointed out, literally meant "dog." This was a "damnable lie." The men on strike were "American citizens, who are endeavoring to make an honorable living," and those who called them "dogs" were themselves "curs of dogs." After going on in this vein for some time, McBride proposed a way to solve the difficulties facing the nation, in the form of a resolution calling upon the president to convene Congress immediately for the purpose of "appropriating $100,000,000 or more of the people's money to save the people's lives by giving them work." The proposal concluded:

Resolved, That while we are in favor of law and order and of maintaining the legal rights of property, we are also in favor of bread and meat, and of maintaining the natural right of man to "life, liberty and the pursuit of happiness."

Resolved, That our motto is Right! Might will sustain the Right against the power of every foe!

Amid cheers, the resolution was adopted unanimously.

The climax of the meeting came when Henry Allen, in the name of the executive committee, introduced a series of resolutions which began by cautioning against violence and then asserted that "every man willing to perform a use to society" was "entitled to a living," and that if the "present system of production and distribution fails to provide for our wants, it then becomes the duty of the government to enact such laws as will insure equal justice to all the peoples of the nation." The resolutions closed with the recommendation of the executive committee for

. . . a general strike of all branches of industry, for eight hours as a day's work, and we call on the legislature for the immediate enactment of an eight-hour law and the enforcement and severe penalty for its violation, and that the employment of all children under fourteen years of age be prohibited.

After the resolution calling for a general strike was adopted "amidst loud cheers," the meeting adjourned. The crowd then formed a procession and, preceded by a band, marched through the principal streets carrying torchlights. They crossed the bridge to the railroaders' strike headquarters in East St. Louis, where there were more speeches and the reading of the resolution adopted in St. Louis calling for the general strike.[38]

"A more orderly procession has seldom been seen," said the *Globe-Democrat* in its report on the parade to East St. Louis.[39] But the British consul in St. Louis had a different opinion. That very day, he reported to his superiors in London:

The city was practically in the hands of a mob, while the inhabitants were in perpetual terror of some outbreak which should excel in horror the stories that were hourly coming from the City of Pittsburgh. . . . Parades of the discontented were permitted on all principal streets without a show of countervailing force, and nightly mass meetings were held in the most public places, where thousands of the most ignorant and depraved in the community were made riotous by the incendiary speeches of their orators.

Yet the sergeant in charge of the U.S. Signal Service in St. Louis, in a wire to Washington following the mass meeting at Lucas Market, noted that despite the "incendiary speeches," the most the proposed general strike called for was an eight-hour law, and that the railroad workers, who were primarily interested in rescinding the wage cuts, were probably not even ready to endorse this new demand.[40]

However, the St. Louis business community was not interested in such fine distinctions. That same day—Tuesday, July 24— Mayor Overstolz had called a secret meeting of businessmen and other "respectable elements," and made it clear that neither the police nor the militia could cope with the situation long planned by "thirty thousand fully armed socialists," bent upon overthrowing the city government. The following morning, Sheriff John Finn raised a posse of five thousand men. A "Committee of Public Safety" was organized, and the Four Courts building was taken over for its headquarters. (The committee itself consisted of a judge and five ex-generals.) Governor John S. Phelps sent the committee arms and ammunition from the state arsenal at Jefferson City, but the committee, frightened by the scope and vigor of the Lucas Market mass meeting, wired the secretary of war for ten thousand stands of rifles, two thousand revolvers, a battery of artillery, and ammunition. This request was rejected when it was learned that there were simply not enough arms available in Washington to meet it.[41]

The day following the Lucas Market meeting, the resolutions calling for the general strike were printed in the form of a "Proclamation" in English and German, and distributed throughout the city. They were preceded by a statement addressed to "Fellow-Citizens," which was the first of a series of contradictory policy statements issued by the executive committee. After pointing to the widespread unemployment that existed in the city, and the failure of the government to do anything to aid those who were suffering, the statement declared boldly: "Therefore, fellow-workingmen, we MUST act ourselves, unless we want starvation to stare to our faces the coming winter. There is only one way— HELP YOURSELF!" The rest of the statement, however, emphasized the importance of avoiding violence and that the executive committee was determined to make sure that only peaceful and lawful means were employed in the battle that was developing.[42]

The executive committee that was organized by the Workingmen's Party to guide the general strike was never identified with the party in the handbills and proclamations issued in its name. Moreover, its composition changed after the party decided to enlarge the group and include representatives of different unions and strikers' groups. Nevertheless, Morris Hillquit exaggerated when he wrote in his *History of Socialism in the United States* that the committee "seems to have been a rather loose body composed of whomsoever chanced to come in and take part in its deliberations." Throughout the strike, the committee consisted in the main of six of the more active party members: Albert Currlin, Peter Lofgreen, James E. Cope, Thomas Curtis, William B. Fischer, and Henry F. Allen. Of the six, only Curtis, an elderly bookseller, denied that he had been a member of the party. Fischer, a German printer, was the younger brother of Adolph Fischer, who was one of the eight Haymarket martyrs. Allen, a Welshman, was a sign painter and a self-taught physician.[43]

Along with the "Proclamation" that it issued in English and German, the executive committee distributed circulars calling upon laboring men to assemble at Lucas Market that afternoon— July 25—for a grand parade "to demonstrate their strength and to induce all who were still in the ranks of non-strikers to lend their assistance for the common interest." While the procession was being prepared, the general strike was getting under way. The employees of a beef cannery announced on a banner that they would strike for an increase in wages from $.75 to $1.75 a day—thereby earning for themselves the description of "Mad Strikers" in the *Missouri Republican*.[44] The steamer *Centennial* was fully loaded, ready to leave for New Orleans, but a few minutes before its departure, several hundred strikers—"the negroes predominating"—boarded the vessel and demanded that the wages of roustabouts be increased from $25 to $40 per month, and that the wages of deckhands and firemen be increased from $30 to $45 per month. "He [the captain] was completely in their power and had to make the concessions demanded," a reporter wrote. With their numbers considerably increased, the victorious workers visited other boats, forcing the captains and officers of the packet companies to grant their demands. Summing up the situation at one o'clock in the afternoon, the *Globe-Democrat* reported: "Thus far, the river men have gained all of their demands."[45]

At precisely that hour, these workers "of all colors," waving a huge American flag, headed triumphantly for Lucas Market to join the great procession. The march got under way at two o'clock in the afternoon. Four abreast and stretching for nearly four blocks, the workers moved along. Six hundred factory workers marched up behind a brass band and carried a huge transparency with the words: "NO MONOPOLY—WORKINGMEN'S RIGHTS." A company of railroad strikers came bearing coupling pins, brake rods, red signal flags, and other "irons and implements emblematic of their calling." The red signal flags carried by the railroaders as emblems of their trade were the only flags of that color in the parade. During the march, someone ran into a bakery, came out with a loaf of bread, stuck it on a flagstaff, and bore it aloft to the cheers of the crowd. What followed was reported in the *Globe-Democrat:*

> When the men saw it they cheered again and again. "That is what we are fighting for," said one.
> "Let it be the symbol of the strike," said another.

The procession, headed by the English, German, and Bohemian sections of the Workingmen's Party, marched through the streets. Strikers' committees went out ahead to call out those who were still working, and as the march came by, workers in foundries, bagging companies, flour mills, bakeries, and chemical plants all poured out of the shops and into the crowd.

In Carondelet, on the extreme south end of the city, a similar march developed as a crowd of ironworkers closed down the zinc works, the steel works, and other plants. A reporter telegraphed to a Pennsylvania paper:

> . . . Great crowds of strikers and some 300 negro laborers on the levee visited a large number of manufacturing establishments in the southern part of the city, compelling all employees to stop work, putting out all fires in the engine rooms and closing the building.

In Carondelet, too, the railroad strikers carried red signal flags, but there, the red flags of the "Internationals" also appeared, as members of the Workingmen's Party held their banners aloft. A reporter for the *St. Louis Times* conceded that the red flags of the "Internationals" were "always greeted with a round of cheers." In East St. Louis, there was a parade of women in support of the strikers.[46]

The parade continued for three hours, during which the marchers' numbers were swelled into the thousands. Not even the rain could dampen the marchers' determination to close down all establishments. "Through the pelting rain they went, closed shop after shop, and making threats of what would be done if the work resumed before the strike was over," reported the *Globe-Democrat*. By sundown, nearly all the manufacturing establishments had been closed; the next morning, the *Daily Market Reporter* announced that "the strike in its effect permeated every branch of trade in St. Louis." That same morning, the *Missouri Republican* conceded that the parade which had closed down St. Louis was generally orderly, and it complimented the Workingmen's Party for its "leadership and organizational qualities."[47]

The grand climax of the exciting day came that evening at a mass meeting at Lucas Market, where an estimated 10,000 people assembled for another WPUS meeting. Peter A. Lofgreen opened the meeting, the largest of its kind held during the strike, with the announcement that the general strike must go on not only until the eight-hour day was achieved, but until the workers obtained control of the government and cleaned it out. This could be accomplished, he declared, if the workingmen sent to Washington as their representatives men of their own class, instead of the "kid glove" lawyers who had so misrepresented them during the last decade. But to achieve this goal, labor must unite behind the Workingmen's Party. Then, just as Lincoln had freed the four million slaves, the nine million white slaves would be emancipated. Finally, in a reference to the defense of the railroad companies' wage-cutting policies, he said that if the railroads could not pay the interest on their bonds, let alone meet their expenses, the managers should resign and put the roads into the hands of the people.

Another party speaker stressed that the movement was "not a strike but a social revolution": "The people are rising up in their might and declaring that they will not longer submit to being oppressed by unproductive capital." "This great movement is rapidly increasing in intensity," said another party spokesman, "and is now so strong that no state, and not even the United States Government can peaceably put a stop to it." He demanded that Congress pass an effective eight-hour law, recall the charters of all national banks, institute a public works program to relieve unemployment, and purchase all railroads with an issue of greenbacks. "I propose," he concluded, "that we make an appeal directly to the President of the United States."

The meeting closed with the adoption of "a platform and plan of action" submitted by the executive committee. Printed later under the title of "Vox Populi Vox Dei" (Voice of the People, Voice of God), the manifesto noted that "the entire labor movement of the USA" was "in a condition of revolution," and that the managers of the railroads had "confessed their inability to make expenses." In view of this, the manifesto demanded that the government "take possession of all the railroads and run them for the general welfare." Three other demands were advanced: for the "recall of all charters of all national banks, together with their whole currency," for a program of public works, and for an eight-hour law. If these demands were granted, the workingmen would pledge that they would "everywhere uphold the government of the people thus established in justice and equity."[48]

That night, the executive committee ruled the city. Nearly all the manufacturing establishments in St. Louis had been closed. Sixty factories were shut down, not including the "mercantile firms from Fifth Street to the river . . . which closed down for prudential reasons." "Business is fairly paralyzed here," said the *Daily Market Reporter*. Such economic activities as continued did so only with the permission of the executive committee. The British consul in St. Louis noted how the railroad strikers had "taken the road into their own hands, running the trains and collecting fares," and added that "it is to be deplored that a large portion of the general public appear to regard such conduct as a legitimate mode of warfare."[49]

A repetition of Wednesday's parade on Thursday moring closed twenty more factories. In order to provide bread, a flour mill was permitted to remain open. When the owner of the Belcher Sugar Refinery applied to the executive committee for permission to operate his plant for forty-eight hours, lest a large quantity of sugar spoil, the executive committee persuaded the refinery workers to go back and work and sent a guard of two hundred men to protect the refinery. David T. Burbank points out that "the Belcher episode revealed . . . the spectacle of the owner of one of the city's largest industrial enterprises recognizing the *de facto* authority of the Executive Committee." Small wonder that some historians later described the situation as "the St. Louis 'Soviet,'" and that the "'Soviet' . . . seems to have taken over most of the functions of government in the city."[50] The contemporary press, however, preferred the title, "St. Louis Commune," and while the St. Louis papers used that term in horror, they still took a certain pride in the claim that it was the "only *genuine* Commune" established during the Great Strikes of 1877.[51]

But reports of a mighty executive committee representing at least 22,000 workingmen and carrying through a "real revolution" unhesitatingly and unswervingly, until crushed by overwhelming police and military force, were hardly accurate. In truth, having shattered the authority of the city and temporarily paralyzed the wealthy classes, the executive committee vacillated, hesitated, and fell back, unsure of what to do next. At the same time, it revealed that it feared the very mass movement it had helped to create. The committee was actually a mass of contradictions. In a handbill issued on July 25, it raised the threat of mob violence, and at the same time repudiated it. The handbill expressed the workingmen's desire to gain their demands "without spilling one drop of blood"; yet it demanded "justice . . . or death!" Again: "We shall do all in our power to keep down the mob, but fear we can no longer restrain the starving millions of our once happy land." A further contradiction was in the declaration: "We are united in purpose," but "are undecided what course to pursue."[52]

The next day, July 26, the executive committee issued a proclamation to employers, through the mayor of St. Louis, suggesting that they feed the strikers and hinting that in this way they could "avoid plunder, arson or violence by persons made desperate by destitution. . . ." The proclamation assured the mayor of the executive committee's desire to assist "in maintaining order and protecting property," and concluded with this revealing statement:

Further, in order to avoid riot, we have determined to have no large processions until our organization is so complete as to positively assure the citizens of St. Louis of a perfect maintenance of order and full protection of property.[53]

Yet it was precisely those "large processions" that had been the main source of the committee's strength, and its decision to hold no further meetings was fatal, for it practically guaranteed that the great upheaval would disintegrate. There were no strong trade unions left in St. Louis, so that it was only through the mass meetings that the committee had been able to maintain contact with the workers.

The decision was motivated by a variety of reasons, but the chief one was the fear that the mass meetings could quickly get out of control as speakers pressed for a more militant policy than that advocated by the executive committee. When a speaker at a mass meeting on July 25 began talking of "commencing the work of organizing and arming" so as to be prepared for an armed attack against the strikers by the police and the federal troops, the executive committee tried to have him arrested. However, he vanished before the police could lay their hands on him.

Racism, too, played an important part in the committee's decision. When the Black steamboat man had asked at the very outset of the strike whether the crowd would stand behind the strikers regardless of color, he had good reason to raise the question. Since the end of slavery, neither the trade unions nor the socialist organizations of St. Louis had ever displayed any willingness to cooperate with Black workers, and during its year of existence the Workingmen's Party of St. Louis had not made the slightest effort to recruit Blacks. The answer of the crowd— "We will"—had encouraged the Black workers, and, as we have seen, they began to play a prominent role in the general strike. Indeed, a reporter for the *New York Sun* noted that the Black participation with white workers in the general strike was "a novel feature of the times."[54]

But the "novel feature" soon began to disturb both camps in the St. Louis struggle. The establishment, of course, was shocked at the notion that Blacks were forgetting their assigned role of "contented banjo-strummers," and were beginning to assert their rights just as if they were white. In its description of the Black strikers who had paraded on the levee before joining the great procession, the *Missouri Republican* had labeled them "a dangerous-looking set of men," and had observed almost in terror that "there was something blood-curdling in the manner in which they shouldered their clubs and started up the levee whooping." And the *St. Louis Times* kept insisting that women workers in the factories were holding back from joining the general strike because they were "frightened at the scent and wild-eyed look of the black race."[55]

As Blacks began to appear in the processions and at the mass meetings sponsored by the Workingmen's Party, the press—and particularly the *Missouri Republican*—began to paint pictures of a movement that was being taken over by "notorious Negroes." It was all due, it charged, to the "insidious influence of the International," and the Workingmen's Party was accused of being responsible for these "outrages" against the social values of the community.[56]

This was enough for the white supremacists in the Workingmen's Party. After the strike, Albert Currlin, a leader of the German section and a prominent member of the executive committee, was interviewed by the *St. Louis Times*. In the course of the interview, Currlin emphasized that the executive committee had been shocked by the part the "niggers" had assumed in the parades and mass meetings, and that it viewed with horror the thought of having them as members. "A gang of niggers, it looked like about 500, came to Turner Hall, and sent word that they wanted to join our party. We replied that we wanted nothing to do with them." Thereafter, he said, the party leadership tried "to dissuade any white men from going with the niggers."[57] [The use of the derogatory term is Currlin's.] One sure way of keeping Blacks out of mass meetings, and white workers from joining the Black workers, was not to hold any mass meetings at all!

Another factor contributing to the weakness of the WPUS during the general strike was the influence of Lassalleanism, which resulted in a reluctance to link the struggle more closely to trade unionism. Not much was done to involve whatever unions still existed in organizing the strikers, the vast majority of whom were unorganized, into unions or to mobilize them to fight jointly for demands that would give the workers concrete, immediate benefits. Instead, the party and executive committee speakers, and their literature, raised only national and state legislative demands, such as those for a state law for the eight-hour day, for the prohibition of child labor, for a national law for the issuance of greenbacks with which to purchase the railroads, for a national law for the recall of the charters of all national banks, and for a national eight-hour law. Aside from the fact that the demand for currency reform had little in common with the WPUS platform, it was hardly a program that the workers could turn to for their immediate benefit.

Whatever the reasons—fear, racism, internal dissension, or the lack of a concrete program—the executive committee of the Workingmen's Party of the United States in St. Louis simply lost contact with the people it had organized and led. David T. Burbank put it aptly:

At the very point in the strike when the Committee should have exercised the strictest control of its forces, and should have stated its objectives, policies and strategies in the clearest manner, it virtually abdicated.[58]

Having abandoned the holding of mass meetings, the executive committee was reduced to appealing to the authorities, and its appeals were couched in the type of contradictory language already cited, which opposed mob violence while at the same time threatening that only the adoption of its demands would forestall it. It urged Governor Phelps to convene the legislature and speak out for the passage of an eight-hour law and for a measure prohibiting the employment of children under fourteen years of age. "Nothing short of compliance to the above just demand," the committee declared, "will arrest the tidal wave of revolution."[59]

At an earlier stage in the general strike, such a declaration might have produced results; state and city authorities had practically left the executive committee in control of the city, and when the receivers of the St. Louis & Southeastern Railroad had asked Mayor Overstolz to arrest the strikers, he had refused because of his "inability to do so."[60] But by the time the executive committee pleaded with the governor, the authorities had decided that the general strike was already in the process of disintegrating and that there were other ways of arresting "the tidal wave of revolution" than by making concessions to the executive committee.

On Friday, July 27, the executive committee issued a "Proclamation to the Citizens of St. Louis" assuring them that reports that the committee favored "arming" the workers were "villainous falsehoods." As usual, it denounced "mob violence" and declared itself ready to assist the city authorities in preventing "mobs" from parading through the streets. It called upon the businessmen to "further the passage of an eight-hour law."[61]

Even as the executive committee was denying the charge that it intended to arm the workers, St. Louis merchants had raised $20,000 to arm a citizens' militia; the swank St. Louis Gun Club had contributed shotguns and 1,500 rifles had arrived from the state arsenal, while small arms were being shipped from the federal arsenal at Rock Island to arm the citizens. Three companies of the United States Infantry came in from Kansas to buttress the St. Louis police and its citizen militia. Mayor Overstolz, having been raked over the coals by the press for attending a WPUS meeting, albeit only as a bystander at the edge of the crowd, took steps to make amends. He issued a proclamation warning the "Communists" to desist from closing factories, and ordered all business to resume operations. Governor Phelps, who had not even been to the city, issued his own proclamation instructing all "riotous" elements to desist.[62]

Receiver Wilson was pleased. "Time has come," he wired Schurz, "when the President should stamp out mob now rampant. . . . The law can be found for it after order is restored."[63]

Thus, while the executive committee was issuing proclamations and handbills affirming its devotion to peaceful activities and its abhorrence of violence in any form, powerful forces in the city, undeterred by any such scruples, were mobilizing to crush the strike by whatever means might be necessary.

During the morning of Friday, July 27, "a very large crowd," estimated at over two thousand, congregated outside Schuler's Hall, where the executive committee (having been ousted from Turner Hall) was meeting. A *Globe-Democrat* reporter circulating among the Black and white workers found them growing impatient with the executive committee's failure to act. They expressed the fear that unless the strikers were organized as rapidly as the citizens' militia was organizing, it would soon be over, and that it was "now or never."[64] A *Missouri Republican* reporter on the scene quoted a Black striker as expressing the wish that arms might be turned over to "a company of colored men," and he guaranteed that the strike would end quickly and victoriously. The crowd agreed, and cried out that the issue was "whether the poor man was going to get any show at all for his rights." Occasionally, the reporter noted, Lofgreen of the executive committee would emerge from the committee room in his shirtsleeves and take a walk among the workers, "beaming benignly on a few and scowling at those who demanded to know whether they were to have nothing better than finger-nails for long-range fighting."[65] At this point, the *Globe-Democrat* reporter added: "The crowd would not leave the vicinity of the communist headquarters. They certainly expected arms and orders, and that is the reason why they waited patiently."[66]

But all they received from the executive committee was a posted notice reading:

To the Workingmen: Have patience. The Executive Committee are now busily organizing the various trades-unions. Delegations from the unions will report tonight, when the facts will be given to the public. No man of spirit will disturb the Executive Committee.[67]

Albert Currlin later claimed that detectives mingling with the crowd had spread the report that the executive committee had seven thousand stands of arms and plenty of ammunition, which would be distributed for a fight to the finish. He described how part of the crowd came up the stairs to the committee room and "threatened to throw us out of the window if we didn't give them arms." Currlin proudly related to the reporter for the *Times* that he told the gang that the committee had no arms and had no intention of fighting—"that if the police came . . . we would give up right away."[68]

At three o'clock in the afternoon, someone came into the hall and shouted, "The soldiers are coming!" The alarm had been given several times earlier that day, and a good many of those present paid no attention to the new notice. About a hundred workers, however, moved downstairs to the street. The *Missouri Republican* reporter climbed out upon the balcony, on top of the second story awning, from which point he commanded a long view of Fifth Street south. As he described it:

The scene of Fifth Street was a pretty one. The police cavalry, led by Captain Fox and Sergeant Florerich, came northward at a moderate gait, occupying nearly the full width of the street. Just behind them the two files of foot police, led by Captain Lee, mounted, and with Captain Hueber and Sergeants Body and Powell, afoot, moving with a quick step, their bayoneted muskets at a "carry arms." The cannon showed grimly near the middle of the force. The rear of the company was brought up by Mayor Overstolz and three citizens who marched well, regardless of mud.

A half block behind these, the soldiers, with their forest of bayonets, advanced with regular, measured tread, presenting a very pretty column.[69]

This "pretty scene" was quickly followed by a bloody one, as the police drove their horses into the crowd outside Schuler's Hall, swinging their clubs viciously at the heads of anyone in sight, encouraged by Captain Fox's cry, "They have no business here. Cut 'em down, if they don't go."[70]

The attack of the mounted police drove workers away from outside the hall and caused a general stampede among those inside. The *Missouri Republican* reporter, viewing it from his vantage point, wrote:

Some jumped from the third-story porch on the south side of the building, and running over a couple of roofs, made a descent. Many shinned down the pillars of the porches. A score of others got up on the second floor balcony at the east side of the building, and letting themselves down their full length, dropped upon the sidewalk, all in a heap. Several of these jumpers suffered severe sprains.

The foot soldiers arrested those strikers who remained in the building. Not a shot had been fired. The reporter closed his account:

The fort was taken, the mob was dispersed or captured, and a work, great not in itself, but in its influence on future affairs, was completed without bloodshed.[71]

As soon as the strikers came down from the hall, they were marched between two lines of armed police to the Four Courts, where they were locked temporarily in the basement. The arrested parties, the *Globe-Democrat* reported, "conducted themselves very peaceably." The paper observed with some regret that none of the seventy-three arrested were members of the executive committee. Several of the committee members escaped through the windows, while Albert Currlin met the police on the steps as he walked out, but was not recognized. The reporters for the *Missouri Republican* and the *Globe-Democrat* were not that lucky. They, too, were not recognized, but, on the assumption that they had "no business" in the area, they were arrested and marched with the other prisoners to the Four Courts, where they were later released.[72]

Within two days, the entire executive committee, together with a considerable number of other members of the Workingmen's Party, were behind bars.[73] But by that time, the general strike in St. Louis was over. It ended on Friday afternoon, immediately after the police and militia had captured "Fort Schuler" without a struggle. To be sure, there was some hope that if the strike in East St. Louis continued, the strikers on the other side of the river might regain their shattered confidence and renew the struggle. But any hope in that direction ended when the news came in the early hours of Saturday, July 28, that United States troops had poured into East St. Louis and taken over the Relay Depot, without meeting any more resistance from the railroad strikers than the police and militia had encountered in St. Louis. The last flare-up of the strike in East St. Louis came on Sunday, July 29, when the railroad strikers made a final but futile effort to enforce the freight blockade. United States troops helped Marshal Edward Roe arrest scores of strikers, and the strike was over.[74]

In ending a report on the Great Strike in East St. Louis and St. Louis, the British vice-consul commented caustically that "the illegal arrest of a few men met together to talk in a hall was sufficient to bring the whole affair to an end."[75] This tone was reflected also in the St. Louis press, which had a field day ridiculing the very same Workingmen's Party and its executive committee, which for over a week the press had painted as all-powerful, and as strong enough to engineer a revolution in the nation. "Communism in St. Louis received a very black eye . . . ," sneered the *Globe-Democrat.* "After all the brag and bluster of 'the Executive Committee,' it took only a small squad of police to disperse the mob of more than 1,000 within five minutes, and without a shot being fired." However, the paper did concede that the forces of law and order in St. Louis had had to face a strike unprecedented in American history, and it published a list of sixty factories that had been closed by the strike, not including the "mercantile firms from Fifth Street to the river . . . which closed down for prudential reasons." Had there been an effective leadership, it admitted, the stricken city could truly have been transformed into "the first American Commune."[76] The *Times* agreed that St. Louis had just barely escaped the revolution: "Had a single man of good executive ability taken hold of the movement, it could never have been crushed so easily."[77] But it was the *Missouri Republican* that had the last word. The strikers, it declared, had proclaimed "a revolution, and it *was* a revolution."[78]

THE FRENZY, AND WHAT CAME OF IT.—[Drawn by E. A. Abbey.]

Antistrike drawing from Harper's Weekly: The Frenzy, and What
Came of It.

X

The End of the Great Strike

The speed with which the Great Strike moved across the country was positively breathtaking. On July 18 the strike, which had begun in West Virginia, spread to Ohio; one day later, it reached Pennsylvania, and a day after that, New York. On Sunday and Monday, July 22 and 23, thousands of workers throughout the eastern and midwestern sections of the country went on strike. By noon on Tuesday, July 24, the Great Strike had ripped through West Virginia, Maryland, Pennsylvania, New York, New Jersey, Ohio, Indiana, Kentucky, Missouri, and even Iowa. The *New York World* estimated that day that it involved more than eighty thousand railroad workers and over five hundred thousand workers in other occupations.[1] Aside from the walkouts of workers in sympathy with the railroad men, thousands of businesses that were dependent upon the railroads for their supplies—factories, mills, coal mines, and oil refineries— were forced to shut down. In Cleveland, for example, the effects of the stoppage on the Pennsylvania Railroad system were felt as early as Monday morning, July 22, and the *Cleveland Leader* noted that the closing down of the Cleveland & Pittsburgh line (a subsidiary of the Pennsylvania Railroad) by "rioters" had cut off an "important source of supply for fuel":

As a direct consequence of this, all the mills and furnaces of the Cleveland Rolling Mill Company and the Northern Ohio Iron Company are shut down. The Standard Oil Company, with its legion of employees, will stop work this morning for lack of transportation. No less than six foundries in this city will be forced to suspend operations today. . . .[2]

By Wednesday, July 25, all the main railway lines were affected, and employees of some Canadian roads were also joining the strike.[3] By this time, it was a thoroughly national event. Business in many cities was feeling the effect of the freight blockade; for example, New York's supply of western grain and cattle had been completely cut off. There were strike reports from such scattered points as Kansas City, Chicago, Indianapolis, Terre Haute, Columbus, Cincinnati, Louisville, Pittsburgh, Baltimore, East St. Louis, and St. Louis. Illinois Central trains were stopped at Effingham, Malltown, Decatur, and Carbondale, Illinois. Governor Cullom of that state declared in his 1879 biennial message that "the railway trains and machine shops and factories in Chicago, Peoria, Galesburg, Decatur, and East St. Louis were in the hands of the mob, as well as the mines at Bradwood, La Salle, and some other places."[4] The *New York Sun* felt that the decision of railroad workers on the line controlled by the Delaware & Hudson Canal Company *not* to walk out was so unusual a piece of news that it placed it on its front page under the headline, "Where There Was No Strike."[5]

On Wednesday, July 25, John Hay confided to his father-in-law that the railroads would probably have to surrender to the demands of the strikers, even though he felt that it was disgraceful.[6] Others in his class had reached the same conclusion, and that evening quite a few public officials throughout the United States felt more genuine alarm at the possibility of imminent social revolution than on any occasion before—and probably since.[7]

But that same day, Andrew C. Cameron, long-time editor of the *Chicago Workingman's Advocate*, took a more realistic view of the situation. He noted that if the corporations really wanted to, they could easily bring the struggle to a peaceful end. While it was true that the Great Strike had sprung from a reservoir of accumulated grievances, as far as the railroad workers were concerned, the one grievance that was universally cited was the 10 percent wage reduction, and it was this that bound workers in Baltimore to those in Chicago and made them all part of the tremendous labor upheaval. Therefore, the speedy rescinding of the wage cut, reasoned Cameron, could restore peace on the railroads, and this would influence other employers to make concessions and bring the nation back to normalcy.

But, Cameron continued, the railroad managers had proclaimed that the demand for the restoration of the wage cut was an infringement on their management rights, and they were determined not to allow the slightest interference with their total domination over the lives of their workers. In this, they were receiving the backing of the nation's press, for those few railroad managers who had rescinded the wage cut were being pilloried as traitors to the nation. Instead of settling the conflict on reasonable terms, the capitalists were relying on their "puppets" in city and state governments to do the work for them of breaking the strike and forcing the workers to live at a starvation level. Thus, while they appeared to be paralyzed and helpless, their agents were drowning "the grand uprising of labor" in blood:

Already two hundred lives have been sacrificed. The military powers in different states have been used to shoot like dogs men claiming their God-given rights: at Reading, Pittsburgh, Baltimore, Chicago and other points, men, women and helpless children have been massacred by citizen soldiery, employed to enforce the demands of the railroad companies.

"The end is not yet," Cameron went on. The strikers were yet to feel the full power of the federal, state, and city governments, as President Hayes did the bidding of the capitalists who had put him in the White House. Against such a massive array of force, he concluded, the Great Strike could not possibly end in victory.[8]

Cameron proved a more accurate prophet than Hay. His evaluation of the situation that Wednesday, July 25, was based on reality. It is true that a few railroad managers had yielded to the workers' demands. Even as Cameron was writing, a strike was being avoided on the "Bee Line"—the Cleveland, Columbus, Cincinnati & Indianapolis Railroad—when President J. H. Deveraux rescinded the 10 percent reduction. A few other railroads joined this move, and some miners in Pennsylvania were rehired at the old wage, not the proposed reduction—or even, in the case of those in Wilkes-Barre, at a ten percent increase.[9] But these were few indeed, and the newspapers bitterly listed the names of the companies and wrote vitriolic editorials about the dire consequences of their action. Under no circumstances, the press warned, should the railroads give in to the demands of the strikers, for such a surrender would only encourage future outbreaks. Typical was the view of the *Nation,* a journal which, although small in circulation, spoke for an influential section of the population:

What is most to be feared now is that through some weakness on the part of the companies, the strikers may come out of the struggle with an appearance of victory. This would result either from a concession as to wages or the retention of persons engaged in the strike at any wages; and it would be a national calamity, for it would be virtually the surrender to a body of day laborers of the lowest grade of power, whenever they were discontented with their conditions, to block all the great highways in the country. . . .[10]

All but a few of the newspapers and periodicals offered advice to the railroads on how to deal with the strikers, and the vast majority called for the most brutal form of repression. It may not have come as a surprise that the *Railroad Gazette,* the trade journal, should demand that the strikers be "shot on the spot like highway robbers."[11] But it certainly was not to be expected that Lucy Stone, a leading women's rights advocate, should write in the *Woman's Journal:* "The insurrection must be suppressed, if it costs a hundred thousand lives and the destruction of every railroad in the country."[12] The *Independent,* a religious weekly, gave similar callous advice:

If the club of the policeman, knocking out the brains of the rioter, will answer, then well and good; but if it does not promptly meet the exigency, then bullets and bayonets, canister and grape—with no shame or pretense, in order to frighten men, but with fearful and destructive reality— constitute the one remedy and one duty of the hour. . . . Rioters are worse than mad dogs. . . . Napoleon was right when he said that the way to deal with a mob is to exterminate it.[13]

This advice was accepted by governors, mayors, judges, and even by the president of the United States. But then, said the *Martinsville Statesman* (one of the few papers to defend the strikers from beginning to end), such action was really not too surprising: "Presidents, judges, governors, mayors and legislators are but cats' paws nowadays in the interest of rings and corporations."[14]

Cameron was realistic, too, when he predicted that the strikers could not possibly win in the face of the kind of power massed by the federal, state, and city governments. To cite but one example: by Tuesday afternoon, July 24, the Pennsylvania Railroad had at its disposal for use against the strikers in Philadelphia a total of 1,400 armed police, 400 armed firemen, 700 United States regulars, 125 marines, 2,000 special police, and 500 men of the Veteran Corps. Because the city had no means of paying this force, it sought help from the business community. They arranged for a loan of $518.40 from each of the thirty-five local financial institutions, for a total of $18,144, which the city repaid in October.[15]

Within the space of eight days, nine governors, under the influence of railroad managers and owners, defined the strike as an insurrection and called for federal troops. After some slight hesitation, the administration accepted their definition and yielded control of the federal troops to the governors. "The failure to distinguish between an 'insurrection' and a genuine work stoppage placed the federal government in league with the railroads," observes Jean Martin Cooper in his study of the federal military intervention. Pointing out that the army did not kill one striker in 1877, Cooper notes that by the time the federal troops arrived at any point in the upheaval, "violence had run its course or local officials had become organized enough to restore order." But he makes this significant point:

> . . . the Army remained on duty related to the railroad strike through mid-August in some states, and until the end of August in others. It was during this time that they performed the most important part of their duty, strikebreaking. Federal troops opened rail traffic in West Virginia, Maryland, Pennsylvania, Indiana, Illinois, and Missouri. By protecting non-striking train crews, maintaining peace along the line of traffic, in the rail yards and in train stations, the Army guaranteed management the kind of protection state and local governments could not give.[16]

While the governors were pleading for federal troops, they were dispatching National Guard divisions and "reading the riot act" to strikers. One governor went so far as to threaten strikers with prosecution for first-degree murder if they misplaced a rail or obstructed a track in any way, and a federal judge did his part by insisting that a strike against a road in receivership constituted contempt of court, and backed up this astounding new claim with federal troops.[17]

The decision to send troops against strikers on railroads that were in receivership was unprecedented. Up to that time, federal forces had been used during the strike to guard United States property, and then only upon formal requests from state governors. The new decision was made at a cabinet meeting on Thursday, July 26. The day before, there had been a serious discussion about the calling out of volunteers, a move that Pennsylvania Railroad President Thomas Scott had been urging upon Hayes since Saturday, on the ground that the United States Army was being spread dangerously thin.[18] But as much as Hayes would have liked to oblige the man who had put him into the White House, he was influenced more by a letter that Secretary of the Treasury John Sherman had received that morning from a friend in Cincinnati: "Tell the President a call for volunteers will precipitate a revolution. Tell him I speak advisedly."[19] Although this correspondence is not mentioned in

Hayes's notes of that day's cabinet meeting, the president and his cabinet members must have seen the wisdom of its advice, for the idea of calling out volunteers was finally overruled.[20] That night, Charles Nordhoff, "the best-informed and most influential Washington correspondent of his day," wrote Secretary of the Interior Schurz, advancing another argument against the calling out of volunteers: "If you should call for troops, there are signs that you would only get a lot of riffraff who would mutiny on your hands."[21]

The following night, Schurz received a telegram from Parkersburg, Pennsylvania, informing the secretary: "Should the President intercede if the strikers should submit an honorable proposition of compromise to the Balt[im]o.[re] Road I believe it can be obtained. Large oil interests here have requested me to ask. I will go to Wash[ingto]n. if favorable."[22] It is hardly surprising that the "oil interests" should have been interested in bringing the strike to a speedy end. Supplies of fuel were running short in a number of cities, and the companies were unable to furnish any oil.[23] But even though the workers on the Baltimore & Ohio made an offer to "compromise," no summons to Washington was sent to the party who had sent the wire. The president and his cabinet were clearly not interested in ending the strike by "compromise" if it meant yielding to any of the strikers' demands.

By contrast, a reply was sent to frantic wires from United States District Judge Walter Q. Gresham informing Hayes that the situation in Indianapolis was "most critical and dangerous," that the "mob" was the "supreme authority," and that there was "so much sympathy with the strike," and "so much distrust of local authorities" in that city that it was urgent that federal troops be sent there immediately. Hayes knew very well from the Signal Corps in Indianapolis that Gresham's hysterical report was not true—in fact that, on the contrary, there was "not the least sign of mob violence" in Indianapolis.[24] But he hardly hesitated in meeting Gresham's request. The pressure of the strike was now beginning to let up. Calls for soldiers were coming in less frequently, as were reports of violence. It was apparent that the troops could be spared. Four batteries of regulars had just finished their job in Reading; General Getty and the Second U.S. Artillery had met with success in breaking the blockade in West Virginia and Maryland; and the crises had passed in Hornellsville, Albany, Buffalo, Columbus, Cincinnati, and other places. True, Chicago and St. Louis were still raging, but Hayes was not worried.

The cabinet shared Hayes's optimism, and the atmosphere at the meeting grew lighthearted. Much pleasure was derived from the frantic suggestion of the governor of Wisconsin that three residents of the Old Soldiers' Home in Milwaukee be mustered in to save the city from "the labor insurrection." Two days earlier, this proposition might have been taken seriously. But now Hayes recorded: "[Secretary of State William M.] Evarts laughs: 'Old Home men had better be called out to keep open the drives in the Park.' "[25]

It was in this good-humored atmosphere that Hayes made the precedent-setting decision that was to plague the labor movement for years to come. "It looks now as if our expectations of getting through without extraordinary measures would not be disappointed," observed Evarts.[26] Therefore, casually, confidently, and without much deliberation, the decision was made to send federal troops to sustain and support Gresham's claim that striking against a road in receivership constituted contempt of court. It only remained for the courts to give legal sanction to Hayes's decision, and on August 1 and 2 Judge Thomas Drummond—a man who shared Gresham's view on labor—did this almost automatically.

Gresham wired Judge Drummond asking him to come down from Chicago to try the persons arrested during the strike. He did this, his wife explained, because he had been so involved in the events that he was afraid he would not be able to adjudicate the issue impartially,[27] but since he and Drummond shared the same prejudices, it actually made no difference who tried the cases.[28] In the end, both of them did—jointly. On August 1, fifteen strikers were brought before the judges. They were presumed guilty of contempt and were asked if they could prove their innocence. A jury trial was not even considered. The prosecution rested its entire case on the testimony of the company officials, and after they had finished, the strikers were brought up to answer for themselves. The outcome was inevitable: thirteen of them were found guilty and sentenced to from one to six months in jail. One striker was acquitted, and the other was permitted to go free for one year on good behavior on a $5,000 bond.[29]

The unprecedented technical ground for the decision in these cases was that the strikers had disobeyed the court's orders to the receivers to operate the railroads involved. In other words,

Drummond had turned receivership orders into standing injunctions against strikes, and had made violators liable to automatic imprisonment without due process of law. Actually, in his casual compliance with Gresham's frantic request for troops, Hayes set a precedent which was to be used in later years not only for the benefit of receivers, but for all other businessmen as well. Thus, the strike injunction, backed by the power of the U.S. Army—one of the most effective weapons to be used against the labor movement—emerged out of the cases in 1877.[30]

In the same decision in Indianapolis, Judge Drummond forged another antistrike weapon by holding that the strikers had obstructed the mails because they "arrested the trains by which they were carried." This decision was ironical as well as tragic. When the strikers had allowed mail trains to go through, the companies stopped running any trains, hoping to get the men convicted for interfering with the mails. The superintendent of the Pittsburgh, Cincinnati & St. Louis Line refused to allow the mail to go out, although the strikers had said they would take it; he then blamed the strikers for stopping it, and demanded that the federal courts arrest them for contempt of court. As he explained: "The mail always has gone with the passenger trains, and if the strikers don't let them go, the mail don't go. That's the strikers' fault, not ours."

When the strikers pleaded with Postmaster General David M. Key to order the companies to send the mail through, they were ignored. But when the companies placed mail on passenger trains and these trains were delayed even slightly, the Hayes administration charged that federal postal laws had been violated, and threatened the strikers with jail if they did not allow the trains to go through. Even though the strikers agreed to these terms—signifying their recognition that they could not hold out against such open government hostility—they were later "vigorously prosecuted" in the courts for having delayed the mails. This, too, would establish a serious precedent for breaking important strikes of American workers in the future.[31]

At the time, however, the railroad strikers were concerned with their own struggles rather than with those that lay ahead for them and their descendants. With the enormous power of the federal government now fully joined to that of the city and state, many of them were convinced that their defeat was inevitable and gave up the struggle. But by no means all of them, for, even though many of the strikers began to drift back, seeking their jobs, others were holding out—stubbornly, if vainly, resisting the breaking up of the freight blockade, battling the police in Chicago, and impatiently pleading for arms with which to fight back in St. Louis. And on July 27—the very day that the railroad blockade was wholly or partially raised at several of the major transportation centers, and the day the crisis passed in Chicago and the general strike was broken in St. Louis—the Great Strike came to Galveston, Texas. The headline in the *Galveston Daily News* of July 28 read: "IT IS HERE!"[32] Hundreds of Black (and a few Irish) laborers went on strike against a cut in their wages from $2.00 to $1.50 per day. For the next several days, the strikers paraded through the streets of the city, moving from job to job and asking all workers who made less than $2.00 a day to join them. At the Narrow Gauge Railroad, the strikers told the men engaged in laying the track that "they were not being justly compensated for their labor, and that no measure could repair the wrongs to which they were subjected except that to which the body before them had resorted. They urged them to lay down their tools and to 'stand by their rights' until the price of $2 per day was paid them." The reporter for the *Galveston Daily News,* who was following the strikers as they moved from place to place, described the response:

All the hands employed at this point immediately assented to the proposition and filled out the strength of the column that was leading the revolutionary movement against a low rate of wages.[33]

After the strikers had succeeded in closing down the majority of Galveston's business establishments, they marched to the courthouse and, "without a dissenting voice," adopted a series of resolutions. In view of the temper of the nation and the treatment that strikers were receiving in communities all over the country, the resolutions of the laborers of Galveston are remarkable for their courage. Moreover, they were probably the last resolutions adopted at a strikers' meeting during the Great Strike. One of them read:

Whereas the reduction of wages paid to the laboring classes, without any corresponding reduction in the cost of living, we believe to be a wrong that should not be tamely and quietly submitted to by those most deeply and vitally interested in securing a fair and just compensation for their labor; and

Whereas the necessity of revolutionizing the rates paid for labor has demonstrated itself in countless strikes which have occurred in all parts of the country, visiting only those places and affecting only those institutions which have pressed the question of reduction to the point where further toleration could result in the absolute starvation of the laboring classes; therefore be it

Resolved, That it is not the intention or desire of the workingmen of Galveston to do violence to either the persons or property of its people.

Resolved, That in inaugurating the strike which has taken practical form and existence today, we have but yielded to the popular manner of expression of our condemnation of the oppressions to which we have been subjected in the reduction of the prices paid for our labor. . . .

Resolved, That so long as the price of rates that now prevail continue, and the cost of the necessary elements of subsistence remain at the prices they now demand, that we deem $2 per diem for manual labor as a rate sufficiently low; and that we pledge ourselves by all honorable means to secure this rate for this city, and that we agree to work for no less under any circumstances.

The third resolution, after asserting that "the law should be respected, and that all peaceable means . . . be exhausted by the laboring classes to vindicate their claims for wages sufficient to meet the ordinary wants of life," asked for the cooperation of the civil authorities in the achievement of the goal set by the strikers, and "in establishing permanently a fairer schedule in the price of honest labor."[34]

But the authorities were more interested in breaking the strike, and after a Black striker had been shot by the police, they trotted out Norris Wright Cuney, a Black longshoreman leader, to persuade the strikers to give up the battle. Cuney told a crowd of several hundred strikers that they had no chance of winning, since they would speedily learn, as had the railroad strikers all over the country, that they could not hold out against armed soldiers:

There are over 700 armed men—trained soldiers—in this city, who will annihilate you in an hour, and if they don't quite succeed, in the city of Houston, there are 1,000 men under arms who could be brought to this city in two hours and accomplish that bloody work.[35]

Since the *Galveston Daily News* had been reporting on its front page how soldiers had broken the resistance of railroad strikers who were still holding out at a few points in Indiana, Missouri, Ohio, Pennsylvania, and West Virginia, and arrested them by the hundreds,[36] Cuney's warnings had to be taken seriously.

Nevertheless, as the paper reported angrily, the strikers rejected the Black longshoreman's advice "with contempt," and continued to fight for the wage scale they demanded.[37] By Tuesday, July 31, the majority of the employers, after meeting with a committee of five strikers who had been elected at the courthouse meeting, signed agreements to pay $2.00 a day.[38]

As the male laborers were returning victoriously to their jobs, another strike broke out, this time among "the washerwomen, all colored." The *Galveston Daily News* explained:

The colored women, emboldened by the liberties allowed their fathers, husbands, and brothers, and being of a jealous nature, determined to have a public hurrah of their own, and as the men had now gained two dollars a day for a day's labor, they would ask for $1.50 or $9 per week.[39]

Following the pattern set by "their fathers, husbands, and brothers," the Black washerwomen went from laundry to laundry, urging the women at work to demand $9.00 a week and to join the strike if their employer rejected the new wage scale:

So down Market Street they went, led by a portly colored lady. On the way many expressions as to their contentions were heard, such as "We will starve no longer." Success awaited them as many laundries, including those owned by the Chinese, granted their demands while at those which did not, the women were forced to leave and join the strikers.

The women proceeded through Market to Eighteenth Street where they scattered after avowing they would meet again at 4 o'clock on the corner of Market and Eleventh Streets, and visit each place where women are hired, and if they receive less than $1.50 per day or $9.00 per week they would force them to quit.[40]

On Tuesday, July 31, President Hayes held his last important meeting during the Great Strike. Reports from all over the country indicated that the labor uprising was just about over; the militia was formally disbanded in St. Louis with a great parade throughout the city, and elsewhere citizens' committees of safety were hailing the victory over strikers with toast after toast in saloons and taverns that had been allowed to resume business as usual.[41] But the president was still being pressed to make further use of United States troops by Thomas Scott, who wired from the Pennsylvania Railroad's headquarters in Philadelphia:

Please do not be misled by any news of peaceable settlement of existing troubles having been reached. The removal of the military in all probability will be followed by renewed outbreaks such as have occurred within the past week. You may depend upon it that riotous organizations will insist as opportunity offers upon their claim to set aside all laws until they are taught by experience that the government and the country are both determined and able to maintain law and protect property. They evidently regard themselves today as virtual masters of several points in Indiana and they have again stopped the transportation of the military stores of the U.S. and the commerce between the states and with foreign countries. This whole matter is so grave and important and requires such careful consideration that I have taken the liberty of sending this message to you.[42]

Since the Pennsylvania had resumed normal operations on July 31, since Governor Hartranft of Pennsylvania was cleaning up resistance everywhere in that state with federal and state troops equipped with Gatling guns, and since reports from the U.S. Signal Service completely contradicted Scott's wire with respect to the existing dangers, the telegram was filed and forgotten.

On August 5, General Meyer, the chief signal officer, reported to the president and the secretary of war: *"Pax semper ubique"* (Peace always and everywhere).[43]

Actually, it was not until the latter part of the month that all the isolated pockets of resistance gave in; in the case of the Scranton miners, even though their strike was broken early in August, they did not return to work on their employers' terms until two months later.[44] But by the end of July, newspapers throughout the country were carrying such headlines as: "THE REIGN OF THE COMMUNE DRAWING TO AN END." From August 1 on, the legend was: "LAW AND ORDER. THE COUNTRY HAS COME BACK TO THAT CONDITION ONCE MORE."

The Great Strike occurred after a number of struggles between workers and factory owners in the depression years of the 1870s, touched off by declining wages and unemployment. In a surprising number of instances, the workingmen in small towns, without the benefit of trade unions or outside support, prevailed over the mill owner. And in the few cases in which workingmen suffered defeat, it was largely because the employer was able to obtain aid—strikebreakers or state militiamen—from outside the town and impose his will on the populace arrayed against him.

Herbert Gutman, in his study of a dozen or so communities beset by industrial conflict during the 1870s, found that workingmen gained widespread support from local shopkeepers, lawyers, and professional people. Shopkeepers and tavern keepers extended credit to striking workers. City officials refused to endorse the mill owner's request for state troops. Police officers arrested strikebreakers on fabricated charges of trespassing or carrying a weapon.

Gutman also found that in the large commercial centers of New York and Chicago, the situation was different. In struggles between workers and employers, workingmen gained little or no support from the middle class elements that extended aid to workingmen in the small towns. The press, pulpit, police, and courts sided with the capitalists. Demands for public works were refused. Strikers and demonstrators were arrested, intimidated, and terrorized. The press portrayed them as dangerous foreigners, radicals, and troublemakers. The pulpit intoned against them, while the middle class in general, from fear or anger, applauded at every turn.[45]

The experience of the railroad strikers and their allies in the Great Strike followed this pattern. But in the end it mattered little whether the struggle occurred in a small town or a big city. The decisive power was wielded by the president of the United States at the head of the federal troops, and the various state governors at the head of the state militias.

On August 5, 1877, the Great Strike passed into history. As President Hayes wrote in his diary: "The strikers have been put down by *force.* . . ."[46]

XI

Epilogue

"There is not much new to be told concerning the railroad strike," declared the *Pittsburgh Post* on August 1, 1877, as it proceeded to move the Russo-Turkish War into first place in the news. Nevertheless, for some time the *Post* and all other papers in the nation continued to devote a good deal of space to discussions of the Great Strike, both on a local and national level. Some papers ran columns entitled "Novelties of the Strike," which included such items as the fact that the strikers on the Vandalia line had told the manager that they would run passenger trains without pay, but had been refused; that in Newark, Ohio, the strikers and some businessmen had paid the Licking Valley Hotel bills of the soldiers who had left town out of sympathy with the strikers; that the railroad strikers in that same city, upon learning that eleven carloads of Shawnee and Straitsville miners were coming to do battle with four companies of militia brought in by Governor Thomas Young, had appointed a committee which intercepted the miners at Thornport (a Newark suburb) and persuaded them to go home; that striking railroaders in Columbus, Ohio, had proposed that if the strikers succeeded in winning their demands, they should contribute, on a national scale, thirty-five to forty cents each per month to help pay for the millions of dollars worth of property destroyed during the upheaval; and that workingmen in various cities had posted notices outside the factories in which they worked, informing "tramps and dead beats" that they had volunteered to protect the property, and that the men warned should "keep clear of this place."[1] One paper even published a column entitled "Humors of the Strike." An example was the letter sent by "Many Employes" of the Union Railway and Transit Company of St. Louis to their superintendent, who happened to be named R. H. Shoemaker. It went:

Dear Sir: "Awl" of the employes of this company do not wish to "strike," but will keep "pegging" away, provided you restore the "cut." Knowing

203

you to be a whole "soled" fellow, we desire to "stick" to you to the "last." We know you belong to the "upper ten" of society and are, therefore, well "heeled." Now, in view of said facts, do not "tread" on our "toes." If you do, you may find it a "bootless" "task," for we shall "wax" wroth and the "end" is not yet. The boys East have "capped" the "business" and if they "tip" us the wink, we will "stretch" our "legs" and "foot" it across the "bridge," and lend them a helping hand. "Shoe" us soon what you intend to do.[2]

There was no humor, however, when the country looked back at the trail of bloodshed. Baltimore buried eleven of its citizens; Pittsburgh, forty-two; Reading, twelve; and in other cities and towns, funerals were held for citizens killed by police, militia, and federal troops. Over one hundred lives were lost, many of them innocent bystanders.[3]

For the living, too, there was little humor as the victors proceeded to punish the vanquished. During the first days of August, most workers returned to work. With few exceptions, they returned at the starvation wages that had triggered the Great Strike. Judged purely as a strike movement against wage cuts, the great upheaval of 1877 had to be considered a dismal failure. In other respects, too, the labor rebellion seemed to have ended in what could only be called a defeat for the workers. On almost every railroad and in many shops and factories, strikers were fired and their leaders blacklisted. The New York Central, the Chicago, Burlington & Quincy, the Baltimore & Ohio, and the Pennsylvania Railroad alone fired hundreds of workers specifically for being strikers.[4]

Nor were the strikers the only ones to feel this type of repression. After they had refused to shoot down strikers, members of the Reading militia were dismissed by Governor Hartranft for "insubordination, cowardice and mutinous conduct," and newspapers reported gleefully that "these cowards have been dismissed by their employers."[5] The *New York Evening Post* called upon the federal government to mete out the same punishment to members of the Columbia Typographical Union, "composed almost exclusively of printers employed in the government printing office," because the union had dared to denounce the railroad corporations for their attempt "to reduce to a system of starvation a worthy class of employes, by cutting down to a small figure their present salaries," and had extended

. . . a message of sympathy to all workingmen affected by the strike, and that we will sustain them by all legitimate means in our power to the final end, and wish them success in their great efforts to break down the barrier now sought to be erected by capital in order that labor may be degraded and crushed.

The *Evening Post* assured its readers: "The attention of President Hayes has been called to this, and to the fact that, while United States troops were trying to suppress rioting and anarchy, these printers in the employ of the government are encouraging the mob."[6]

Not content with dismissals and blacklists, however, the companies set about punishing the strikers in the courts. The Pennsylvania Railroad had more than a hundred of them arrested and thrown into jail. The Baltimore & Ohio prosecuted thirteen of its workers for "inciting to riot," and the Philadelphia & Reading brought eight to trial. Railroads in receivership prosecuted several scores of strikers. The railroad companies, possessing as they did considerable influence over the appointment of judges, many of whom had been railroad lawyers, envisioned little difficulty in having these men put away for years. In this, they had the support of many of the nation's newspapers and periodicals. The *Independent*, whose role as a leading religious journal had not prevented it from calling for the wholesale slaughter of strikers during the Great Strike, now demanded years of "hard labor in state prisons" for the arrested men, "to furnish an example of the punitive power of the law."[7] But the *New York Sun*, in an editorial (probably written by John Swinton), called for a different policy:

There is a strong disposition in some quarters to pursue these working men through the courts, and to make examples of all who can be reached, as a means of inspiring terror hereafter. He greatly misjudges American character who urges this kind of policy as wise. It would be the very height of unwisdom. Charges of conspiracy are easy to make and hard to prove. If made by the corporations against the laborers, the laborers might retaliate against the corporations, and in nine cases out of ten, the sympathy of the juries would be with them.

This is a time for forbearance and conciliation. Both sides must give up something for the general good and for the peace of the community at large. Any vindictive prosecution which may aim to inspire alarm, will not only fail of the mark, but will leave a dangerous remembrance. Generosity will win more friends and secure better results than a stern assertion of the letter of the law against men who honestly believed they were contending for the bread of their wives and children.

Labor, a weekly journal published in Pittsburgh, was more to the point:

> Pittsburgh has taught the monopolists a lesson they will never forget. And the more they arrest, punish, imprison and persecute the men engaged in the late strikes, the worse it will be for them in the end. Every man that is unjustly punished for these offenses, has a thousand outside of prison walls pledged to avenge the outrages. The railroad managers had better employ the men at an increase of wages, than to arrest and imprison them. They are ten times more dangerous in the prison walls than they are outside at work. If these monopolists think they can promote their prosperity, and secure support of the people by such means, let them go on, and they will have something to learn yet.[8]

It appears that the judges took such warnings seriously. The situation was still too tense, and the sympathizers with the arrested men too numerous, to permit harsh punishments. While district attorneys charged that the defendants, exhibiting intelligence superior to that of the "lower class," were responsible for the labor upheaval and should be severely punished, judges sought not to exacerbate tensions—especially once the legal precedents for future action in strikes had been set. Thus, strikers arrested in Indianapolis and Chicago for halting freight traffic on railroads in receivership were given lectures by Judge Drummond on the meaning of contempt of court and, much to the fury of the railroad managers, were clapped into jail for only three months. Several strikers were charged by Drummond with the felony of interfering with the United States mails, but they got off lightly because he decided they had not done so with criminal intent. Strikers on the Indianapolis, Bloomington & Western Railway at Urbana, Illinois, were tried before Judge Samuel Hubbel Treat in Springfield. He found them guilty of criminal contempt (although he considered them guilty of criminal conspiracy, since they had by an *"unlawful combination"* stopped "the running of trains" in receivership) and sentenced them to ninety days in jail. The men arrested in East St. Louis were also tried before Judge Treat. Several of them had the charges against them nolle-prossed. Six others received ninety-day sentences. Barney Donahue, the leader of the Erie strikers in Hornellsville, was convicted by Judge Jennings in New York City, not of contempt (although the Erie was in receivership), but of conspiracy, and sentenced to three months' imprisonment.

But none of the men involved in the cases of railroads in receivership remained in prison for long. On August 29 and 31, Drummond released the men convicted in Indianapolis and Chicago, and Treat and Jennings followed his example. All the convicted strikers were released on $500 recognizance each, with the requirement that they refrain for one year from interfering with property in control of the federal courts.

Where juries were involved, the outcome was even more lenient. Of the hundreds arrested in Pittsburgh, most were discharged at preliminary hearings, and all but a few of the remainder were given short terms in the workhouse. Of sixty-three indicted in Reading, only three were convicted. Hiram Nachtrieb, a discharged engineer, was acquitted. Franklin B. Gowen, determined to put Nachtrieb behind bars, had alleged him to be a ringleader of the strike. A week later, thirteen of the fourteen men accused of inciting to riot were acquitted, while the convicted man received a light sentence. As Ronald L. Filippeli points out in explaining the outcome in Reading, "The people of Reading knew that the behavior of the workers was the anguished cry of ordinary men, their neighbors, asserting their rights as human beings and free American citizens in the face of a corporate monopoly which in 1877 still seemed alien to the American spirit."[9]

In Harrisburg, where over sixty strikers had been arrested, all were only fined. The arrested members of the Carondelet executive committee were fined $100 each on such charges as "disturbing the peace" and "resisting an officer." Of the rank-and-file strikers arrested in St. Louis on riot charges, some were fined and, being unable to pay, were sentenced to short terms in the workhouse. A number of the cases were dismissed.[10]

On July 31, a warrant was sworn out charging Albert Currlin, Peter Lofgreen, and the other arrested leaders of the St. Louis strike with the felony of riot "by forcibly compelling peaceful laboring men to quit their employment" on Tuesday, July 24, the day on which the executive committee of the Workingmen's Party had introduced the resolution for a general strike. Bail was set at $3,000 each, which their attorneys termed exorbitant. Currlin and Cope were released on bail, while the others remained in jail awaiting trial.[11]

After his release, Currlin was interviewed in his home by a reporter for the *St. Louis Times*. The interview was headed "Albert the Agitator," but it might more correctly have been labeled "Albert the Racist Condemns the Working Masses of St.

Louis." Currlin's remarks during this interview, which have been referred to earlier, were shot through with insulting attacks on "niggers" who, he charged, had pushed their way, uninvited, into the ranks of the strikers, had forgotten their "place" in St. Louis society, and had tried to play a leading role in the processions. As a result, the community had received the impression that the general strike, led by the Workingmen's Party, was a plot to undermine white supremacy. As indicated above, Currlin proudly told the reporter that the party had worked hard to influence the white strikers to break off all connections with them.

Currlin defended the decision to call off all mass meetings with the claim that the executive committee had had no intention of allowing the general strike to turn into a violent uprising. When this tendency began to manifest itself, he and other members of the committee had gone to Mayor Overstolz and assured him that the party would not allow "the mob" to take over and push the strike in a violent direction—"that we, as a committee, and our party, as an organization, had nothing to do with them; that we were not responsible for such acts; and our principles opposed such. We told him that we were anxious, for the credit of ourselves and the party, to suppress such outrages." This was the reason, Currlin said, that the committee had decided to put an end to all mass meetings.

Finally, in keeping with this outlook, Currlin reported, the executive committee had informed the mass of workers gathered at the Friday, July 27, meeting at Schuler's Hall that "we were not thinking of fighting; that if the police came—and everybody was saying they were coming—we would give up right away. We didn't mean to fight, and wouldn't fight, and that our principles taught us different."[12]

A somewhat different note was struck by Joseph N. Glenn, one of the executive committee members still in jail. In a letter to the *National Labor Tribune* headed "St Louis Jail, Aug. 8, 1877," he began:

I am incarcerated here for addressing workingmen in St. Louis on the importance of "Trade Unions," and lecturing on the principles and platform of the W[orkingmen's] P[arty]. I addressed sixteen different meetings during the strike and had detectives on my track all the time. The charges preferred against me are "inciting to riot," and I am held in $3,000 bond. I am to be tried Friday and expect to be acquitted. After our arrest the military fired a salute in honor of the victory of capital over labor.[13]

In mid-August, the members of the executive committee were brought to trial. The court proceedings were brief. The prosecuting attorney asked for more time to round up witnesses, whereupon counsel for the defense objected that the ten days already elapsed since the warrants had been served were time enough. The court upheld this contention. Thereupon, the prosecuting attorney declared that he was obliged to enter a *nolle prosequi* in all the cases. This had the effect of freeing the defendants, but was not equivalent to acquittal, nor did it bar the possibility of future action against them. In October, the grand jury was instructed to look into the disturbances of the past summer to see if further legal action was warranted. That body reported that it was "compelled, although reluctantly, to see those who were most guilty, and who had been instrumental in bringing all this trouble upon the city, escape any punishment whatsoever." The jury explained its inability to act on the ground that grave doubt existed as to the constitutionality of the law that had been relied upon to punish the strike leaders.[14]

At President Hayes's last important cabinet meeting during the Great Strike, on Tuesday, July 31, the discussion had turned to possible remedies. That very morning, the *Chicago Tribune,* in an editorial entitled "National Legislation for Railroads," had broached the issue of a federal law to assist the railroads during strikes. In it, it emphasized how public the nation's roads had become, and how great, therefore, was their need for such legislation.[15] The cabinet decided to discuss the matter after Secretary of the Treasury John Sherman had brought it up. He explained the extent and importance of the country's railroad network and said that both demonstrated "a need for national action."[16] Secretary of the Navy Richard W. Thompson suggested that contracts be entered into between the government and the railroad magnates, but Secretary of State Evarts quickly pointed out the social pitfalls involved in this suggestion, and the idea was shelved. Evarts did concede, however, that "the country is ready for an exertion of this power,"[17] but no one seemed willing to say just what form the "exertion" should take.

Hayes sat listening quietly. The meeting adjourned without reaching a decision, but later, on August 5, he wrote in his diary, after his previously cited observation that the strikers had been put down *"by force"*:

. . . but now for the real remedy. Can't something [be] done by education of the strikers, by judicious control of the capitalists, by wise general policy to end or diminish the evil? The railroad strikers as a rule are good men, sober, intelligent and industrious.[18]

This was the only conclusion drawn by the president of the United States after the greatest labor upheaval that had taken place up to that time in American history, and even then, he never elaborated on these ideas in public.

But with the strike over, with the dead buried and the ashes swept away, with the stock market on the rise once again, and with "financial people abroad" assured "that the U.S. Government . . . can and will maintain order," the issues raised by the upheaval still kept making themselves felt. For several weeks, two questions ran like a refrain through the press: "What did it mean?" and "How can we prevent similar upheavals in the future?" Some saw the Great Strike only in terms of the loss of wages and the future taxes that the strikers and others would have to pay for the destruction they had wrought. The *St. Louis Missouri Republican,* for example, noted with considerable glee: "Society is but an endless circle, and the losses which the mob have inflicted upon the railroads . . . will but follow the circle around to return with force upon the originators." Temperance organizations blamed the upheaval on "idle and vicious young men" who were alcohol corrupted.[19] But most of the nation's press viewed the events of the latter part of July as reflecting the dangers of trade unionism and communism, which it linked together. "The formidable insurrection of different classes of laborers along the principal railroads in the Northern and Middle States," the *Galveston Daily News* declared in an editorial entitled "Trade Union Fallacies," "may be regarded as a logical outcome of ideas inculcated and habits acquired in the trade unions to which the insurgents belong." The fact that most of the strikers did not belong to any trade unions made no difference to the Texas paper, and it concluded that "the trade unions which spread the ideas that had given birth to the insurrection were themselves infiltrated by Communists."[20] The *Philadelphia Ledger* congratulated its southern colleague on its astuteness, and pointed out that the police of the City of Brotherly Love had concrete evidence to prove the charge. It was clear, it went on, "that when the whole history of the uprising becomes to be known, it will be found that the secret inspiration of it will be discovered in the famous International Society, which played such havoc in Paris when they had the upper hand there."[21] If the Great Strike proved anything, declared the *Washington National Republican,* it was that "Communistic ideas are now widely entertained in America."[22]

But there were both groups and individuals who rejected such simplistic interpretations. "The Commune Nonsense," insisted the *Pittsburgh Post,* was simply a way of "alarming timid people, by insinuating that the American working classes are influenced by the teachings of the Paris Commune." The truth was that "the strike originated in well ascertained grievances," and, as far as Pittsburgh was concerned, no evidence had ever been furnished to prove that a single communist had had anything to do with it.[23] A writer who had journeyed through the states in which the troubles had occurred made the same point in an article on "The Truth About the Strike" in the *Galaxy.* He was convinced that if "the readers of daily newspapers could only see the leaders of these movements [the local strikes] shorn of the coloring of special dispatches, the 'terrible communist element in the United States' would serve only to scare children and stir up alarm in the hearts of nervous old ladies." And he concluded: "To construe the uprising as the result of the presence of a communistic element . . . is something that the facts in the case do not warrant."[24]

In answer to an article by W. W. Grosvenor entitled "The Communist and the Railway," in which the writer had attacked the striking workingmen as being communists, a correspondent who described himself as "A Red-Hot Striker," retorted graphically:

You challenge me to compare "the Communist and the Railway." The way to do it is, first to see what is the idea of both, what each of them demands. Now, I say,—and I challenge you, or any other fellow like you, to show I'm not right,—I say the "Commune" *represents the cause of the poor in this: that its object is to give every human born into this world a chance to live; live long, and die well.* And I say of the "Railway," it *represents the few rich who don't want everybody to have a chance for a decent living, but intend to grind out of the rest of the world all the wealth possible for their own special benefit.* I say this, and don't fear you can show the contrary. The difference is, the one is struggling to make it possible for all the world to get on; the other is doing its damnedest to make it impossible for anybody to get on, save the few rich it represents. Let the public judge which side is most worthy,—as it will judge in good time, and don't you forget it.[25]

Another colorful reply by a striker appeared in the "Working-men's Ten Commandments," "as written down in the statute book of railroad officials, idle monopolies and Jay Gould aristocrats." The third commandment read:

> Thou shalt not serve any other master, neither work for any more pay than I give, for I am a jealous master; I will have you discharged on the least provocation, and half starve your wife and children, *and have you punished as a communist*, and not treat you as becomes an American citizen, but as a tramp and a vagabond.[26]

While the debate over trade unionism and communism raged in the press, business leaders and chambers of commerce were busy drawing up proposals calling for more restrictive legislation against "tramps," the poor, and strikers, and for greater limitations upon the suffrage. They also demanded a strengthening of the police, the state militia, and the United States Army in preparation for future conflicts. Within two weeks of the Great Strike, plans were under way to augment the Chicago police and the Illinois militia. Governor Hartranft of Pennsylvania completely reorganized that state's National Guard, discarding fancy uniforms and increasing the expenditures for Gatling guns. He also took the precaution of weeding out companies that might be sympathetic to strikers in the future, and mustered out a few major generals as well. Other states followed suit. In November, the War Department published a manual on "Riot Duty," and one private citizen issued, at his own expense, a pamphlet called *Suggestions Upon the Strategy of Street Fighting*.[27]

One labor advocate wrote exultantly: "More sacred in history than Lexington or Yorktown will be the ground where militia men stacked their arms, refusing to fire on the insurgents."[28] Business groups and their spokesmen did not share his enthusiasm. Of the 45,000 militia in eleven states estimated to have been involved in suppressing the Great Strike they had praise for only a small fraction.[29] Such prominent Americans as Horace White, Carl Schurz, and Thomas N. Scott all united in emphasizing the inadequacy of the local militia and the need for a large standing army if the United States was to avoid the horrors of the Paris Commune. The *Nation* pointed out that the militia was no substitute for a well-trained army, for in many cases the local militia had sympathized with the strikers. This theme received sensational support in a small booklet published shortly after the strike entitled *The Commune in 1880: Downfall of the Republic*. Its author ("Spectator") described in fiction to his father, who had left the country early in 1877, "the dreadful story" of the

Great Strike that had led to the establishment of a Commune in the United States. The fatal weakness of the forces fighting the communist strikers, according to "Spectator," was that the militia was infiltrated with their agents and sympathizers:

> If we could only have had a free well-drilled anti-communist militia! Our greatest safety, however, would have been the regulars. With a regular army of one hundred thousand men that uprising would never have taken place. One thousand regular troops in the city of New York would have been a more efficient force than ten thousand militia. Militia are good, but the real safety of a country lies in her regular army.[30]

But there was by no means unanimous support for the demand for a large standing army. The labor press bitterly opposed it. "Labor refuses to be fettered with the shackles with which capital seeks to enthrall it," cried the *Locomotive Firemen's Magazine*, in explaining the move to strengthen the army. The *National Labor Tribune* added:

> What they demand is a well organized body of trained soldiers, who know and care nothing about the grievances of the people, and who stand ready to defend railroad and other corporations in their career of plunder and oppression.

The *Philadelphia Commonwealth* dubbed the proposal by "Mr. Hayes and his railway managers" nothing but a means of getting ready to crush out all types of protest. The *Pittsburgh Post* called the "cry for a large army" a "superficial" way of solving deep-rooted social evils; the *New York Sun* characterized it as "nothing less than a radical revolution of our whole republican system of government"; and even the *Commercial and Financial Chronicle* came out against the whole idea, fearing that a large, permanent standing army could be used as a weapon "against business itself." The sharpest criticism appears to have come from the *Cincinnati Enquirer*, which expressed its own shock at the fact that the idea of raising and equipping a standing army "for the sole purpose of suppressing strikes nowhere seems to create a shock":

> The sad spectacle is presented in this broad, free land, longing for labor, of a government with one hand driving laboring men to desperation, with the other bayoneting back their acts of despair, of a Congress enacting laws, whose results it must raise a standing army to

smother; of a great and peaceful republic whose legislation necessarily leads to insurrection and anarchy unless supported by arms! How long will our Congress continue to enact starvation and send it forth in statutes only to be compelled to raise an army to batter down the consequences of the hunger and want it has enacted?

Mark Twain put it more tersely when he wrote to Mrs. Fairbanks on August 6, 1877: "Pittsburgh and the riots neither surprised nor disturbed me; for where the government is a sham, one must expect such things."[31]

But there were also other reactions to the events of the Great Strike. As early as 1875, a small group of German socialists in Chicago had formed an armed club, *Lehr und Wehr Verein*, to defend workers from attacks by the police. Now, after the brutal attack on the cabinetmakers in Chicago's Turner Hall and the proposals for the strengthening of the police and the militia, the armed club movement was expanded to meet the new threat. However, by an act of 1879, the state put an end to these activities by making it illegal for any "unofficial" body to form a military organization. The legislation did nothing to impede the right of "official" bodies, sponsored by the wealthy classes, to organize armed units. Thus, a "Military Committee" formed by Chicago's businessmen raised $30,000 by 1880, built an armory, and levied taxes for its support. This was a reflection of a national trend. The move to strengthen the United States Army and to hasten the construction of numerous well-equipped armories in the large urban areas of the United States dates from 1877.[32]

The advocates of a larger army and more effective militias were largely successful in their efforts, but some conservatives began to ask whether military preparations alone were enough to serve as a "preventive cure." The *Railroad Gazette* advanced the idea that American businessmen were deluding themselves if they believed that repressive measures would guarantee them security from future labor struggles:

There is a delusion prevalent among railroad officials and the community generally that a strike is an abnormal condition of things, somewhat like a pestilence or an invasion of potato bugs, and that if we could only employ sufficiently destructive means to kill the bugs . . . we would always be free from the evil.

While the *Gazette* took the position that nothing really could prevent strikes in the future ("Strikes are inseparably associated with our present economy and must be regarded as the natural outgrowth of the existing relations between employers and employed"),[33] there were those who believed that armory-building, strengthening the militias and the army for riot duty, and other repressive measures must be accompanied by a program to improve labor morale, both spiritually and materially. A Chicago minister who served on a committee to strengthen the militia sermonized: "These laboring men, so narrow and selfish in their views and so violent in their proceedings, these tramps and bummers and thieves, the very sight of whom are a disgust, are . . . members of the same communities with us. In some sense we are responsible for their souls; responsible, at least, to do all we can to raise them out of ignorance and woe." Within a year after the Great Strike, the Chicago middle class had mobilized a broad reform movement involving the church, temperance organizations, Christian missions, and educational reformers, as a "preventive cure" to accompany their military preparations.[34]

The railroads were quick to pick up the idea. Thomas Scott acknowledged that the Great Strike had brought new issues to the fore, and in a letter to the *North American Review* in August 1877 he pointed out: "Now, for the first time in American history, has an organized mob learned its power to terrorize the law-abiding citizens of great communities."[35] Even as he was pleading for greater federal assistance to railroads to meet this threat, Scott himself set aside $3,000 to distribute among those employees who had remained "loyal" during the strike.[36] To be sure, this was a paltry sum compared with Vanderbilt's $100,000, but then, unlike Vanderbilt, Scott had deluded neither himself nor others concerning the number of his "loyal employees." Vanderbilt, for his part, rescinded half of the 10 percent wage cut in October. President Robert Harris, of the Chicago, Burlington & Quincy Railroad, over the protests of his subordinates, proposed a graduated wage scale for engineers according to length of service, as an incentive. He further suggested that the company should provide a ninety-day notice before discharging any worker, and then only for violations of a contract which the workers would sign upon being hired. Finally, Harris sought to abandon Sunday freight service in order to give his workers a day of rest.[37] Other companies made similar proposals. The Lehigh Valley set up a workers' relief fund and matched the employees' contributions. The Central Pacific opened a hospital for sick or injured employees, and Charles Francis Adams argued for sickness and accident insurance plans as a means of eliminating the need for unions.[38] Vice-President William Ackerman of the Illinois Central even began arguing for an eight-hour day for his men, and went so far as to propose both life tenure and compensation for accidents for all classes of employees.[39]

On the political front, too, both parties began proposing measures aimed at ameliorating the conditions of the working-men as a protection against future outbreaks. The Ohio Republican platform for the fall election of 1877 included a plank for the establishment of a national bureau of industry. The measure, proposed by Senator Stanley Mathews, would enable workers to communicate their views to the government without fear of being regarded as outlaws or outcasts, and Congress would enforce such reasonable regulations as would tend to secure a fair return for invested capital, while at the same time ensuring equitable wages for employees. Judge West, the Republican nominee for governor of Ohio, went even further and called for a minimum wage for labor, which would be supplement-ed at the end of each year by a dividend out of the profits of the business. The Democrats, for their part, put forth a suggestion the following spring for a law "for the ventilation of coal mines—one that would be just to the miner and to the owner."[40]

These proposals were too much for a press that still believed that repression was the only valid way to prevent future upheavals. The *Nation,* a typical representative of this viewpoint, condemned equally the Ohio Republican platform, Senator Mathews, and Judge West. The latter was portrayed as advocat-ing measures that were "the essence of the doctrines proclaimed by the bedlamites of the several French Revolutions, and their last expression—the last before the regime of street barricades and petroleum." Turning to Senator Mathews, the journal inquired sarcastically whether he also wished to support those who were doing nothing, in addition to helping those whose wages were low:

Taxing all for the support of all is a principle in which any communard of the Old World can serve as preceptor to Senator Mathews, and one which the people of Ohio should be warned not to import in any of the disguises which candidates for office may seek to array it.

Harper's Weekly also attacked the Ohio senator on the ground that his measures were "un-American," because they involved "a total misconception of the function of government and of the conditions of a republic. They logically end in 'national workshops and Communism.'"[41]

Meanwhile, a number of midwest Republicans, including Riley McKeen, president of the Vandalia line, Secretary of the Navy Richard W. Thompson, and Judge Walter Q. Gresham, were privately discussing the possibility of capturing the 1880 Republican presidential nomination for Ulysses S. Grant, since they felt they needed a strong military president to meet the problem of future labor unrest.[42]

As one student of the Great Strike has pointed out, the policies of the railroad companies and the legislative proposals following the upheaval are indicative of a dawning recognition of the need to move "in the direction of assisting the worker."[43] Yet it is clear that there were still powerful forces that feared such concessions and that clung to the view that repression alone could prevent future outbreaks. What the railroad managers and politicians like Mathews and West understood, and what the spokesmen for the "repression school" failed to grasp, was that even though the Great Strike had ended in what appeared to be total defeat for the workers, the uprising had actually strengthened the labor and socialist movements. Therefore, the interests of the capitalists would be better served by a policy of granting some concessions to the workers than by one that relied upon repression alone.

In an editorial entitled "The Dangerous Classes," published a few days after the strikes were crushed, the *Chicago Tribune* argued that the upheaval had revealed that the American social order was developing in a manner similar to those of European industrial societies:

We, too, have our crowded tenement houses, and our entire streets and neighborhoods occupied by paupers and thieves. . . . The extremes of wealth and poverty are now to be seen here as abroad: the rich growing richer and the poor poorer—a fact to tempt disorder.

And—most important of all—"We now have the Communists on our soil."[44]

Of course, they had been there long before, but they had been unable, to any great extent, to reach the American workers. Speaking of the situation in the Workingmen's Party of the United States before the strikes of 1877, Robert Schilling wrote a decade later:

We called public meetings in all parts of the country, but the masses were slow to move. Oft-times, after posting bills and paying for advertising, we were also compelled to contribute our last nickel for hall rent and walk home instead of ride.[45]

To a marked degree, the Great Strike changed all this. "The industrial disturbances of 1877, the first great manifestation of industrial and social unrest in this country," wrote Thomas J. Morgan of the Chicago WPUS, "gave us the sympathetic ear of the discontented toiler."[46]

In the course of the strikes, as we have seen, party leaders addressed large audiences—sometimes as many as ten thousand—and were able to reach more American workers in two weeks than socialists in this country had in two-score years before. Moreover, the party speakers made it quite clear that they were speaking for a socialist movement. "I would have you understand that what I say tonight," declared Albert R. Parsons to more than ten thousand workers at the Chicago meeting of July 24, "is not as an individual, but as a member of the Workingmen's Party of the United States. (*Loud applause.*) What I say represents the principles, platform, and performances of the Workingmen's Party of the United States."[47] For the first time, many workers heard discussions about the nature of the capitalist system and how socialism intended to solve many of these problems; how the government was controlled by the capitalists; and how the press served the interests of the corporations. The workers' own experiences during the Great Strike lent credence to the analysis provided by the WPUS spokesmen. Small wonder, then, that the party enjoyed both an increase in enrollment and a growth in its press circulation.[48] However, the ones who profited most from this development were the Lassalleans.

During the strikes, the Marxists had presented resolutions at WPUS meetings which, after expressing sympathy for the strikers and opposition to the use of force against them, declared

That it is the imperative duty of all workmen to organize in trade unions and to aid in establishing a National Federation of all trades so that combined capital can be successfully resisted and overcome.[49]

Once the strikes were over, the Marxists insisted that the next immediate task was to create such a national federation of trade unions, with the eight-hour day as the unifying issue. Executive committees set up during the struggle, and scattered mass meetings were not enough, they argued. Strikers with hungry families to feed required swift relief payments, and hastily established committees could not meet this need. The strikes had demonstrated the indispensability of trade unions capable of holding out against the combined employer-government offensive.

The Marxists also maintained that the strikes had also proven that skilled and unskilled, employed and unemployed, Black and white, American- and foreign-born, men and women—all could join together in a common struggle against the common enemy. Thus, it was possible to build a labor movement that would unite these different sections of the working class for the first time in American history.[50]

But the Marxists were aware of the fact that the strike experience had also given impetus to the "political socialists," to the advocates of greenbacks, and to other reformers. J. P. McDonnell warned the workers not to lend an ear to

> . . . the men who, in this favored hour, take hurried steps to catch the rising tide, who talk politics, claptrap and labor buncombe and refer to trade unions with faint praise, and who a few months ago held them up to public condemnation. Stand by the tried and true who never fail in darkness or in storm, stand by the Labor Press, and above all stand by your unions. There are no organizations so feared as the trades unions.[51]

McDonnell, however, was whistling in the dark. The rush into politics was on, and nothing the Marxists said could halt it. Nor is this surprising. In the aftermath of the strikes, employers throughout the nation used the blacklist with great effect in weeding out strikers and union members from their labor force. The fledgling unions had no resources with which to fight organized capital, and many simply disintegrated before the employer onslaught. In late 1877, the *Labor Standard* was able to list only nine national unions as still functioning, and most of them existed more in name than in fact. Yet the forces unleashed by the strike could not wait for a new resurgence of unions. What good would it do to build unions if the government remained under the complete control of the capitalists? the Lassalleans asked. "The strikes have demonstrated more clearly than ever," wrote one of their organs, "that the corporations have the law on their side; they own the legislatures, they control most of the newspapers, and manufacture public opinion." Of what value would unions be if the corporations, by means of this control, were able to bring in armed forces to crush labor's struggles? The Lassalleans also argued that even without unions, the Great Strike could have been won if the workers had had political power: "Had the governors of the states kept their hands off for a few days, the strikers would have forced the railroads to pay them living wages." But since the strikers had no effective political influence, these officials had felt free to rescue the railroads from certain defeat.[52]

But, the argument continued, greater danger lay ahead for the workers unless they gained political power. Already the capitalists were strengthening the police, the state militias, and the United States Army. Already there was increased talk of limiting the suffrage to the educated, and businessmen were applauding George Vest of Missouri for having said that "universal suffrage is a standing menace to all stable and good government. Its twin sister is the Commune with its labor unions, etc., etc." If the workers waited for a new union resurgence, they would find themselves so limited in what they could do that the unions would prove to be useless. In short, working class control of government was a prelude to effective trade unionism, rather than the other way around, as the Marxists claimed.[53]

It is not surprising, then, that in the context of the atmosphere existing in the period after the 1877 strike, the trend in the WPUS was toward political action. Within a few weeks after the Great Strike, sections of the party began preparing for the upcoming campaigns of the summer and fall of 1877.

The Louisville sections were the first to act. On August 1, barely a week before the election for members of the state legislature, they held a mass meeting, drew up a platform, and nominated candidates. The platform began with the statement that since "the two political parties of the United States, within the past eight or ten years, have failed to legislate in behalf of the working class of people," the working people of the city of Louisville have decided to "repudiate the Democratic and Republican Parties," and recommended similar action by "the industrial classes of the Union." Specifically, the platform called for an eight-hour day; the arbitration of disputes between capital and labor; prohibition of the use of prison labor by private employers; prohibition of labor by children under fourteen years of age; compulsory education with "the liberal application of funds for educational purposes"; reduction of taxation and

economy in all governmental expenses—federal, state, or municipal; a tariff for revenue only, and "an absolute abolition of duties
upon the necessities of life, the burden of which is borne by the
poorer classes"; opposition to class legislation; and a firm refusal
to support professional politicians. But the first plank in the
platform read: "A better financial policy than the one which has
impoverished the masses, brought utter stagnation upon commerce, and thrown out of employment millions of people." The
plank was inserted at the insistence of the greenbackers, who had
joined forces with the Workingmen's Party, and was readily
accepted by the Lassalleans who dominated the local WPUS. The
Marxists were unable to keep this plank out of the platform, but
they did succeed in having a plank included that read: "No man
shall be put in nomination save he be a workingman."⁵⁴
Consequently, all of the candidates nominated for the state
legislature were workers, and they ran on the Workingmen's
ticket.

The immense mass meeting which adopted the platform and
fielded the candidates of the Workingmen's Party amazed the
Louisville Courier-Journal, and it began to devote almost its
entire editorial page until election day to appeals to the
workingmen not to support the "New Political Party." At first it
relied on reason and logic. "The effort of workingmen to seek
improvement of their condition by an appeal to the ballot rather
than by appeal to violence is certainly a manifestation of
intelligence and right feeling," it editorialized. It even conceded
that "some grievous error lies at the bottom of the present
condition of affairs in this country," and acknowledged that some
of the new party's planks had something one could "commend,"
insofar as they were directed toward correcting aspects of this
"grievous error." But it insisted that the best way to achieve
reform was through the existing parties, which, after all, had the
power to enact such legislation. For the workingman to place his
reliance on an inexperienced political entity would be a "grave
mistake."⁵⁵

But as election day approached and the response to the
Workingmen's Party in Louisville's working class districts
appeared to be increasing, the *Courier-Journal* threw logic and
reason to the winds and concentrated exclusively on the danger
that a victory for the Workingmen's ticket would be followed by a
"Kentucky Commune": "Its success will be the signal for all the
secret societies of Communists in this country and abroad to head
for our fair state and begin their work of wreckage. The duty of

the peace-promoting and order-loving citizens is plain. They must vote for men who are upholders of civilization."[56]

When the returns were in, it was clear that the workingmen of Louisville had not been intimidated. "The Workingmen Win," read the horrified headline in the *Courier-Journal,* and its report continued: "The returns show that the workingmen swept the city save in two wards." A few days later, it reported the official vote: "The total vote cast in the city was 13,578, this being in the Legislative race, in which the Workingmen cast 8,850 votes to 4,728 by the opposition, leaving a total majority for the Workingmen of 4,132." The Workingmen's Party elected five out of seven candidates, and its vote placed it ahead of the Democrats.[57]

The *Courier-Journal* blamed "the criminal apathy of conservative men" for the victory "of what is essentially a mob movement." In a calmer mood, it observed:

Its victory followed on the heels of the late strike, of which it is the representative and is a reflection of the bitterness of the defeated strikers. It will surely, unfortunately, have a profound effect wherever the strike made itself felt.[58]

It was an accurate prediction. Inspired by the news from Louisville, Workingmen's Party tickets were nominated in city after city, especially where there were socialist sections. A somewhat astounded *St. Louis Globe-Democrat* reported on its front page:

The Democrats were disastrously defeated in Louisville . . . , the Workingmen's ticket carrying five out of seven districts in the race for the next Legislature. . . . Workingmen turned out *en masse,* and carried the day handsomely. They allowed no buying of votes, either bluffing off or arresting anyone so attempting.

The *Globe-Democrat* predicted that it would not be long before the shattered Workingmen's Party would renew its activities in St. Louis.[59]

Once again, the prediction proved accurate. On September 3, under the same leadership that had led the general strike, the party held a mass meeting at Lucas Market, which attracted a crowd of two or three thousand, and announced that it would place a ticket in the field during the October city election of school directors.[60]

The headlines in the newspapers of cities that had been centers of the Great Strike read: "The political striker has taken the place of the railroad striker," and "Workingmen Earnestly Preparing and Organizing for Thorough Work at the Ballot Box." One interesting headline read: "Hayes Denounced At Home." The dispatch was from Columbus, Ohio, Hayes's home state, and reported:

A mass meeting of workingmen adopted resolutions denouncing the Republican and Democratic parties and Hayes' administration, and appointed an Executive Committee to take steps toward calling state and county conventions, to nominate a full Workingmen's ticket.[61]

In several cities, socialists and other groups nominated joint tickets. Most often, the socialists and greenbackers joined forces, and the platform which resulted included a demand for green-backs as well as planks calling for the eight-hour day, abolition of child labor, compulsory education, and several others patterned after the Louisville platform.[62] In Chicago, the Workingmen's Party united with reformers who advocated a change in taxation procedures of the city so that wealthy citizens would not escape their fair share.[63]

An interesting feature of the WPUS electoral campaigns in 1877 was the effort to establish Black-white unity. In Maryland, the Workingmen's Party appealed to workers and all other citizens "without regard to race, nationality or political creed," to support its candidates.[64] In Cincinnati, the party nominated Peter H. Clark for state superintendent of schools. The other candidates on the socialist ticket were an American-born white, a Bohemian, a German cigarmaker, and an Irish stonecutter. But the socialist *Emancipator* called for special efforts to pile up a big vote for the Black candidate:

Peter H. Clark, of all the candidates on the ticket, most thoroughly represents the contest between laborers and capitalists, of the proscribed race, whose sorrows made the name of the United States the synonym of robbery and murder throughout the world; his nomination is therefore above all the finest vindication of the claim that the Workingmen's Party is a purely cosmopolitan organization.

But a long time since this man of learning and culture, now the principal of our colored schools, was a youth, on the streets of Cincinnati battling for a living as a newspaper carrier, hated and proscribed because he belonged to a class whose labors had opened every field in the South, and whose woes and miseries had ladened every breeze with appeals to the hearts of the just for the wrong and injustice of slavery, to be lifted off of Africa's outraged sons and daughters. . . . [65]

Clark campaigned enthusiastically for the Workingmen's Party. That summer and fall, he spoke for the socialists in Louisville and in Jeffersonville, Indiana. A Louisville socialist wrote: "Clark for reasoning can't be beat." Clark's "reasoning" consisted of pointing out to working class audiences that the Great Strike had proved the socialist contention that the local, state, and national governments of the United States were controlled by, of, and for the capitalists, and that, just as the capitalists were preparing for future labor conflicts by building up the armed forces, so the workers should prepare by electing socialists to office to guarantee that these forces would not be used to break strikes.[66]

The candidates nominated for the autumn election by the WPUS local sections met with considerable success at the polls. The approximate vote was: in Chicago, 7,000; Cincinnati (where Clark ran ahead of the entire ticket), 9,000; Buffalo, 6,000; Milwaukee, 1,500; New York, 1,800; Brooklyn, 1,200; New Haven, 1,600; and Detroit, 800.[67] In St. Louis, the Workingmen's Party elected its candidates in five of the twenty-eight wards—"a surprising victory for a Party which only two months previously had been denounced as beyond the pale of civilized society!"[68]

However, it was the emerging Greenback-Labor Party, and not the WPUS, that reaped the greatest benefit from the working class's turn to independent political action following the Great Strike. The workers' parties which sprang up all over the country, in almost every industrial center between New York and San Francisco, were at first independent of the Greenback Party, founded in 1875. Soon, however, a great many of them merged with the greenbackers because of the close relationships that had been built up during the strikes between the workers, farmers, and small businessmen. The farmers had demonstrated their solidarity with the strikers in their battle against the hated railroad corporations by supplying strikers' relief stores with food in several communities.[69]

The first Greenback-Labor fusion took place in Pennsylvania, in the very heart of the district where the strike had been most extensive and violent. On August 13, 1877, a meeting in Pittsburgh, sponsored by trade unions, formed the United Labor Party. Its platform included the typical demand of the greenbackers—currency reform—and called for protective tariff legislation, labor bureaus in the state and national governments, the abolition of contract convict labor, workmen's compensation legislation, child labor laws, the abolition of conspiracy laws applying to labor organizations, the distribution of public lands to settlers only, and the establishment of courts of arbitration for the settlement of disputes between labor and capital.[70]

Late in August, the Greenback Party of Pennsylvania and the United Labor Party appointed a joint committee to merge the two parties and write a common platform. The platform that emerged from this conference kept the original financial demands of the Greenback Party and added a number of the labor demands raised by the United Labor Party. The two parties then fused. Most of the candidates nominated for office had been nominated a few weeks earlier by the Greenback Party, but a number of labor men were added to the ticket. Most of the labor candidates who ran for office under the Greenback-Labor emblem had been strike leaders.[71]

A similar fusion movement was taking place in Ohio. On September 13, a convention called by the executive committee of the Workingmen's Party of Columbus, Ohio, met in that city. The convention voted to merge with the Greenback Party and form a national party, provided that the greenbackers agreed to certain conditions: the Greenback candidates nominated the previous June were to be withdrawn, new candidates were to be selected by a joint convention, and labor demands were to be added to the Greenback platform. The Greenback Party accepted these conditions, and a new convention was held. Stephen Johnson, whom the party had nominated for governor, was renominated, but the other candidates were selected from the ranks of the workingmen. A new platform was drawn up advocating repeal of the Resumption Act and the National Banking Act, and restrictions on the issuance of money by the government, a graduated income tax, complete control by the government over all corporate bodies, and the abolition of wages paid in store scrip.[72]

In New York, a Labor Reform Convention was held in Troy on October 9, which nominated an independent ticket for state officers and drew up a platform of labor reforms. John J. Junio of Syracuse, a cigarmaker and trade union leader, was nominated for the office of secretary of state; George A. Blair of New York City, a leader of the Knights of Labor, for state controller; and Ralph Beaumont, a shoemaker, for state senator. The labor demands in the platform called for a reduction in the hours of labor, abolition of the contract system of prison labor, prohibition of tenement house manufacturing, establishment of a bureau of labor statistics, and state ownership and management of railways. The financial plank favored "a currency of gold, silver, and United States Treasury notes, which should be a full legal tender for all debts, public and private, and the retirement of national-bank bills."[73] Such a mild proposal for currency reform prevented the greenbackers from proposing merger, although at their state convention, they did place some of the Labor Reform candidates on their ticket. One of the questions asked of all candidates by both the Labor Reform and Greenback parties was the attitude they had taken during the railroad strikes.[74]

An analysis of the election returns in 1877 reveals the impetus that the Great Strike had given to the movement for independent political action by labor. The vote polled by Stephen Johnson, the Greenback-Labor candidate for governor of Ohio, was almost 17,000, more than five times the Greenback vote of the preceding year. More than half of the votes were polled in those counties which covered the industrial cities of Toledo, Cleveland, Youngstown, Canton, and Columbus; another quarter of the vote came from railway towns and industrial counties in the northeastern area of the state. In Toledo, scene of an abbreviated general strike during the July upheaval, the city ticket and some of the candidates on the county ticket were swept into office. Toledo also sent two Greenback-Labor men to the lower house of the legislature.

In Pennsylvania, the Greenback-Labor Party polled 52,854 votes, seven times more than the Greenback vote of the preceding year and nearly 10 percent of the total vote cast. The vote came mainly from the anthracite and bituminous counties, from the counties through which the Pennsylvania Railroad ran, and from those adjacent to New York, the territory of the Erie Railroad. A young labor leader named Terence V. Powderly was elected mayor of Scranton on the Greenback-Labor ticket. In 1879, he would head the Knights of Labor.

The Labor Reform Party of New York polled over 20,000 votes, ten times the vote of the Greenback Party in 1876. Steuben County, which contained the town of Hornellsville, center of the Erie strike, and Chemung County, which included nearby Elmira, gave the party 4,666 votes, or a little less than one-quarter of the total vote. Rochester, another highly industrialized area, and one of the centers of the strike on the New York Central, contributed 23 percent of the total vote.[75]

Within a year, the independent political movement stimulated by the Great Strike was to lead to the formation of a Greenback-Labor (or National) Party on a nationwide basis. It also decided the outcome of the struggle between the Marxists and Lassalleans for control of the Workingmen's Party of the United States. Dazzled by the election returns in the fall of 1877, the Lassalleans were determined to rid the party of any limitations on political action. Even though a referendum on the need for a new convention to revise the party's attitude toward political action had been rejected on October 14, 1877, the Lassallean-dominated executive committee and the Board of Control jointly issued a call for a convention to take place in Newark, New Jersey, on November 11. By the time the convention actually met, on December 26, the electoral results had strengthened the Lassalleans' position in the various sections of the Party.[76]

The "political action" socialists had a free hand at the convention, for the Marxists refused to attend. The *Labor Standard* and *Vorbote* were stricken from the list of party organs because of their pro-trade union position, and the Constitution and Declaration of Principles were completely revamped. All obstacles to immediate campaigning were removed, and the main purpose of the party, it was now asserted, was the mobilization of the working class for political action. In a subsidiary statement, it was affirmed that the party "should maintain friendly relations with the trade unions and should promote their formation upon socialistic principles." But it was made quite clear that the chief function of the party was the organization of political campaigns. Its guiding principle would be: *"Science the Arsenal, Reason the Weapon, the Ballot the Missile."*

At the Newark convention, too, the name of the party was changed to the Socialist Labor Party, bringing to an end the career of the Workingmen's Party of the United States.[77]

At its convention in September 1877, the Brotherhood of Locomotive Firemen denounced the attacks on the strikers as "banditti," and assured the public that workingmen were not "deliberating about Springfield rifles and Gatling guns as a means of preserving their rights: They have a more powerful and effective weapon—the ballot box." At the same time, however, the Brotherhood stressed that it was necessary to strengthen labor's other weapon—the trade union.[78]

The Brotherhood had good reason to raise this point. In the aftermath of the Great Strike, the railroad brotherhoods came close to disintegrating completely. Those members who had actively supported the strike had been discharged and blacklisted, and most of the others were confused and disheartened.[79] But slowly, along with other labor organizations, the brotherhoods began to revive. Indeed, during the very same period in which workers were so busily engaged in independent political action, the trade unions, inspired by the stirring strikes, started to attract new members. The situation described by the Cigar Makers' Union of St. Louis was typical: "The recent troubles of the country have aroused the cigarmakers of this city from their lethargy, and quite a number have joined our Association." Within a few weeks after the strike, the union was holding public meetings in St. Louis at which a campaign against tenement-house work was announced. At the same time, the trade unions of East St. Louis began to openly recruit new members at open-air meetings, to which some of the leaders of the railroad strike and the general strike in St. Louis were invited as speakers.[80]

In September 1877, the cigarmakers of New York City launched a bitter strike against the tenement-house system, for higher wages, and for recognition of the union. The police, applying the same tactics they had used in July, sided openly with the manufacturers, arresting strikers freely without placing charges against them, and beating them unmercifully on their way to jail. When the strike was broken, the Manufacturers Association publicly thanked the police commissioner.

Although the strike did not achieve its objective, it did reduce the number of cigars manufactured in the tenements and brought the issue of tenement-house manufacture to the attention of the public, preparing the ground for the final struggle against the system. In addition, the "Great Uprising" of 1877, as it was called by the union, gained wide support among cigarmakers throughout the country and checked the relentless wage-cutting policy that had been pursued for several years in every city. It was a tremendous stimulus to organization and marked the beginning of a rapid increase in the membership of the Cigar Makers' International Union.[81]

Despite the threat of swift retaliation in the form of dismissals and blacklisting in many industries, the months following the Great Strike witnessed meetings of workers where they laid plans to rebuild their unions, shattered by four years of paralyzing depression, and even to start new ones. Yet, because of the widespread reprisals, in many cases they had to meet and operate secretly. "The recent troubles," a Pittsburgh paper reported in mid-August 1877, "have given a great impetus to the growth of secret labor organizations and workingmen by the hundreds are paying their necessary dues and taking strange oaths—but all in secrecy." Such organizations, it noted, had names like Sovereigns of Industry, and Junior Sons of '76, but the most prominent of them was called the Noble and Holy Order of the Knights of Labor.[82]

Although it had played no role in the Great Strike, the Knights of Labor had benefited considerably in growth from the labor uprising. At its General Assembly in January 1878, the order established its first permanent national organization and began the drive to organize workers regardless of skill, sex, race, color, or nationality, which was to make it the dominant labor organization of the 1880s.[83] That same year, the Marxists, who had left the WPUS, established the International Labor Union, together with eight-hour advocates Ira Steward and George E. McNeill, to organize the unskilled workers, especially those in the textile industry, unite them with the skilled workers, and together build a new American labor movement.[84] At the same time, the Marxists played a significant role in the revival of the national trade unions, the organization of new national trade unions, and their federation for collective action. These efforts laid the foundation for the modern labor movement and produced, among other things, a federation of trade unions that has continued, although in a different form, up to the present day—the American Federation of Labor.[85]

It is clear that although the strikers returned to work without wage increases, they did not return demoralized. At the end of the Great Strike, the British ambassador wrote to his government from Washington, D.C.: "The power wielded by the great corporations in this country is almost incredible and in their treatment of their subordinates they ignore entirely the principle that property has its duties as well as its privileges. Unless the lesson which they have now received should open the eyes of those corporations to the necessity of some radical improvement in the relations of capital to labour, I much fear that the only result of this strike will be to show the labouring classes their strength and to enable them still further to improve for future use the organization which it has now cost so much trouble and bloodshed to subdue."[86] As we have seen, this proved to be an accurate prediction. The Great Strike, which was described in the WPUS journal, *Labor Standard,* as "The Second American Revolution,"[87] became the springboard for political and trade union action by the American working class. It was able to assume this character because it was more than a strike movement against wage cuts. It was a social rebellion, the first assertion by a national working class of a common anger against a variety of grievances—years of brutal exploitation, and a system of industrialization which viewed the worker as little more than part of the machine, who could be discarded the moment he was no longer needed, and which required him to adjust to a deadening routine of work that made him practically part of the machine. It was the first real evidence of working class collective power capable of imposing its own will upon future social developments. Workers from New York to San Francisco understood, for the first time, their potential power.

"Pittsburgh," George Schilling wrote, ". . . was the calcium light which illumined the skies of our social and industrial life."[88] Writing to Friedrich Engels, Karl Marx called the Great Strike "the first uprising against the oligarchy of capital which had developed since the Civil War," and predicted that while it would be suppressed, it "could very well be the point of origin for the creation of a serious workers' party in the United States."[89] Other contemporaries also understood the broader implications of the vast labor upheaval, but the *Washington Capital* probably put it best just a month after it ended:

The late strike was not the work of a mob nor the working of a riot, but a revolution that is making itself felt throughout the land. The afterbirth indicates the serious nature of a nativity. Capitalists may stuff cotton in their ears, the subsidized press may write with apparent indifference, as boys whistle when passing a graveyard, but those who understand the forces at work in society know already that America will never be the same again. For decades, yes centuries to come, our nation will feel the effects of the tidal wave that swept over it for two weeks in July.[90]

APPENDIX
A Chronology of the Great Strike

May 15

Representatives of the four great eastern trunk lines—Pennsylvania, New York Central & Hudson, Erie, and Baltimore & Ohio—meet in Chicago and conclude a pooling agreement, including an agreement to reduce wages of their employees by another 10 percent.

June 1

Pennsylvania Railroad announces a 10 percent wage cut for its employees, and also that additional doubleheader freight trains will be introduced.

June 2

One hundred longshoremen employed by the Pennsylvania Railroad on New York docks walk out in protest against the June 1 wage cut. They return to work after three weeks, accepting compromise offer from the company.

Grievance committee of between thirty and forty railroad workers on the Pennsylvania Railroad meets with President Thomas A. Scott in Philadelphia and pleads for rescinding of the wage cut, pointing out that it is reducing their wages to the starvation level. Scott rejects their plea, arguing that the railroad is being kept in operation to provide jobs for the men, even though it is not making any profit.

Trainmen's Union is organized in Allegheny City, Pennsylvania, as a union of all railroad workers, with plans to strike on June 27 to force employers to rescind the 10 percent wage cut. Robert Ammon, freight brakeman on the Pittsburgh, Fort Wayne & Chicago Railroad, becomes the union's head and chief organizer. In three weeks, it has 500 members in its Pittsburgh–Allegheny City local and has locals organized on the Baltimore & Ohio line from Pittsburgh to Baltimore; on the Fort Wayne line from Pittsburgh to Chicago; on the Northern Central, the Atlantic & Great Western, and the Erie lines, and on the entire Pennsylvania line, covering more than 2,000 miles.

June 27   General strike on railraods scheduled by the Trainmen's Union to start at noon, but canceled when informers lead to the discharge of many members, and dissension breaks out in the union's ranks.

July 1   All leading railroads in the country reduce wages of their employees by 10 percent, except the Baltimore & Ohio, which did not immediately join the wage-cutting drive.

July 11   President John W. Garrett of the Baltimore & Ohio Railroad announces a 10 percent wage cut for all employees, to take effect on the following Monday, July 16.

Monday,   Ten percent wage reduction for all employees
July 16   goes into effect on the entire Baltimore & Ohio Line.

Strike begins on the Baltimore & Ohio Railroad, two miles out of Baltimore at Camden Junction, in opposition to the 10 percent wage reduction. Baltimore police arrest strikers.

Strike begins at Martinsburg, West Virginia, on Baltimore & Ohio Railroad, in opposition to the 10 percent wage reduction.

Robert Pitcairn, general superintendent of the Pennsylvania Railroad's western division, in Pittsburgh, posts notice that starting Thursday, July 19, all eastbound trains going as far as Altoona will be doubleheaders.

Tuesday,   Militia sent to Martinsburg, West Virginia, by
July 17   Governor Henry M. Mathews to put down strike.

First striker wounded: William Vandergriff shot by militia at Martinsburg and dies a few days later.

Strike breaks out in every city on the Baltimore & Ohio main line.

Wednesday,
July 18

Governor Mathews and President Garrett of the Baltimore & Ohio ask President Rutherford B. Hayes to send federal troops to Martinsburg. President Hayes issues proclamation admonishing all in Martinsburg against aiding or taking part in "such unlawful proceedings," and orders General William H. French to proceed to Martinsburg with the Second U.S. Artillery to enforce his proclamation.

Strike breaks out on the Baltimore & Ohio at Cumberland, Maryland.

Strike breaks out on the Baltimore & Ohio at Newark, Ohio.

Thursday,
July 19

Strike begins on the Pennsylvania Railroad at Pittsburgh in opposition to the doubleheader policy. Strikers stop freight trains attempting to move out.

John Scott, general solicitor for the Pennsylvania Railroad, sends telegram in the name of Sheriff Fife to Adjutant General Latta, asking for militia. Governor John F. Hartranft, on vacation, has authorized Latta to act in his name, and the Adjutant General orders a regiment of the Sixth Division in Pittsburgh to the scene of the strike.

Strike on the Baltimore & Ohio becomes general, extending all along the line from Martinsburg to Chicago.

Friday,
July 20

Strike broken on the Baltimore & Ohio at Martinsburg by federal troops. Freight traffic resumes.

Strikers at Cumberland stop freight trains from going through and are aided by boatmen of the Chesapeake & Ohio Canal.

Governor John Lee Carroll of Maryland calls out the Baltimore Fiftieth and Sixth Militia regiments to go to Cumberland.

En route to Camden Depot in Baltimore, militia is attacked by crowd and fires into it, killing eleven innocent people and wounding many others. Enraged crowds burn Baltimore & Ohio Railroad property at Camden Depot and prevent militia from going to Cumberland. Governor Carroll calls on President Hayes to send federal troops to Baltimore, and at 11:30 p.m. Hayes orders three companies of regulars from New York Harbor, under command of General Winfield Hancock, to leave for Baltimore.

After Pittsburgh militia fraternizes with strikers, First Division of National Guard in Philadelphia is ordered to Pittsburgh.

Pittsburgh strikers present demands to officials of the Pennsylvania Railroad, asking for rescinding of 10 percent wage cut and doubleheader order. They are rejected.

Strike extends to the Erie, Union Pacific, and other lines. Erie workers at Hornellsville, New York, walk out.

Saturday, July 21

Philadelphia militia shoots into crowd in Pittsburgh, killing ten and wounding eleven. Infuriated crowd drives militia into roundhouse in Pennsylvania Railroad Company freight yard and sets fire to railroad's property. Fire extends for three miles to city limits and burns through Saturday night and Sunday, destroying 39 buildings of the Pennsylvania Railroad, 104 engines, 45 passenger cars, and over 1,200 freight cars.

Marines from Washington Naval Yard are stationed in Baltimore with three pieces of artillery from Fort McHenry, as well as soldiers from New York Harbor and a regiment from Fortress Monroe, Virginia.

Strike spreads almost from the Atlantic to the Pacific.

Workers on the Pittsburgh, Fort Wayne & Chicago line in Allegheny City walk out.

Sunday, July 22

Committee of Safety formed in Pittsburgh.

Philadelphia militia escapes from roundhouse and shoots way out of Pittsburgh, killing twenty more people on the way. Several militiamen are killed and more are wounded.

Pennsylvania Railroad employees in Philadelphia join the strike, as do workmen on the Delaware Railroad and New Jersey Central.

At Hornellsville, on the Erie Railroad, men prevent trains from going out, despite military.

Strike begins at Columbus, Ohio, on the Pittsburgh, Cincinnati, St. Louis & Chicago line.

Strike in Buffalo on Lake Shore Road, Erie, and New York Central.

Strike begins at Harrisburg, Pennsylvania, on Pennsylvania Railroad.

Main line of Pennsylvania Railroad from Philadelphia to Pittsburgh is virtually paralyzed.

Strike begins in Reading, Pennsylvania, on Philadelphia & Reading Railroad.

Robert Ammon takes control of Pittsburgh, Fort Wayne & Chicago Railroad's dispatcher's office and conducts its passenger traffic until Tuesday, July 24.

Workers in East St. Louis, Illinois, go out on strike on all railroads leading into the city.

President Hayes holds first special cabinet meeting on the strike.

Philip Van Patten, national secretary of the Workingmen's Party of the United States, sends letters from Chicago to all sections of the party, urging aid for the railroad strikers, and emphasizing the party's chief demands: government ownership of the railroads and telegraph lines, and an eight-hour day in all industry.

Monday, July 23

Strikers in East St. Louis take possession of the Relay Depot and strikers' executive committee issues "General Order No. 1," forbidding freight trains to leave any yard.

Mass meeting held in the heart of St. Louis, at Lucas Market, called by the Workingmen's Party of St. Louis, to voice sympathy with railroad strikers.

Six companies of Fourth National Guard arrive in Reading, Pennsylvania, and militiamen shoot into crowd, killing eleven innocent people.

Strike begins in Rochester, New York, on New York Central.

Strike begins on Vandalia line in Terre Haute, Indiana, and on Pittsburgh, Cincinnati & St. Louis and Cleveland, Columbus, Cincinnati & Indianapolis lines in Indianapolis.

Strike begins in Toledo, Ohio, on Cincinnati, Ohio & Mississippi line.

Mass meeting held in Chicago at Market Square, called by the Workingmen's Party of Chicago in support of railroad strikers.

Strike begins in Chicago when switchmen of Michigan Central line strike for more pay.

One hundred twenty-five marines from Baltimore arrive in Philadelphia under General Winfield Hancock.

General John Pope leaves Leavenworth, Kansas, for St. Louis, with six companies of regulars of the U.S. Twenty-third Infantry.

Sixty-fifth Regiment called to Buffalo, New York, by Governor Robinson.

General William Getty, with federal troops, starts to break the strike on the Baltimore & Ohio at Cumberland, Maryland, by opening the freight blockade at every point.

Four pieces of cannon are brought to the New York City Post Office.

Mass meeting held in San Francisco, called by the Workingmen's Party of San Francisco in support of eastern strikers, but it is taken over by anti-Chinese rioters, leading to prolonged rioting against dwellings of Chinese.

"Monster meeting" of railroad workers in Kansas City declares a general strike, to begin at noon, Tuesday, July 24, demanding restoration of wages to January 1, 1874, level.

Tuesday,
July 24

Resolution passed at mass meeting in St. Louis, called by the Workingmen's Party of St. Louis, for a general strike with two principal objectives: an eight-hour day, and the prohibition of child labor.

Committee of Public Safety formed in St. Louis

by conservative forces after meeting of business-men in mayor's office.

Chicago strike spreads to all railroads, and strikers are joined by workers in other industries.

Mayor Becker of Buffalo, New York, issues proclamation that anyone found on streets after ten o'clock will be arrested.

General strike fails to develop in Kansas City.

Up to this date, strikes have occurred on the following lines: Baltimore & Ohio; Pennsylvania; New York Central; Erie; Lake Shore; Michigan Southern; Pittsburgh, Fort Wayne & Chicago; Pittsburgh, St. Louis & Cincinnati; Vandalia; Ohio & Mississippi; Cleveland, Columbus, Cincinnati & Indianapolis; Philadelphia & Reading; Philadelphia & Erie; Erie & Pittsburgh; Chicago, Alton & St. Louis; Canadian Southern; and some minor roads.

Wednesday, July 25

Great parade of strikers in St. Louis, including many Blacks, closes down business establishments and practically achieves a general strike.

Strike spreads all over Chicago. Many clashes between police and crowds. Police attack and fire into crowds, killing workers. Police attack peaceful meeting of the Workingmen's Party and break it up.

President Hayes orders six companies of Ninth Division to go to Chicago, if needed.

Striking laborers, many of them Blacks, march through Louisville, and business is completely suspended. Mayor, with over a thousand men enrolled in the militia, anxiously awaits arrival of U.S. troops.

Governor Hartranft of Pennsylvania wires President Hayes that in his opinion the disturbances have "assumed the character of a general insurrection," which cannot be suppressed by the "organized forces" of either state or federal government. He urges the president to consider calling in volunteers. It is decided late that day that state and federal troops in Pennsylvania will begin on Thursday to "open the road" to Pittsburgh.

Traffic is blocked on all lines in Indianapolis.

Citizens' militia is enrolled by United States District Judge Walter Q. Gresham, who wires President Hayes urging that federal troops be sent in. Although U.S. Signal Service in Indianapolis reports no violence, Hayes sends in troops.

Committee of Safety is formed by businessmen in San Francisco to battle anti-Chinese rioters. Governor of California urges president to order U.S. naval vessels to take positions in the harbor in front of the city and hold their forces in readiness, subject to governor's call.

Night meeting of 20,000 people in Tompkins Square, New York City, called by the Workingmen's Party of New York. Meeting is surrounded by 1,400 police and the Seventh Regiment of the National Guard, with loaded guns, ready to fire. Expected riot does not occur.

Thursday, July 26

General strike is complete in St. Louis, with business at a standstill.

Robert Ammon urges strikers in Allegheny City to give up strike and return to work. He is hissed and jeered, and resigns his leadership.

Strike ends in Hornellsville, New York, and is virtually over in Buffalo, Philadelphia, and Baltimore.

Militia and United States troops proceed to open the road to Pittsburgh, where rail traffic is still blocked.

Reading is occupied by United States troops.

Eight out of ten roads operating out of Indianapolis are running only one passenger and one mail train each way per day.

At Cincinnati, passenger and mail trains (but no freight trains) are running regularly on all lines, except the Ohio & Mississippi, on which no trains of any kind are running.

Crowds of strikers and others surge through the streets of Chicago, and a great battle takes place between police and workers (including many women), in which a number of workers are killed and wounded. Peaceful meeting of cabinetmakers is broken into by police, with one worker killed and others brutally beaten.

Police and militia, with the backing of U.S. troops, are gaining control in some cities, but strike movement is still spreading through the middle west.

Supplies of food and fuel are running short in a number of cities.

Friday, July 27

General strike in St. Louis is crushed by police and citizens' militia, and many strikers are arrested.

Strike in Toledo, which also took on the aspect of a general strike, ends.

Governor Hartranft breaks strikes in Harrisburg and Altoona, Pennsylvania, with federal and state troops. Railroad blockade is wholly or partially raised at several of the major transportation centers in the East.

Strike ends in Chicago.

At Indianapolis, the secretary of the Brotherhood of Locomotive Firemen and others are arrested on charge of interfering with operation of railroads in federal receivership. However, strikers continue their stand at Terre Haute and Vincennes, Indiana.

Strike of Black and some Irish laborers begins in Galveston, Texas.

Strike is complete in Scranton, Pennsylvania, with miners and railroad workers out.

Saturday, July 28

Strike in East St. Louis is broken by United States troops.

Governor Hartranft refuses to meet with strikers in Pittsburgh and breaks blocade in that area.

Call of strikers in Baltimore for ending of strike by accepting their demand for ending wage reduction, etc., is rejected.

Sunday, July 29

Last flare-up of strike in East St. Louis is ended when many strikers are arrested.

Pennsylvania Railroad sends trains on to Altoona.

Great Strike is practically over, although railroad strikers still hold out at a few points in Indiana, Ohio, Pennsylvania, and West Virginia, and miners in northern coal fields of Pennsylvania still continue their strike.

Monday,
July 30

Pennsylvania and Philadelphia & Reading Railroads announce they will resume normal operations on July 31.

Tuesday,
July 31

Vice-president King announces that main line of Baltimore & Ohio is open for traffic.

President Hayes holds last cabinet meeting during the strike.

Strikers returning everywhere on lines all over the country, seeking to regain their jobs.

Laborers in Galveston (mainly Black) win agreements giving them $2.00 a day in place of $1.50. Black washerwomen in Galveston win agreements in strike against laundries for $1.50 per day, or $9.00 per week.

Wednesday,
August 1

William H. Vanderbilt announces that New York Central has resumed normal operations, and distributes $100,000 among workers of the railroad as a reward for their "loyalty."

Strike broken at Scranton, Pennsylvania, by federal and state troops.

Sunday,
August 5

General Meyer, Chief Signal Officer, reports to President Hayes: *"Pax semper ubique."*

REFERENCE NOTES

Preface

1. Herbert G. Gutman, "The Tompkins Square 'Riot' in New York City on January 31, 1874," *Labor History,* vol. VI, Winter 1965, pp. 63-64; *New York Tribune,* January 13-14, 1877; *New York Sun,* January 13, 1877.

2. *National Labor Tribune,* December 12, 1874, June 26, July 17, 1875.

3. *Workingman's Advocate,* July 1, 1876. *See also* Philip S. Foner, ed., *We, the Other People: Alternative Declarations of Independence by Labor Groups, Farmers, Women's Rights Advocates, Socialists, and Blacks, 1829-1975,* Urbana, Illinois, 1976, pp. 18-19.

4. Tyler Dennett, *John Hay,* New York, 1933, p. 122.

5. Quoted in John S. Bass, *The Harmonists. A Personal History,* Harrisburg, Pa., 1943, pp. 184-86.

6. *Labor Standard,* August 4, 1877.

7. Chicago, 1877, p. 22.

8. *New York Sun,* July 26, 1877.

9. George Rudé, *The Crowd in History: A Study of Popular Disturbances in France and England, 1730-1848,* New York, 1964; E. P. Thompson, *The Making of the English Working Class,* New York, 1963; Eric Hobsbawm, *Primitive Rebels: Studies in Archaic Forms of Social Movement in the 19th and 20th Centuries,* New York, 1959.

The Great Strike exemplifies the two general theories of violent protest set forth in *The Rebellious Century, 1830-1930,* by Charles, Louise, and Richard Tilly. These are the "Breakdown Theories" (caused by large changes in the economic and social structure of society, like industrialization and urbanization), and the "Solidarity Theories" (the perception by workers of the class lines that divide industrial society).

10. This tendency began with Edward Winslow Martin's *The History of the Great Riots,* published soon after the Great Strike.

11. A good example of this tendency is O. D. Boyle's chapter on the 1877 strike in his *History of Railroad Strikes,* published by the Brotherhood Publishing Company, Washington, D.C., 1932. In discussing the strike situation in East St. Louis, Boyle does not once mention the general strike in St. Louis just across the river.

12. Norman J. Ware, *The Labor Movement in the United States, 1860-1885,* New York, 1929, p. 45.

13. *See,* for example, Robert V. Bruce, *1877: Year of Violence,* Indianapolis, 1959, pp. 27 and 233-53.

14. Samuel Yellen, *American Labor Struggles,* New York, 1935, Chapter I.

15. Rudé, *op. cit.,* p. 9.

16. *See,* in this connection, Jeremy Brecher, *Strike,* Greenwich, Conn., 1972, Chapter I.

17. Herbert Gutman, "Work, Culture and Society in Industrializing America, 1865-1919," *American Historical Review,* vol. LV, June 1973, pp. 569-71.

Gutman adds: "It had specific purposes and was the product of long-standing grievances that accompanied the transformation of old America into new America." According to Gutman, the chief grievance was resentment against being forced to adjust to an industrial routine, and he sees the labor violence in the Great Strike as flowing in large measure from the "contact and conflict between diverse preindustrial cultures and a changing and increasingly bureaucratized industrial society."

Chapter I: Prologue

1. Charles Francis Adams, Jr., *Chapters of Erie and Other Essays,* New York, 1886, p. 136.

Much as he detested these two "robber barons," Charles Francis Adams, Jr., hated the railroad workers even more, especially when they exercised their right to organize for a decent livelihood. He even went so far as to draft a law imposing a heavy fine or a year or more in jail for any railroad worker who refused to handle the rolling stock of any road on strike. Even peaceful discussion of strikebreakers on company property would bring a $300 fine or three months in prison. As a member of the three-man Massachusetts Board of Railroad Commissioners, Adams hoped to see his proposed strike law enacted. But it was too bloodthirsty for the Massachusetts legislature, and was never enacted. (Charles Francis Adams, *Charles Francis Adams, 1835-1915, An Autobiography,* Boston, 1916, pp. 170-71; Bruce, *op. cit.* p. 36.

2. Thomas C. Cochran and William Miller, *Age of Enterprise,* New York, 1942, pp. 131-33; Leland H. Jenks, "Railroads as an Economic Force in American Development," *Journal of Economic History,* vol. IV, May 1944, pp. 13-18; George Rogers Taylor, *The Transportation Revolution, 1815-1860,* New York, 1951, pp. 102-3; Alfred D. Chandler, ed., *The Railroads, The Nation's First Big Business,* New York, 1965, pp. 8-9; Herman E. Kross, *American Economic Development,* Englewood Cliffs, N.J., 1955, pp. 438-40; *Poor's Manual of the Railroads of the United States,* New York, 1877, p. 11.

For the view of the "new economic historians," *see* Robert V. Fogel, *Railroads and American Economic Growth: Essays in Economic History,* Baltimore, 1964.

3. Quoted in Joseph Dorfman, *The Economic Mind in American Civilization,* vol. III, 1865-1918, New York, 1949, p. 23.

4. Eggert, *op. cit.,* pp. 5-6; Clifton K. Yearley, Jr., "The Baltimore and Ohio Railroad Strike of 1877," *Maryland Historical Magazine,* vol. LI, April 1956, p. 191.

5. C. Vann Woodward, *Reunion and Reaction: The Compromise of 1877 and the End of Reconstruction,* Boston, 1951, pp. 204-25.

6. Harry Barnard, *Rutherford B. Hayes and His America,* Indianapolis, 1954, p. 403.

7. *New York Sun,* June 25, 1877.

8. The strike resulted when laborers quit work after a contractor on the third division absconded, leaving them unpaid. It was crushed by the state militia. There is a detailed story on the strike in the *Baltimore Gazette,* July 18, 1877. For an account of a "Railroad Riot" four years later which "originated in a determination on the part of a considerable number of the Dutch laborers (on the Washington and Baltimore Railroad) to obtain higher wages," *see New York Working Man's Advocate,* March 14, 1835.

9. *Locomotive Firemen's Magazine,* vol. I, December 1876, p. 2.

10. George E. McNeill, ed., *The Labor Movement: The Problem of Today,* New York, 1891, pp. 321-32; John B. Commons and Associates, *History of Labor in the United States,* New York, 1918, vol. II, pp. 63-66; George Stephenson, *The Brotherhood of Locomotive Engineers,* Princeton, N.J., 1964, pp. 23-45.

11. *Journal of the Brotherhood of Locomotive Engineers,* vol. VII, April 1873, p. 162.

12. *Cincinnati Daily Gazette,* July 25, 1877; *Baltimore American,* July 18, 20, 1877; *Cleveland Leader,* July 27, 1877; Bruce, *op. cit.,* pp. 65, 77; Yellen, *op. cit.,* pp. 7-8; Edward Hungerford, *The Story of the Baltimore and Ohio Railroad,* New York, 1928, vol. II, p. 134; Edith Abbott, "The Wages of Unskilled Labor in the United States," *Journal of Political Economy,* vol. XIII, June 1905, p. 363; "Railroad Wages," *Nation,* vol. XXV, August 16, 1877, p. 99. According to the *Nation,* engineers were earning more than $3 a day.

13. *New York Times,* July 22, 25, 1877.

14. *"Resolutions of the Susquehanna Depot, Pa., Strikers,"* printed in *Workingman's Advocate,* March 14, 1874; interviews with unidentified locomotive engineers, *Chicago Tribune,* December 29, 1873, and *Chicago Times,* December 31, 1873.

15. *New York Times,* December 30, 1873.

16. *Workingman's Advocate,* February 21, 1874; Bruce, *op. cit.,* pp. 42-47; Morton J. Horowitz, *The Transformation of American Law, 1780-1860,* Cambridge, Mass., 1977, p. 132.

17. Philip S. Foner, *History of the Labor Movement in the United States,* vol. I, New York, 1947, pp. 439-42.

18. V. Poor, *Poor's Manual for Railroads,* for 1877, 1878-79; *Commercial and Financial Chronicle,* July 14, 1877, p. 30; August 11, 1877, p. 126; August 18, 1877, p. 149; *Harper's Weekly,* vol. XVII, November 1, 1873, p. 963; *Railroad Gazette,* vol. IX, August 10, 1877, p. 365; "Railroad Wages," *Nation,* vol. XXV, August 16, 1877, p. 99; *Baltimore American,* July 18, 20, 1877.

19. "Interview with J. M. McCullough," in *Chicago Times,* December 28, 1873.

20. *New York Times,* November 19, December 29, 1873.

21. The only study of these railroad strikes is the excellent article by Herbert G. Gutman, "Trouble on the Railroads in 1873-1874; Prelude to the 1877 Crisis?" *Labor History,* vol. II, Spring 1961, pp. 215-35.

22. *Ibid.,* pp. 218-23; *New York Times,* December 30, 1873.

23. *New York Times,* December 5, 1873. *See also* Marvin E. Schlegel, *Ruler of the Reading: The Life of Franklin B. Gowen, 1836-1889,* Harrisburg, Pa., 1937, p. 69.

24. Gutman, "Trouble on the Railroads," pp. 225-28; General E. S. Osbourne, Susquehanna Depot, to Gov. J. F. Hartranft, Harrisburg, March 29, 1874, printed in Adjutant General of Pennsylvania, *Annual Report, 1874,* Harrisburg, 1875, p. 20; *Scranton Times,* March 30, 31, 1874; *Scranton Republican,* March 30, 31, 1874.

25. David T. Burbank, *Reign of the Rabble: The St. Louis General Strike of 1877,* New York, 1966, p. 14.

26. *Scranton Republican,* April 2, 1874.

27. Gutman, "Trouble on the Railroads," p. 233.

28. *Montgomery* (Ala.) *Advertiser,* November 22, 1873; *Journal of the Brotherhood of Locomotive Engineers,* vol. VII, December 1875, pp. 579-80, and vol. IX, January 1875, pp. 33-34.

29. *New York Times,* November 9, 1873; *Workingman's Advocate,* December 27, 1873, January 3, 1874; Gutman, "Trouble on the Railroads," p. 234n.

30. *Journal of the Brotherhood of Locomotive Engineers,* vol. XI, February 1877, pp. 66-78, June 1877, p. 263.

31. *San Francisco Mail,* December 24, 1877; Foner, *History of the Labor Movement,* vol. I, p. 443; Alan Calmer, *Labor Agitator: The Story of Albert R. Parsons,* New York, 1937, p. 24.

32. J. W. J. in *New Orleans Daily Picayune,* April 15, 1877.

33. *Cigar Makers' Journal,* May 1877, p. 23.

34. Foner, *History of the Labor Movement,* vol. I, pp. 439-41; Commons, *op. cit.,* vol. II, pp. 176-77.

35. The *New York Herald* which cited the Brotherhood's membership added the information: "Candidates for admission to the Brotherhood must be white men, not less than twenty-one years old, able to read and write, of temperate habits, and good moral character, and with at least one year's experience as an engineer." (August 1, 1877. *See also Louisville Courier-Journal,* August 3, 1877.)

36. *Boston Advertiser,* February 13, 14, 1877; *Boston Transcript,* February 13, 14, 1877.
The one bright spot in the otherwise tragic outcome was the support the engineers received from the *Locomotive Firemen's Magazine.* Abandoning its reluctance to deal with anything but insurance and intemperance, the magazine fully supported the engineers' strike, arguing that it was "brought about by the conspiracy refusing to pay the men an honest price for their labor." Those who refused to strike were considered to be "thus violating their obligation to God and man." (*Locomotive Firemen's Magazine,* vol. I, March 1877, p. 106.)

37. *Journal of the Brotherhood of Locomotive Engineers,* vol. XII, April 1877, p. 135; June 1877, pp. 259-61; *Railroad Gazette,* vol. IX, March 23, 1877, p. 135; April 13, 1877, p. 170; Charles Francis Adams, "The Brotherhood of Locomotive Engineers," *Nation,* vol. XXIV.

38. Foner, *History of the Labor Movement,* vol. I, pp. 455-60.

39. Philadelphia, 1970, p. 265.

Recent studies have exploded the myth that there were actually terrorist groups such as the Molly Maguires in the coal fields, and that there is any connection between individual terrorists and coal unionism. (*See* Thomas Barrett, *The Mollies Were Men,* New York, 1969; Charles McCarthy, *The Great Molly Maguire Hoax,* Wyoming, Pa., 1969.) For an earlier expression of this viewpoint, *see* Anthony Bimba, *The Molly Maguires,* New York, 1932, and for a summary of the story of the Molly Maguires episode, *see* Foner, *History of the Labor Movement,* vol. I, pp. 460-64.

40. Schlegel, *op. cit.,* p. 21.

41. *Journal of the Brotherhood of Locomotive Engineers,* vol. XI, April 1877, pp. 161-67, May 1877, pp. 219-20, June 1877, pp. 267-69, July 1877, pp. 310-18; *Report of the Committee Appointed to Investigate the Railroad Riots in July, 1877,* Harrisburg, Pa., 1878, pp. 901-06 (testimony of Franklin B. Gowen). (Hereinafter cited as *Report of the Committee . . . to Investigate . . . Railroad Riots.) See also* Schlegel, *op. cit.,* pp. 63, 76, 151, 152, 158-61.

42. Other executions followed within a year, and the legal murders were over on January 14, 1879, when the last two were hanged.

43. In 1874 the presidents of three eastern trunk lines met in Saratoga, New York, and concluded an agreement by which each promised to stop cutting freight and passenger rates between Chicago and the East Coast. But the Baltimore & Ohio Railroad refused to sign the agreement, and a war of rates got under way which continued until the pooling agreement of 1877. (*See* "The Freight Competition of 1874." "The Freight Competition of 1876," *Sixth Annual Report of the Board of Railroad Commissioners,* Boston, January 1875, pp. 39-44; *Seventh Annual Report . . . ,* Boston, 1876, pp. 60-71; *Eighth Annual Report . . . ,* Boston, January 1877, pp. 46-55.)

44. *Report of the Committee . . . to Investigate . . . Railroad Riots,* p. 928 (testimony of Thomas A. Scott); "The Pooling Combination of 1877," *Ninth Annual Report of the Board of Railroad Commissioners,* Boston, 1878, p. 65.

45. *New York Times,* May 16, 17, 18, 20, 1877; Yearley, *op. cit.,* p. 191.

46. Pittsburgh Post, May 15, 1877.

47. *Ibid.,* June 7, 1877; Tom Scott, "The Recent Strikes," *North American Review,* vol. CXXV, September 1877, pp. 352-53.

48. *New York Times,* June 2, 3, 5, 1877; *Irish World and Industrial Liberator,* June 30, 1877; *Commercial and Financial Chronicle* quoted in *Appleton's Annual Cyclopedia,* n.s., vol. II, 1877, p. 231.

49. *Report of the Committee . . . to Investigate . . . Railroad Riots*, pp. 671, 673-74; *Chicago Inter-Ocean*, August 2, 1877.

50. *Report of the Committee . . . to Investigate . . . Railroad Riots*, p. 671.

51. *Ibid.*, pp. 681-82.

52. *Ibid.*, pp. 683-84; Bruce, *op. cit.*, p. 61.

53. *Report of the Committee . . . to Investigate . . . Railroad Riots*, pp. 671-72.

54. *Ibid.*, p. 672.

55. *Ibid.*, p. 675.

56. Christopher Hoyt, "The Labor Explosion of 1877: A Study of the Great Railroad Strike of 1877," unpublished Senior Thesis, History, Princeton University, 1960, p.32.

57. *Report of the Committee . . . to Investigate . . . Railroad Riots*, p. 684.

58. *Baltimore Sun*, July 6, 1877; *Martinsburg Statesman*, July 8, 1877.

Chapter II: The Strike on the Baltimore & Ohio Railroad

1. Hungerford, *op. cit.*, vol. I, p. 133; *Baltimore Sun*, July 15-17, 1877; *Baltimore America*, July 14, 18, 1877.

2. *Baltimore Sun*, July 20, 1877.

3. *Ibid.*, July 15, 16, 1877.

4. *Baltimore American*, July 17-18, 1877; *Baltimore Sun*, July 17-18, 1877; Yearley, Jr., *op. cit.*, pp. 193-94. For connections of the Latrobe family with the B & O, *see Dictionary of American Biography*, New York, 1957, vol. XI, pp. 20-21.

5. *Baltimore American*, July 18, 1877; *Baltimore Sun*, July 18, 1877.

6. *Report of the Committee . . . to Investigate . . . Railroad Riots*, pp. 683-84.

7. *Martinsville Statesman*, July 17, 24, 1877.

8. *Wheeling Intelligencer*, July 17-18, 1877.

9. *Ibid.*, July 18, 1877.

10. *Baltimore American*, July 17, 1877; *Baltimore Sun*, July 17, 18, 1877; *Biennial Message of Governor M. Mathews with accompanying documents to the Legislature of West Virginia*, Wheeling, 1879, pp. 1-2. Hereinafter cited as Mathews, *Documents*.

11. *Martinsburg Statesman*, July 31, 1877.

12. *Ibid.*, July 24, 1877; Mathews, *Documents*, p. 3.

13. Mathews, *Documents*, p. 4; Gerald G. Eggert, *Railroad Labor Disputes: The Beginnings of Federal Strike Policy*, Ann Arbor, 1967, p. 26.

14. *Ibid.*, pp. 3-4; Bruce, *op. cit.*, pp. 80-82.

15. *Baltimore Gazette*, reprinted in *Scranton Republican*, July 29, 1877; *Labor Standard*, August 14, 1877.

16. *Wheeling Intelligencer*, July 20, 1877.

17. *Ibid.,* July 21, 1877.

18. *Baltimore Sun,* July 22, 1877.

19. *Ibid.,* July 19, 1877.

20. *Ibid.,* Mathews, *Documents,* p. 4.

21. Eggert, *op. cit.,* p. 26.

22. Copies of Correspondence, Reports, Orders, Etc., relating to . . . Labor Disturbances, . . . 1877, file #4042, Adjutant General's Office, Early Wars Branch, Record Group 94, National Archives. Hereinafter cited as AGO Strike Papers. *See also* Eggert, *op. cit.,* p. 27.

23. *New York World,* July 23, 1877.

24. *Wheeling Register,* July 21, 1877; Bruce, *op. cit.,* p. 85; AGO Strike Papers.

25. *See* Richard B. Morris, "Andrew Jackson, Strikebreaker," *American Historical Review,* vol. LV, October 1949, pp. 54-68; Foner, *History of the Labor Movement,* vol. I, pp. 328-29.

26. *Labor Standard,* July 28, 1877.

27. Eggert, *op. cit.,* pp. 27-28; Charles L. Barrows, *William M. Evarts, Lawyer, Diplomat, Statesman,* Chapel Hill, N. Car., 1941, pp. 184-88, 258; Van Woodward, *op. cit.,* p. 190; Shelby M. Cullom, *Fifty Years of Public Service,* Chicago, 1911, p. 325.

Upon leaving public service, McCrary immediately became a leading corporation lawyer and member of a firm which served the Atcheson, Topeka & Santa Fe Railroad. (*Dictionary of American Biography,* vol. XII, p. 3.)

28. *See Baltimore Sun, New York Tribune,* July 17, 1877.

29. Eggert, *op. cit.,* p. 38; Charles R. Williams, ed., *Diary and Letters of Rutherford B. Hayes,* Columbus, Ohio, 1922-26, vol. III, pp. 314-19; Rutherford B. Hayes to James A. Garfield, May 17, 1876; Marcus A. Hanna to Rutherford B. Hayes, June 16, 1876, Rutherford B. Hayes Papers, Rutherford B. Hayes Library, Fremont, Ohio. Hereinafter cited as Hayes Papers.

30. Bruce, *op. cit.,* pp. 87-89; James A. Garfield, "The Army of the United States," *North American Review,* vol. CXXVI, April 1878, pp. 195-96.

31. Adjutant General's Office, Letters Received, 1877 #4064, National Archives (hereinafter cited as AGO, L'ttrs Rec'd); *Baltimore Sun,* July 19, 1877; James A. Dacus, *Annals of the Great Strikes,* St. Louis, 1877, pp. 39-41; Charles Phillips Anson, "History of the Labor Movement in West Virginia," unpublished Ph.D. thesis, University of North Carolina, 1940, p. 193*n;* Bruce, *op. cit.,* p. 93; Eggert, *op. cit.,* p. 30.

32. *New York Sun,* July 20, 1877; *Wheeling Register,* July 20, 21, 1877.

33. *New York Sun,* July 20, 1877.

34. *Ibid.; Wheeling Register,* July 20, 1877.

35. *New York Sun,* July 20, 1877; *Wheeling Register,* July 20, 21, 1877.

36. *Baltimore Sun,* July 20, 1877.

37. *Wheeling Register,* July 21, 1877; *New York Herald,* July 20, 1877.

38. *Reading Daily Eagle,* July 21, 1877. The document was reprinted in *The Alarm,* the anarchist weekly published in Chicago by Albert R.

Parsons in the 1880s, "to refresh our readers with the stirring events of those stormy days." (June 27, 1885.)

39. *Baltimore Sun,* July 21, 1877; Hungerford, *op. cit.,* vol. I, p. 328.

40. *Baltimore Sun,* July 18, 20, 1877; *Baltimore American,* July 19, 20, 1877; *Baltimore Evening Bulletin,* July 18, 19, 20, 1877.

41. *Philadelphia Inquirer,* July 23, 1877.

42. *Baltimore Sun,* July 16, 1877; *Baltimore American,* July 17, 18, 20, 1877; *Baltimore News,* July 20, 1877; Bruce, *op. cit.,* pp. 100, 214.

43. The description of the events of Friday, July 20, 1877, are based on reports in the *Baltimore Sun, Baltimore American, Baltimore News,* July 21, 22, 1877, and the hearings of the coroner's jury in Baltimore, *Baltimore Sun,* July 31–August 4, 1877.

44. *Baltimore Sun,* July 21, 1877; *Baltimore News,* July 21, 1877; *Baltimore American,* July 21, 1877.

45. *Baltimore Sun,* July 22, 1877.

46. *Baltimore American,* July 23, 1877.

47. See *Baltimore Sun,* July 22, 1877; *Baltimore American,* July 23, 1877.

48. *Baltimore Sun,* July 22, 1877; *Baltimore American,* July 22, 1877.

49. *Baltimore Sun,* July 27, 1877; Yearley, *op. cit.,* p. 203.

50. *Baltimore Sun,* July 27, 1877.
Evidently the strikers had been under the impression that the governor asked to see their committee, but Carroll denied this.

51. *Baltimore Sun,* July 28, 1877.

52. *Ibid.*

53. French asked to be relieved of his command after the Baltimore & Ohio's Master of Transportation called him "a drunkard and a lout." "If I cannot act independent of them [B & O officials]," he wrote to Secretary of War McCrary asking to be relieved, "it would be preferable to have another officer who would be less objectionable to that corporation."

54. *Report of the Committee . . . to Investigate . . . Railroad Riots,* p. 769.

55. Christopher Hoyt, "The Labor Explosion of 1877: A Study of the Great Strike of 1877," Senior Thesis, History, Princeton University, 1960, p. 35.

56. *Report of the Committee . . . to Investigate . . . Railroad Riots,* p. 789.

Chapter III: The Strike on the Pennsylvania and Philadelphia & Reading Railroads

1. *Report of the Committee . . . to Investigate . . . Railroad Riots,* pp. 63, 273, 274, 558, 674, 818.

2. William B. Sipes, *The Pennsylvania Railroad, Its Origins, Construction, and Connections,* Philadelphia, 1875, p. 255.

3. *Pittsburgh Post,* July 20, 1877; *Report of the Committee . . . to Investigate . . . Railroad Riots,* p. 63.

4. *Report of the Committee . . . to Investigate . . . Railroad Riots,* pp. 59-60, 674.

5. *Ibid.*, pp. 140, 444-46; *Pittsburgh Post,* July 20, 1877.

6. *Pittsburgh Post,* July 20, 1877; *Report of the Committee . . . to Investigate . . . Railroad Riots,* pp. 76, 143, 389.

7. *Report of the Committee . . . to Investigate . . . Railroad Riots,* pp. 60, 79, 176, 374.

8. *Pittsburgh Post,* July 20, 1877.

9. *Ibid.,* July 21, 1877; *Report of the Committee . . . to Investigate . . . Railroad Riots, pp. 77, 78, 139, 144.*

10. *Pittsburgh Critic,* reprinted in *Report of the Committee . . . to Investigate . . . Railroad Riots,* pp. 817-18, and p. 18 for the comment of committee.

11. *Report of the Committee . . . to Investigate . . . Railroad Riots,* pp. 52, 174-76, 184-85, 594; *Pittsburgh Post,* July 21, 22, 1877; *Pittsburgh Dispatch,* July 21, 22, 1877.

12. *Report of the Committee . . . to Investigate . . . Railroad Riots,* pp. 7-8, 19-20, 698; *Pittsburgh Post,* July 21, 1877.

13. *New York Times,* July 22, 1877.

14. *Pittsburgh Critic,* reprinted in *Report of the Committee . . . to Investigate . . . Railroad Riots,* p. 818.

15. Joseph S. Clark, Jr., "The Railroad Struggle for Pittsburgh," *Pennsylvania Magazine of History and Biography,* vol. XLVIII, April 1924; pp. 1-27.

16. *Army Journal,* August 4, 1877. *See also New York Times,* July 22, 1877.

17. *Report of the Committee . . . to Investigate . . . Railroad Riots,* p. 10.

18. *Pittsburgh Post,* July 22, 23, 1877.

19. *Pittsburgh Post,* July 22, 1877; *Report of the Committee . . . to Investigate . . . Railroad Riots,* pp. 788-820; *National Labor Tribune,* July 28, 1877.

20. *Irish World and Industrial Liberator,* December 1, 1877.

21. Reprinted in *Report of the Committee . . . to Investigate . . . Railroad Riots,* p. 806.

22. *Pittsburgh Post,* July 22, 23, 1877; *Pittsburgh Dispatch,* July 22, 23, 1877.

23. *Report of the Committee . . . to Investigate . . . Railroad Riots,* p. 93.

24. James A. Henderson, "The Railroad Riots in Pittsburgh: Saturday and Sunday, April 21st and 22nd, 1877," *Western Pennsylvania Historical Magazine,* vol. XL, July 1928, pp. 195-96. *See also Report of the Committee . . . to Investigate . . . Railroad Riots,* pp. 253-54, 326-27, 882-90.

25. *Report of the Committee . . . to Investigate . . . Railroad Riots,* pp. 15, 68, 69, 252-53, 326, 976-78.

The *National Labor Tribune* insisted that grocers, farmers, and businessmen also hauled away goods from the freight cars, and condemned the practice of blaming such conduct only "upon the poor." The labor weekly went so far as to assert that "in nine cases out of ten, though starving, [the poor] would scorn to eat stolen meat and bread." (July 28, 1877.)

26. *Pittsburgh Post*, July 23, 1877; *New York Herald*, July 23, 1877.

27. George H. Burgess and Miles C. Kennedy, *Centennial History of the Pennsylvania Railroad Company: 1846-1946*, Philadelphia, 1949, pp. 370-73; *Report of the Committee . . . to Investigate . . . Railroad Riots*, pp. 254-55; Henderson, *op. cit.*, p. 196.

On July 28, 1877, the *Cleveland Leader* figured out that just paying the interest on this debt would cost every man, woman, and child in Pittsburgh $32.15 apiece in taxes. The article was entitled, "The Cost of a Mistake."

28. *Pittsburgh Post*, July 23, 1877; *Philadelphia Times*, July 24, 1877; *Report of the Committee . . . to Investigate . . . Railroad Riots*, pp. 978-82.

29. *Missouri Republican*, July 23, 1877; *Washington National Republican*, July 24, 1877; *Chicago Inter-Ocean*, July 23, 1877; *New York Times*, July 23, 1877.

30. *Pittsburgh Post*, July 24, 25, 1877; *New York Sun*, July 24, 1877; *Report of the Committee . . . to Investigate . . . Railroad Riots*, pp. 493-94.

31. *Pittsburgh Post*, July 24, 25, 1877; *National Labor Tribune*, July 28, 1877.

32. *Pittsburgh Post*, July 26, 1877; *Report of the Committee . . . to Investigate . . . Railroad Riots*, p. 515.

33. *Report of the Committee . . . to Investigate . . . Railroad Riots*, p. 689.

34. *Ibid.*, pp. 21-22, 461-68, 661-90, 791-98.

The committee concluded that Ammon's "extraordinary performance" was really "nothing wonderful." A mob or crowd was always willing to follow anyone who had nerve, and "Ammon had the nerve." The mob always wanted a dictator, and in Ammon, "they had one." Finally, the great railroads of the country were so organized, and the trains run on such a regular system, connected by the telegraph, "that the trains can be run for days without a break if the superintendent should abandon the road entirely." Ammon was thus able to be "a king so long as he led in the direction the crowd wished to go." But when they saw he ran "counter to their opinions, he was dethroned with as little ceremony or compunction as one school boy shows in knocking off the hat of another." (*Ibid.*, pp. 22-23.)

35. *Pittsburgh Post*, July 25, 26, 1877; *Pittsburgh Times*, July 25-26, 1877.

36. Philip English Mackey, "Law and Order, 1877: Philadelphia's Response to the Railroad Riots," *Pennsylvania Magazine of History and Biography*, vol. XCVI, April 1972, p. 189; *Philadelphia Record*, July 23, 1877; *Philadelphia Times*, July 27, 1877; *Altoona Mirror*, July 24-27, 1877; George B. Stitcher, "The Schuylkill County Soldiery in the Industrial Disturbances in 1877, or the Railroad Riot War," *Publications of the Historical Society of Schuylkill County*, vol. I, 1907, pp. 193-215; *Harrisburg Independent*, July 24, 1877.

37. Bruce, *op. cit., pp. 155-56; Harrisburg Independent,* July 24, 1877.

38. Telegram (July 24, 1877), Hayes Papers.

39. *Reading Daily Eagle,* July 23, 1877, reprinted in Ronald L. Filippeli, "The Railroad Strike of 1877 in Reading," *Historical Review of Berks County,* vol. XXXVII, Spring 1972, p. 51. Filippeli's article is the most detailed treatment of the strike in Reading.

40. *Ibid.,* July 23, 1877.

41. *Ibid.,* July 23-24, 1877.

42. *Ibid.,* July 24, 1877; *Report of the Committee . . . to Investigate . . . Railroad Riots,* pp. 486-92.

43. *Reading Daily Eagle,* July 26, 1877.

44. *Ibid.,* July 29, 1877.

45. *Ibid.,* July 27-29, 1877.

46. Telegram (July 22, 1877), Hayes Papers.

47. Telegrams (July 23-25, 1877), Hayes Papers.

48. *Pittsburgh Post,* July 30, 1877.

49. Hancock to Secretary of War, July 30, 1877, AGO, L'ttrs Rec'd., #4304.

50. *Scranton Republican,* July 26-30, 1877.

51. *Ibid.,* July 29, 1877.

52. *Report of the Committee . . . to Investigate . . . Railroad Riots,* pp. 162-63.

53. *Ibid.,* pp. 155-60, 709, 735, 755-58; Hartranft to McCrary, AGO #4042, NA.

54. Jean Marvin Cooper, "The Army and Civil Disorder: Federal Military Intervention in American Labor Disputes, 1877-1900," unpublished Ph. D. thesis, University of Wisconsin, 1971, p. 122.

55. Hancock to Major John Hamilton, Aug. 8, 1877, L'ttrs Rec'd., 1877, Allegheny Arsenal, Pittsburgh, Pa., RG 393, NA, marked *Confidential.*

56. Cooper, *op. cit.,* pp. 122-23.

57. *Scranton Republican,* October 22, 1877.

Chapter IV: The Strike on the Erie and New York Central Railroads

1. *See* Edward H. Mott, *Between the Ocean and the Lakes, A Story of the Erie,* New York, 1901, pp. 123-201; Charles Francis Adams, *op. cit.,* pp. 1-192.

2. Ray V. Brown, "The Erie Railroad Strike of 1877 in Hornellsville, New York," unpublished Senior Thesis, History, Princeton University, 1951, pp. 32-34.

3. A complete account of this meeting was published in the *Hornell Times,* July 4, 1877.

4. Brown, *op. cit.,* pp. 37-39.

5. *Utica Observer,* June 29, 1877.

6. *Hornell Times,* July 4, 1877.

7. Brown, *op. cit.,* pp. 38-40.

8. *Hornell Times,* July 4, 1877.

9. *Ibid.,* July 21, 1877. The description of the shacks is by a former Erie worker who was interviewed by Ray V. Brown (*op. cit.,* p. 50).

10. *Hornell Times,* July 21, 1877.

11. *Elmira Daily Advertiser,* July 21, 1877; *Hornellsville Tribune,* July 23, 1877.

12. *New York Times,* July 23, 1877.

13. The list is compiled in Yellen, *op. cit.,* pp. 21-22.

14. *New York Times,* July 27, 1877.

15. McCabe, *op. cit.,* p. 235; *Buffalo Commercial Advertiser,* July 23, 24, 25, 1877.

16. *Hornell Times,* July 25, 1877.

17. The account is based on *Elmira Daily Advertiser,* July 23, 1877; *Hornell Times,* July 25, 1877; Brown, *op. cit.,* pp. 58-62.

18. Brown, *op. cit.,* p. 62.

19. *New York Times,* July 23, 1877.

20. *Elmira Daily Advertiser,* July 23, 1877.

21. *Ibid.*

22. A full account of this trip may be found in the *New York Tribune,* July 24, 1877.

23. *Elmira Daily Advertiser,* July 24, 1877.

24. Brown, *op. cit.,* pp. 68-69.

25. *Hornell Times,* July 25, 1877.

26. *New York Times,* July 24, 1877; *Hornell Times,* July 25, 1877.

27. *New York Sun,* July 24, 1877.

28. "A Letter from the Boss Striker," *Hornell Times,* August 4, 1877.

29. Brown, *op. cit.,* p. 75.

30. Reports of the meetings of the night of July 25 and of the settlement may be found in the *New York Tribune,* July 26, 1877, *Hornell Times,* July 28, 1877, and Brown, *op. cit.,* pp. 75-81.

31. *Elmira Daily Advertiser,* July 27, 1877.

32. *Buffalo Commercial Advertiser,* July 21, 22, 23, 1877.

33. *Ibid.,* July 24, 25, 26, 27, 28, 29, 30, 1877; *New York Times,* July 25, 1877; *New York World,* July 25, 30, 1877.

34. *New York Times,* July 23, 24, 1877; *Albany Journal,* July 22, 23, 24, 1877; W. A. Croffut, *The Vanderbilts,* Chicago, 1886, p. 305.

35. *New York Times,* July 24, 1877; *Albany Journal,* July 23, 24, 1877.

36. *New York Times,* July 25, 1877.

37. *Ibid.*

38. *Ibid.,* July 28, 1877.

39. *Albany Journal,* July 23, 24, 25, 26, 1877.

40. *Ibid.,* July 25, 26, 1877.

41. *Albany Journal,* July 27, 1877; *New York Times,* July 27, 1877.

42. *Albany Journal,* July 28, 1877.

43. *Ibid.,* July 29, 1877; *New York Times,* July 29, 1877.

44. *Buffalo Commercial Advertiser,* July 29, 30, 31, 1877.

The strikers on the Lake Shore at Buffalo returned to work the following day. (*Buffalo Commercial Advertiser,* July 31, August 1, 1877.)

45. Bruce *op. cit.,* p. 251.

46. *Ibid.*

Chapter V: The Strike on the Vandalia of Terre Haute: The Fruits of Class Harmony

1. For a discussion of cross-class cooperation in early labor struggles, *see* Herbert Gutman, "The Worker's Search for Power," in H. Wayne Morgan, ed., *The Gilded Age: A Reappraisal,* Syracuse, N.Y., 1968, pp. 138-68.

2. *Locomotive Firemen's Magazine,* vol. I, July 1877, p. 238.

3. *Terre Haute Express,* July 23, 1877.

4. *Ibid.,* July 25, 1877; Edward Winslow Martin, *The History of the Great Riots,* Philadelphia, 1877, p. 365.

5. *Terre Haute Express,* July 25, 1877.

The only treatment in detail of the strike in Terre Haute is Nicholas Salvatore, "The Small Town Strike: Terre Haute, Indiana," unpublished paper delivered at 1976 Annual Meeting, American Historical Association, Washington, D.C., December 28, 1976. The paper is part of a full-length biography of Eugene V. Debs being prepared by Mr. Salvatore, sections of which, including the one dealing with the strike in Terre Haute, I have had the opportunity to study. The unpublished manuscript is in the possession of the author.

6. *Terre Haute Express,* July 25-26, 1877.

7. *Ibid.,* July 26, 1877.

8. *Ibid.,* July 27, 1877.

9. *Ibid.,* July 28, 1877.

10. Clinton J. Phillips, *Indiana in Transition: The Emergence of an Industrial Commonwealth, 1880-1920,* Indianapolis, 1968, p. 231; George Irving Reed, *Encyclopedia of Biography of Indiana,* Chicago, 1895, vol. I, p. 80; Salvatore, "The Small Town Strike," in his unpublished work on Eugene V. Debs.

11. *Terre Haute Express,* July 27, 28, 1877.

12. *Chicago Tribune,* July 24, 25, 1877; *Indianapolis Sentinel,* July 25, 26, 27, August 1, 1877.

13. *Indianapolis Sentinel,* July 22, 23, 1877; Matilda Gresham, *The Life of Walter Quintin Gresham,* Chicago, 1919, vol. I, p. 382.

14. *Indianapolis Sentinel,* July 24, 1877.

15. Gresham, *op. cit.,* vol. I, p. 384.

16. *Ibid.,* p. 390; *Indianapolis Sentinel,* July 25, 1877.

17. Bruce, *op. cit.,* p. 289.

18. Gresham, *op. cit.,* vol. I, p. 193; *Indianapolis Sentinel,* July 26, 27, 1877.

19. Bruce, *op. cit.,* p. 269.

20. *Indianapolis Sentinel,* July 28, 1877; Gresham, *op. cit.,* vol. I, pp. 398-99.

21. *Terre Haute Express,* July 29, 1899; Gresham, *op. cit.,* vol. I, pp. 398-99.

22. Gresham, *op. cit.,* vol. I, p. 399.

23. *Terre Haute Express,* July 30, 31, 1877.

24. Richard W. Thompson to Colonel Thomas A. Scott, August 5, 1877, quoted in Salvatore, "The Small Town Strike," in his unpublished work on Eugene V. Debs.

25. Gresham, *op. cit.,* vol. I, p. 490; *Terre Haute Express,* July 30, 31, 1877.

26. Members of the Vico Lodge signed a petition supporting Mark Miller and William Sayer in their court cases. One of the signers was Eugene V. Debs, and Nicholas Salvatore points out that this seems to have been his only public action during the strike. ("The Small Town Strike," in unpublished work on Eugene V. Debs.)

Chapter VI: The Workingmen's Party of the United States

1. For a general discussion of the Communist issue during the Great Strike, *see* Gerald Grob, "The Railroad Strike of 1877," *Midwest Journal,* vol. VI, Winter 1954-55, pp. 16-34. For the Communist issue during the railroad strikes of 1873-74, *see* Gutman, "Trouble on the Railroads," p. 227.

2. *Pittsburgh Critic* reprinted in *Report of the Committee . . . to Investigate . . . Railroad Riots,* p. 819.

3. *Ibid.*

4. *Missouri Republican,* July 19, 1877. *See also* Burbank, *Reign of the Rabble,* pp. 13-14.

5. *Brooklyn Daily Eagle,* July 23, 1877.

6. *National Labor Tribune,* July 28, 1877; *Workingman's Advocate,* August 1, 1877; *Labor Standard,* August 4, 1877.

7. "The Commune in the United States," *New York Tribune,* July 25, 1877. *See also* "The American Commune," Washington *National Republican,* July 21, 1877.

8. *Pittsburgh Leader,* July 20, 1877, reprinted in *Report of the Committee . . . to Investigate . . . Railroad Riots,* pp. 798-80.

9. *Chicago Inter-Ocean,* July 25, 1877; *St. Louis Globe-Democrat,* July 28, 1877.

10. Allan Pinkerton, *Strikers, Communists, Tramps and Detectives,* New York, 1878, p. 88.

11. *St. Louis Globe-Democrat,* July 28, 1877.

12. Pinkerton, *op. cit.,* p. 79. Unfortunately the correspondence in the Allan Pinkerton Papers in the Library of Congress skips from June to November 1877 so that it is impossible to determine the nature of the reports from the Pinkerton Agents. *See* Papers of the Pinkerton National Detective Agency, Library of Congress, Manuscripts Division.

13. Dacus, *op. cit.,* p. 76.

14. New York, 1937, pp. 15-19. *See also* Philip A. Slaner, "The Railroad Strikes of 1877," *Marxist Quarterly,* vol. I, April-June 1937, p. 214.

15. For the full story of the American sections of the International, *see* Samuel Bernstein, *The First International in America,* New York, 1965.

16. *Ibid.*, pp. 109-26, 161-78.

17. For Marx's correspondence with Americans, *see* Karl Marx and Frederick Engels, *Letters to Americans, 1848-1895,* New York, 1958.

18. Foner, *History of the Labor Movement,* vol. I, pp. 448-50; Marx to F. Bolte, November 23, 1871, Karl Marx and Frederick Engels, *Letters to Americans,* pp. 93-94.

19. *Vorbote,* June 5, 1874.

20. *Arbeiter-Zeitung,* May 6, 1874; Foner, *History of the Labor Movement,* vol. I, p. 452.

21. *Vorbote,* June 20, 27, 1874.

22. John R. Commons, ed., *A Documentary History of the American Industrial Society,* vol. IX, Cleveland, 1910, pp. 376-78.

23. Commons and Associates, *op. cit.,* vol. II, p. 233; *Socialist,* May 6, 1876.

24. Bernstein, *op. cit.,* p. 274.

25. The English text of the Declaration appeared in the *Socialist,* May 6, 1876, and the German text was published in *Social-Demokrat,* April 30, 1876, and *Vorbote,* April 29, 1876.

26. Bernstein, *op. cit.,* p. 282; Morris Hillquit, *History of Socialism in the United States,* New York, 1903, p. 206.

27. G. Lukert in *Vorbote,* July 8, 1876.

28. However, the first Black socialist in the United States, Peter H. Clark of Cincinnati, became a member of the Workingmen's Party of the United States. (*See below,* pp. 223-24, 258 note 41.)

29. The proceedings of the Unity Congress may be found in Philip S. Foner, ed., *The Formation of the Workingmen's Party of the United States: Proceedings of the Union Congress Held at Philadelphia, July 19-26, 1876,* Occasional Paper No. 18, American Institute for Marxist Studies, New York, 1976.

30. *Labor Standard,* August 12 and 29, 1876.

31. Friedrich A. Sorge, *Socialism and the Worker,* New York, 1876, pp. 12-13, 19-20.

32. *Labor Standard,* October 28, 1876.

33. *Ibid.*, September 30, December 30, 1876; Bernstein, *op. cit.,* pp. 290-91; *Arbeiter-Stimme,* June 17, 1877.

34. *Labor Standard,* January 27, 1877.

35. Friedrich A. Sorge, "Die Arbeiterbewegung in den Vereinigten Staaten," *Neue Zeit* (Berlin), 1 Band (1891-1892), p. 398.

36. Bruce, *op. cit.,* pp. 228-30.

37. *Socialist,* August 26, 1876; Burbank, *op. cit.,* p. 74.
Barney Donahue, leader of the Erie strikers at Hornellsville, New York,

was charged with being a member of the party, but there is no evidence supporting this.

38. Gabriel Kolko's comments in his work *Main Currents in Modern American History* that ". . . to those in power it (the Great Strike) was a clear harbinger of the arrival of the Marxist First International which was wholly inconsequential before, during and after the strike. . . ." (New York, 1976, p. 174.) This statement is wrong on two counts. First, the International had disbanded a year before, and second, as will be spelled out in the following chapters, the Workingmen's Party of the United States (the organization involved) was anything but "inconsequential" during the strike.

Chapter VII: The WPUS and the Great Strike, I: New York City, Louisville, and Cincinnati

1. *Chicago Tribune*, July 23, 1877.

2. *St. Louis Globe-Democrat*, July 23, 1877.

3. Howard H. Quint, *The Forging of American Socialism*, Columbia, S. Car., 1953, pp. 3, 13-14.

4. *Labor Standard*, July 28, August 4, 1877.

James A. Dacus cites two meetings of the Workingmen's Party in Baltimore during the Great Strike, one by the German section and another by a section of Bohemians and Poles. (*Op. cit.*, pp. 65-66.) But neither the Baltimore press nor the *Labor Standard* mention them.

5. *San Francisco Chronicle*, July 27, 1877; Ira B. Cross, *A History of the Labor Movement in California*, Berkeley, 1935, pp. 89-90.

6. *Boston Globe*, July 24-25, 1877; *Labor Standard*, August 4, 1877; Bruce, *op. cit.*, p. 232.

7. Mackey, "Law and Order: 1877," *op. cit.*, pp. 196-97; *Labor Standard*, August 4, 11, 1877; *Philadelphia Record*, July 27, 1877; *Philadelphia North American*, July 24, 26, 27, 1877; *New York Times*, July 25, 29, 30, 1877.

8. *Philadelphia Record*, July 27, 28, 1877; *Labor Standard*, August 11, 1877; Mackey, "Law and Order," *op. cit.*, pp. 198-200.

9. *New York Sun*, July 24, 1877; *New York World*, July 24, 1877; *New York Times*, July 24, 1877; Bruce *op. cit.*, p. 277.

10. *New York World*, July 24, 1877.

11. *New York Times*, July 26, 1877; *New York World*, July 26, 1877.

12. The *New York Sun* headlined the meeting "The Dreaded Assemblage." For the telegrams to Mayor Ely, *see New York Times*, July 26, 1877.

13. *Brooklyn Daily Eagle*, July 23, 1877; *New York Sun*, July 23, 1877.

14. For John Swinton's role in the Tompkins Square clash between police and the unemployed, January 13, 1874, *see* Marc Ross, "John Swinton, Journalist and Reformer, The Active Years, 1857-1887," unpublished Ph.D. thesis, New York University, 1969, pp. 83-90.

15. *New York Sun*, July 26, 1877; *New York Tribune*, July 26, 1877.

In a sermon the following Sunday, during which thirty police officers in civilian dress were in the congregation at Plymouth Church, Beecher conceded that he had received "swarms of letters" criticizing his sermon of the previous week. He argued in defense that he had been "grossly misrepresented through careless reporting," and then proceeded to disprove his own defense by repeating much of what he had said the previous Sunday. This time, he declared that "a dollar a day" was enough "to give a man bread." He called the idea that the government should aid the poor the viewpoint of "impractical German theorists" which would open the door to communism. Finally, he advised workers to "work more and grumble less." Where they could obtain work did not enter into his sermon. (*New York Sun*, July 30, 1877.)

16. *New York Sun*, July 26, 1877; *New York Tribune*, July 26, 1877.

17. *New York Times*, July 26, 1877.

18. *New York Sun*, July 26, 1877; *New York Tribune*, July 26, 1877; *New York World*, July 26, 1877.

19. *New York World*, July 26, 1877; *St. Louis Globe-Democrat*, July 30, 1877.

The address was signed by B. Kaufman, G. Winter, A. Walster, J. Schwab, E. Hall, and Leander Thompson on behalf of the Workingmen's Party of the United States. The address is not in the Hayes Papers.

20. *New York World*, July 26, 1877; *New York Sun*, July 26, 1877.

21. *New York Times*, July 26, 1877; *New York Tribune*, July 26, 1877; *New York Sun*, July 26, 1877; *New York World*, July 26, 1877.

22. *New York Herald*, July 27, 1877; *Labor Standard*, August 4, 1877.

Samuel Gompers, President of the Cigar Makers' Union, was also mentioned as a speaker, but his speech was not reported.

23. *Louisville Courier-Journal*, July 23, 1877.

24. *Ibid.*, July 25, 1877.

Robert V. Bruce states that Standiford "balked" at the request for a raise in wages, but the *Louisville Courier-Journal* reported that he responded affirmatively, a view which appears to have been accepted by the workers in Louisville. This is also the opinion of Bill I. Weaver, "Louisville's Labor Disturbance, July, 1877," *Filson Club Historical Quarterly*, vol. XLVIII, April 1974, pp. 179-80.

25. *Louisville Courier-Journal*, July 25, 1877.

26. Pinkerton, *op. cit.*, p. 381.

27. *Louisville Courier-Journal*, July 25, 1877.

28. *Ibid.*

29. *Ibid.*

30. *Ibid.*

31. *Ibid.*

32. *Ibid.*, July 26, 27, 1877.

33. *Ibid.*, July 26, 1877; Alpheus T. Mason, *Louis D. Brandeis, A Free Man's Life*, New York, 1946, pp. 47-48.

34. *Louisville Courier-Journal*, July 26, 1877.

35. *Ibid.*

36. *Ibid.*, July 28, 29, 1877; *Louisville Commercial*, July 27, 28, 1877.

37. *Ibid.,* July 30, 1877.

38. A brief reference to the victory of the Workingmen's Party in the August election is the only mention of the party in Weaver's article on the strike in Louisville. (*Op. cit.,* p. 186.)

39. *Cincinnati Gazette,* July 23, 1877.

40. *Ibid.; Cincinnati Commercial,* July 23, 1877.

41. Peter H. Clark, principal of the Colored High School in Cincinnati, was probably the first Black American socialist. He was a Republican until 1877, when, disillusioned with the Republican Party's indifference to the problems of Blacks in the South and concerned over the growing power of the industrial capitalists, he became a member of the English-speaking section of the Workingmen's Party. (*See* my discussion of Peter H. Clark in the forthcoming work, Philip S. Foner, *American Socialism and Black Americans: From the Age of Jackson to World War II.*)

42. *Cincinnati Commercial,* July 23, 1877. The speech is reprinted in Philip S. Foner, ed., *The Voice of Black America: Major Speeches of Blacks in the United States, 1797-1973,* New York, 1975, vol. I, pp. 481-87. Extracts from the speech can be found in Herbert G. Gutman, "Peter H. Clark: Pioneer Negro Socialist, 1877," *Journal of Negro Education,* Fall 1965, pp. 413-18.

43. *The Emancipator,* July 21, 28, 1877.

44. *Cincinnati Commercial,* July 24, 1877.

45. *Ibid.,* July 26, 1877.

46. *The Emancipator,* August 4, 1877.

47. *Cincinnati Enquirer,* July 24, 1877.

48. *Ibid.,* July 24, 25, 1877.

49. *Ibid.,* July 25, 1877.

50. *Ibid.,* July 26, 1877.

51. *Cincinnati Enquirer,* July 24, 25, 1877; Bruce, *op. cit.,* p. 253.

52. *Cincinnati Enquirer,* July 26, 1877; *Cincinnati Daily Gazette,* July 26, 1877.

53. *Cincinnati Enquirer,* July 27, August 1, 1877.

Chapter VII: The WPUS and the Great Strike, II: Chicago

1. Bessie Louise Pierce, *A History of Chicago: 1871-1883,* New York, 1957, vol. III, pp. 243-44; Hoyt, "The Labor Explosion of 1877," *op. cit.,* p. 182.

2. *Chicago Tribune,* July 20, 21, 1877; *Chicago Inter-Ocean,* July 20, 21, 1877; *Chicago Daily News,* July 20, 21, 1877.

3. *Chicago Times,* July 20, 1877.

4. *Ibid.,* July 23, 1877.

5. Bruce, *op. cit.,* p. 237.

6. *Chicago Tribune,* July 23, 1877; *Chicago Times,* July 23, 1877.

7. The statement appeared in a *Chicago Tribune* editorial of July 20, 1877. In the same editorial, the *Tribune* commented: "If the Company should reduce wages to a cent a day, [the strikers] have but one privilege

in the premises. They have the right to step out."

8. *Chicago Tribune,* July 23, 1877; *Chicago Times,* July 23, 1877; *Chicago Inter-Ocean,* July 23, 1877.

9. *Chicago Tribune,* July 23, 1877.

The most recent discussion of the Great Strike in Chicago is Kenneth Kann, "The Big City Riot: Chicago, Illinois," unpublished paper delivered at 1976 Annual Meeting, American Historical Association, Washington, D.C., December 28, 1976. This paper is part of a full-length study by Mr. Kann of the working class and labor movement of Chicago from the end of the Civil War to 1890. Pages 68-100 of this study dealing with the Great Strike in Chicago was made available to me by Mr. Kann, and the unpublished manuscript is in the possession of the author.

10. *Chicago Tribune,* July 23, 1877; *Chicago Daily News,* July 23, 1877; Pierce, *op. cit.,* vol. III, pp. 247-48; Bruce, *op. cit.,* pp. 236-37.

11. *Chicago Tribune,* July 24, 1877.

12. *Ibid., Chicago Tribune,* July 24, 1877.

13. *Chicago Tribune,* July 24, 1877.

14. *Ibid.; Chicago Times,* July 24, 1877; *Chicago Daily News,* July 24, 1877; Kann, *op. cit.,* p. 73.

The full text of Parsons' speech was published in *Labor Standard,* August 11, 1877.

15. *Chicago Times,* July 24, 1877; *Chicago Tribune,* July 24, 1877.

16. *Ibid.*

17. *Chicago Tribune,* July 24, 1877.

18. *Chicago Inter-Ocean,* July 25, 1877.

19. *Chicago Times,* July 25, 1877; *Chicago Tribune,* July 25, 1877; *Chicago Daily News,* July 25, 1877.

20. *Chicago Daily News,* July 25, 1877; *Chicago Inter-Ocean,* July 25, 1877.

21. *Chicago Times,* July 25, 1877; *Chicago Tribune,* July 25, 1877; Kann, *op. cit.,* pp. 74-75.

22. Charles Flynn, *History of the Chicago Police,* Chicago, 1922, pp. 165-66; also quoted in Kann, *op. cit.,* p. 75.

23. *Chicago Tribune,* July 25, 1877; *Chicago Times,* July 25, 1877; *Chicago Inter-Ocean,* July 25, 1877.

24. *See,* for example, *Baltimore Sun,* July 25, 1877.

25. David J. Scharnau, "Thomas J. Morgan, Chicago Socialist," unpublished Ph.D. thesis, University of Illinois, 1968, pp. 34-35; *Chicago Tribune,* July 25, 1877; Kann, *op cit.,* pp. 76-77.

26. *Chicago Inter-Ocean,* July 25, 1877.

27. *Chicago Times,* July 25, 1877.

28. *Chicago Daily News,* July 24, 1877; Bruce, *op. cit.,* pp. 242-43.

29. Ross, "John Swinton," *op. cit.,* pp. 160-61.

30. *Chicago Times,* July 24, 1877.

31. For a discussion of the Haymarket Affair, *see* Henry David, *History of the Haymarket Affair,* New York, 1936, and Philip S. Foner, *History of the Labor Movement in the United States,* vol. II, New York, 1955, pp. 162-85.

32. Philip S. Foner, ed., *The Autobiographies of the Haymarket Martyrs*, New York, 1969, pp. 31-33; *Chicago Tribune*, July 25, 1877; Calmer, *Labor Agitator*, p. 28.

33. *Chicago Tribune*, July 25-26, 1877; *Chicago Times*, July 26, 1877.

34. *Chicago Tribune*, July 25, 1877.

35. *Chicago Tribune*, July 26, 1877; *Chicago Times*, July 26, 1877; *Chicago Inter-Ocean*, July 26, 1877.

36. *Chicago Times*, July 26, 1877; *Chicago Tribune*, July 26, 1877; Kann, *op. cit.*, p. 78.

37. *Chicago Times*, July 26, 1877; *Chicago Tribune*, July 26, 1877. Pierce, *op. cit.*, vol. III, p. 250.

38. *Chicago Tribune*, July 26, 1877; Bruce, *op. cit.*, p. 247.

39. *Chicago Times*, July 26, 1877; *Chicago Tribune*, July 26, 1877.

40. *Chicago Tribune*, July 26, 1877; Bruce, *op. cit.*, p. 247.

41. Albert Day, "To My Children," *Mss.*, Chicago Historical Society, 1924, pp. 36-40; also cited in Kann, *op. cit.*, p. 82.

42. *Chicago Tribune*, July 26, 1877; *Chicago Inter-Ocean*, July 27, 1877; Bruce, *op. cit.*, pp. 247-48.

43. *Chicago Tribune*, July 22, 23, 24, 1877; Kann, *op. cit.*, pp. 84-85.

44. The best contemporary description of the Battle of July 26 is in the *Chicago Times*, July 27, 1877, and the best description in a later historical account is in Kann, *op. cit.*, pp. 84-89. The present account is an amalgamation of details from the *Tribune* and Kann as well as from the *Chicago Times*, *Inter-Ocean*, and *Daily News* of July 27, 1877, and that in Hoyt, *op. cit.*, pp. 190-94, and Bruce, *op. cit.*, pp. 246-50.

45. *Chicago Tribune, Times, Inter-Ocean*, and *Daily News*, July 27, 1877; Pierce, *op. cit.*, vol. III, p. 253; Bruce, *op. cit.*, p. 250.

46. *Chicago Times, Tribune, Inter-Ocean*, and *Daily News*, July 27, 1877.

47. *Ibid.*

48. For a description of a strikingly similar action by American-born women in a ten-hour strike of 1845 in Pittsburgh, *see* Foner, *History of the Labor Movement*, vol. I, pp. 207-8.

49. *Chicago Inter-Ocean*, July 27, 1877 and reprinted in *New York Sun, New York Times*, and *Baltimore Sun*, July 28, 29, 1877. *See also Chicago Tribune* and *Times*, July 27, 1877.

50. *Chicago Times, Tribune, Inter-Ocean, and Daily News*, July 27, 1877.

51. *Ibid.*

52. *Chicago Daily News, Times*, and *Tribune*, July 27, 1877; Flynn, *op. cit.*, p. 167; Bruce, *op. cit.*, pp. 251-52; Kann, *op. cit.*, p. 90.

53. *Chicago Tribune*, July 28-29, 1877; *Inter-Ocean*, July 28-29, 1877; *Daily News*, July 28-29, 1877; *Times*, July 28-29, 1877.

54. *Chicago Inter-Ocean*, July 27, 1877.

55. *Chicago Tribune*, July 28, 1877.

56. *Chicago Times*, July 25, 26, 27, 1877; Hoyt, *op. cit.*, p. 195.

57. Pinkerton, *op. cit.*, pp. 265-66.

58. *Chicago Daily News*, July 27, 1877.

59. Bruce, *op. cit.,* p. 250.

Chapter IX: The WPUS and the Great Strike, III: The St. Louis General Strike

1. "St. Louis Communism," *Chicago Tribune,* July 29, 1877.
2. *Missouri Republican,* July 25, 1877; *New York Sun,* July 26, 1877.
3. *Toledo Commercial,* July 24, 1877, reprinted in Bruce, *op. cit.,* p. 207.
4. *Ibid.,* p. 208; Martin, *op. cit.,* pp. 347-48.
5. *Toledo Blade,* July 26, 1877.
6. *Ibid.,* July 27, 28, 1877.
7. Burbank, *Reign of the Rabble, op. cit.,* pp. 55-56. Burbank acknowledges that the Philadelphia strike of 1835 for the ten-hour day is sometimes referred to as America's first general strike, but he observes that this "was hardly so in the modern sense" (p. 55). In that sense, he is correct.
8. *Ibid.,* p. 19; Bruce, *op. cit.,* pp. 253-54; Hoyt, *op. cit.,* pp. 198-99.
9. *St. Louis Globe-Democrat,* July 22, 1877.
10. *Missouri Republican,* July 22, 1877.
11. Gen. J. H. Wilson to Carl Schurz, marked "Personal," July 22, 1877, Carl Schurz Papers, Library of Congress, Manuscripts Division.
12. Gen. J. H. Wilson to Carl Schurz, telegram, July 12, 1877, *ibid.*
13. Burbank is in error when he writes that in all the reports of the meeting there was "no mention of the established brotherhoods of labor." (P. 16.) The account in the *St. Louis Globe-Democrat* mentions the role of the Brotherhood of Locomotive Firemen. (July 23, 1877.)
14. *St. Louis Globe-Democrat,* July 23, 1877.
15. *Ibid.,* July 22, 1877.
16. The information on Lofgreen's (Gronlund's) record at the University of Copenhagen may be found in *Studenterne Veal Kobehnavens 1829-1880,* ed. H. Frus-Peterson, Aarkus, 1950, vol. I, copy in Kongelige Bibliotek, Copenhagen.

In 1884, under his real name of Laurence Gronlund, he published *The Cooperative Commonwealth,* in which he advocated an evolutionary type of socialism. The book influenced Edward Bellamy in writing *Looking Backward.*

The only study of Lofgreen (Gronlund) in English is Solomon Gemorah, "Laurence Gronlund's Ideas and Influence, 1877-1899," unpublished Ph.D. thesis, New York, 1966. However, it adds nothing to what is already known about Lofgreen's role in the 1877 strike, basing its discussion of the events in St. Louis only on Bruce. The same is true of Gemorah's article, "Laurence Gronlund—Utopian or Reformer?" (*Science & Society,* vol. XXXIII, 1969, pp. 446-58.)

17. *St. Louis Globe-Democrat,* July 23, 1877.
18. *St. Louis Globe-Democrat,* July 23, 1877; *St. Louis Times,* July 23, 1877; *Missouri Republican,* July 23, 1877.
19. *Ibid.*
20. Burbank, *op. cit.,* p. 16.

21. *St. Louis Globe-Democrat,* July 26, 1877; *Missouri Republican,* July 25, 1877; *St. Louis Times,* July 26, 1877.

22. *St. Louis Globe-Democrat,* July 23, 1877.

23. *Ibid.;* Hoyt, *op. cit.,* pp. 199-200.

24. Gen. James H. Wilson to Carl Schurz, July 22, 1877, telegram, Carl Schurz Papers, Library of Congress, Manuscripts Division; Burbank, *op. cit.,* pp. 21-22.

25. *St. Louis Times,* July 24, 1877; *St. Louis Globe-Democrat,* July 24, 1877.

26. *St. Louis Globe-Democrat,* July 24, 1877; *St. Louis Times,* July 24, 1877; *Missouri Republican,* July 24, 1877.

27. In the Minutes of the General Council of the First International, Cope is mentioned on August 15, 1865, as having been elected to the General Council, in February, 1866, as one of the signers of the General Council's "Appeal from the British Members of the Central Council to their Fellow Working Men of the United Kingdom," and also in February 1866, as a member of the bootmakers. Cope served on the General Council from 1865-1867. *See The General Council of the First International 1864-1866, Minutes,* Moscow, n.d., pp. 123, 315, 322.

28. *St. Louis Globe-Democrat,* July 24, 1877; *St. Louis Times,* July 24, 1877; *Missouri Republican,* July 24, 1877.

29. *St. Louis Globe-Democrat,* July 25, 1877.

30. Burbank, *op. cit.,* p. 35.

31. *Missouri Republican,* July 24, 1877; Burbank, *op. cit.,* p. 33.

32. *Missouri Republican,* July 25, 1877.

33. James H. Wilson to Carl Schurz, July 24, 1877, two telegrams, Carl Schurz Papers, Library of Congress, Manuscripts Division.

34. *St. Louis Globe-Democrat,* July 25, 1877; Burbank, *op. cit.,* p. 43.

35. *St. Louis Times,* July 25, 1877.

36. *Ibid.; St. Louis Daily Journal,* July 25, 1877; *St. Louis Globe-Democrat,* July 25, 1877.

37. Burbank, *op. cit.,* p. 43.

38. *St. Louis Globe-Democrat,* July 25, 1877; *St. Louis Times,* July 25, 1877; Hoyt, *op. cit.,* pp. 202-3.

J. J. McBride's translation of the word *canaille* as "dog" is incorrect; *canaille* is derived from *chien,* but the word has lost its original literal meaning and is now translated as "rabble."

39. *St. Louis Globe-Democrat,* July 25, 1877.

40. Burbank, *op. cit.,* pp. 59, 61.

41. *Missouri Republican,* July 26, 1877.

42. *St. Louis Globe-Democrat,* July 26, 1877. A copy of the original leaflet of the Proclamation in English and German is in the files of the International Workingmen's Association, State Historical Society, Madison, Wisconsin. It is reproduced as a frontispiece in Burbank's book, *Reign of the Rabble.*

43. Hillquit, *op. cit.,* p. 202.

44. *Missouri Republican,* July 26, 1877; *St. Louis Globe-Democrat,* July 26, 1877.

45. *St. Louis Globe-Democrat,* July 26, 1877.

46. *Ibid.; Missouri Republican,* July 26, 1877; *St. Louis Times,* July 26, 1877; *Scranton Republican,* July 26, 1877.

47. *St. Louis Globe-Democrat,* July 26, 1877; *Missouri Republican,* July 26, 1877; *St. Louis Daily Market Reporter,* July 26, 1877; Burbank, *op. cit.,* pp. 73-75.

48. *St. Louis Globe-Democrat,* July 26, 1877; *Missouri Republican,* July 26, 1877.

49. Burbank, *op. cit.,* pp. 69-70, 78.

50. *Ibid.,* p. 112; Amy Schechter, "Labor Struggles in 1877," *Daily Worker,* July 17, 1926.

51. Burbank, *op. cit.,* pp. 177-78.

52. *St. Louis Globe-Democrat,* July 26, 1877.

53. *Ibid.,* July 27, 1877.

54. *New York Sun,* reprinted in Burbank, *op.cit.,* p. 73.

55. *Missouri Republican,* July 26, 1877; *St. Louis Times,* July 26, 1877.

56. *St. Louis Times,* July 26, 27, 28, 29, 1877; *Missouri Republican,* July 27, 28, 29, 1877; *St. Louis Globe-Democrat,* July 25, 26, 27, 1877; Russell M. Nolen, "The Labor Movement in St. Louis from 1860 to 1890," *Missouri Historical Review,* vol. XXIV, January, 1940, pp. 170-72.

57. *St. Louis Times,* August 4, 1877.

58. Burbank, *op. cit.,* p. 48.

59. *St. Louis Globe-Democrat,* July 28, 1877.

60. *Ibid.,* July 25, 1877; *Scranton Republican,* July 25, 1877.

61. *St. Louis Globe-Democrat,* July 18, 1877; *New York Times,* July 18, 1877; Hoyt, *op. cit.,* p. 206.

62. *St. Louis Times,* July 22, 1877; *Missouri Republican,* July 27, 1877.

63. James H. Wilson to Carl Schurz, July 27, 1877, Carl Schurz Papers, Library of Congress, Manuscripts Division.

64. *St. Louis Globe-Democrat,* July 28, 1877.

65. *Missouri Republican,* July 28, 1877.

66. *St. Louis Globe-Democrat,* July 28, 1877.

67. *Ibid.; Missouri Republican,* July 28, 1877.

68. *St. Louis Times,* August 4, 1877.

69. *Missouri Republican,* July 28, 1877.

70. *Ibid.; St. Louis Globe-Democrat,* July 28, 1877.

71. *Missouri Republican,* July 28, 1877.

72. *Ibid.; St. Louis Globe-Democrat,* July 28, 1877.

73. *St. Louis Times,* July 30, 31, 1877.
The executive committee had tried to hold three meetings, but two failed completely, and the police routed a third small one.

74. *St. Louis Globe-Democrat,* July 29, 30, 31, 1877; *St. Louis Times,* July 29, 30, 31, 1877; *Missouri Republican,* July 29, 30, 31, 1877.

75. Report by Vice-Consul Bagshare on the Late Industrial Conflicts at St. Louis, *Reports Respecting the Late Industrial Conflicts in the United States,* London, 1877, p. 47.

76. *St. Louis Globe-Democrat,* July 28, 29, 1877.

77. *St. Louis Times,* July 29, 1877.

78. *Missouri Republican,* July 28, 1877.

Chapter X: The End of the Great Strike

1. *New York World,* July 24, 1877.

2. *Cleveland Leader,* July 23, 1877.

3. "The Strike Reaches Canada," *Pottsville Weekly Miners' Journal,* July 27, 1877.

The dispatch, dated July 24, was from St. Thomas, Ontario, and read in part: "The employees in the Canada Southern workshops quit work at noon to-day, and a large number of engineers, firemen and brakemen joined the strikers. . . . All freight trains on the road have stopped running. . . . The striking firemen and brakemen visited the workshops and advised the employees to quit work. . . . Word was also sent along the line to stop the trains where they were."

4. *Biennial Report of the Governor to the Legislature of Illinois,* Springfield, Illinois, 1879, pp. 13-15.

5. *New York Sun,* July 24, 1877.

6. William Roscoe Thayer, *The Life and Letters of John Hay,* Boston, 1908, vol. I, p. 179.

Hay's novel, *The Breadwinners,* published anonymously in 1883, was inspired by the railroad strike of 1877 and was bitterly antilabor.

7. *New York Times,* July 26, 1877.

8. *Workingman's Advocate,* July 28, 1877.

9. *Cleveland Leader,* July 24, 1877; Victor R. Greene, *The Slavic Community on Strike: Immigrant Labor in Pennsylvania Anthracite,* Notre Dame, Indiana, 1968, pp. 72-73.

The news that several of the railroad lines (including the Union Pacific) had rescinded the wage cut was hailed by the *Glasgow Sentinel,* a trade union paper in Scotland, as signalling that the violent upheaval would soon be over. "This event we earnestly hope will have its lessons to the workmen of the [United] States generally, which are that they will combine properly, and only ask to change things by legal and constitutional means." (James D. Young, "Scottish Labor and the American Railway Strike of 1877," *Labor History,* vol. XII, Fall, 1971, p. 604.)

The report of a delegation of mechanics of Paris, part of a larger delegation which visited the United States during the Centennial of 1876, referred to the great railroad strike of 1877 as strengthening their conviction that strikes were not effective as a weapon of the working class. Although the report conceded that the use of the troops to crush the strike was evidence of the brutality of the capitalist class and the government it controlled, the resort to a strike by the railroad workers was a gesture of futility. (*Rapport de Délégués des Ouvriers Mécaniciens de Paris à l'Exposition Universelle de Philadelphia,* Paris, 1877, pp. 186-87; Philip S. Foner, "The French Trade Union Delegation to the Philadelphia Centennial Exposition, 1876," *Science & Society,* vol. XL, Fall 1976, p. 284*n.*)

10. *Nation,* vol. XXV, July 26, 1877, p. 50.

11. *Railroad Gazette,* vol. IX, July 27, 1877, p. 50.

12. Lucy Stone, "The Strikers and the Mob," *Woman's Journal,* July 28, 1877, p. 236.

It is ironical that two years later, the historian Francis Parkman used the Great Strike of 1877 as an argument to justify opposition to woman suffrage. Writing in the *North American Review* on "The Woman Question," Parkman argued: "To give women the suffrage is to expose the most excitable part of the human race to the influence of political passions with no means of defense against possible consequences. . . . There are those who think that the suffrage would act as a safety-valve to political passions; but it has not so acted in the case of men." He clinched his argument as follows: "The bloody riots of 1877 were the work of men in full enjoyment of suffrage. It is to the dread of lead and steel that the friends of order must look in the last resort; and, when this does not exist, political frenzy will have its way." (*North American Review,* vol. CCLXXV, October 1879, p. 319.)

13. *Independent,* vol. XXIX, August 2, 1877, p. 16.

14. *Martinsburg Statesman,* July 31, 1877.

The *Statesman* received many letters from workers congratulating it for its unwavering support of the strikers, and special resolutions were adopted at union meetings asserting that the paper deserved the "support and confidence of every laboring man in West Virginia," and urging them to stand by "that journal which in their own dark hours had stood by them." The *Statesman* gratefully received these tributes, but added: "We want it remembered that the *Statesman* has always stood for the workingmen of the country. It has never cloaked or disguised its sentiments." (August 7, 21, 28, 1877.)

15. *Philadelphia North American,* July 25, 1877; Bruce, *op. cit.,* p. 196; Mackey, *op. cit.,* p. 194; *Journal of the Common Council of the City of Philadelphia for the Year 1877,* Philadelphia, 1877, vol. II, pp. 3, 44, 65-66, 89, and Appendix II, 2, 28.

16. Cooper, "The Army and Civil Disorder," *op. cit.,* pp. 104, 117, 131.

17. *Columbus Dispatch,* July 30, 1877; *Daily Ohio State Journal,* July 30, 1877.

18. Minutes Cabinet Meeting, July 23, 24, 25, 1877, Hayes Papers.

19. Bruce, *op. cit.,* p. 229.

20. Minutes Cabinet Meeting, July 25, 1877, Hayes Papers.

21. Bruce, *op. cit.,* p. 280.

22. M. C. Church to Carl Schurz, July 26, 1877, telegram, Carl Schurz Papers, Library of Congress, Manuscripts Division.

23. *Cleveland Leader,* July 23, 1877.

24. *See above* p. 99.

25. Minutes Cabinet Meeting, July 26, 1877, Hayes Papers.

26. *Ibid.*

27. Gresham, *op. cit.,* vol. II, pp. 230-31.

28. Hoyt, *op. cit.,* p. 172.

29. *Indianapolis Sentinel,* August 2, 1877.

30. Gerald G. Eggert, *Railroad Labor Disputes: The Beginning of Federal Strike Policy,* Ann Arbor, Michigan, 1969, pp. 39-42; Alan Drew Adler, "Federal Courts and Railroad Receivership in the Late Nineteenth Century," unpublished Ph.D. thesis, University of Wisconsin, 1971, pp. 112-16; Bruce, *op. cit.,* pp. 289, 308-09.

31. Eggert, *op. cit.,* pp. 43-44.

32. *Galveston Daily News,* July 28, 1877.

Strikes had broken out on the railroads all over Texas, but as yet Galveston had not been affected by the Great Strike.

33. *Galveston Daily News,* July 28, 29, 30, 31, 1877.

34. *Ibid.,* July 31, 1877.

35. *Ibid.,* August 1, 1877.

For an uncritical study of Cuney's rise to leadership of the Negro longshoremen, *see* Maud Cuney Hare, *Norris Wright Cuney,* New York, 1913.

36. *Galveston Daily News,* July 30, 31, August 1, 1877.

37. *Ibid.,* August 1, 1877.

38. *Ibid.*

39. *Ibid.,* August 1, 1877.

40. *Ibid.,* August 1, 2, 1877.

41. The "Veiled Prophet Parade and Ball," the annual upper class affair in St. Louis, dates from the victory celebration after the crushing of the general strike.

42. Thomas Scott to President R. B. Hayes, July 31, 1877, Hayes Papers.

43. Telegram, Hayes Papers.

In another telegram the same day to the president and the secretary of war, General Meyer wired: "Past nine oclock on Sunday night all along lines and all is well." (Hayes Papers.)

44. *Scranton Republican,* October 5, 1877.

45. Herbert Gutman, "Social and Economic Structure and Depression: American Labor in 1873 and 1874," unpublished Ph.D. thesis, University of Wisconsin, 1959.

46. Charles Richard Williams, *The Diary and Letters of Rutherford Birchard Hayes,* Columbus, 1924, vol. V, p. 440.

Chapter XI: Epilogue

1. *Pittsburgh Post,* August 2, 3, 4, 5, 1877; *St. Louis Globe-Democrat,* August 5, 6, 7, 1877; *Columbus Dispatch,* August 5, 1877. The Ohio items appeared originally in the *Ohio State Journal,* July 24, 1877.

2. *St. Louis Globe-Democrat,* August 6, 1877. The letter to Superintendent Shoemaker was originally published in the *St. Louis Times,* July 24, 1877.

3. *Labor Standard,* August 4, 11, 1877.

4. *National Labor Tribune,* August 4, 11, 18, 25, 1877; *Labor Standard,* August 4, 11, 18, 1877.

5. *Pottsville Weekly Miners' Journal,* August 3, 10, 1877; *Philadelphia North American,* August 9, 1877; *Harrisburg Independent,* August 30, 1877.

6. *New York Evening Post,* July 23, 1877. The text of the resolutions adopted by the Columbia Typographical Union was published in the *Martinsville Statesman,* August 7, 1877.

7. *Independent,* August 2, 1877.

8. *New York Sun,* August 3, 1877; reprinted in *National Labor Tribune,* September 22, 1877.

9. Ronald L. Filippeli, "The Railroad Strike of 1877 in Reading," *Historical Review of Berks County,* vol. XXXVII, Spring 1972, p. 71.

10. Edwin W. Sigmund, "Railroad Strikers in Court: Unreported Contempt Cases in Illinois in 1877," *Illinois State Historical Journal,* vol. XLI, Summer 1956, pp. 190-209; Brown, *op. cit.,* p. 72; Burbank, *op. cit.,* pp. 176-77; *Chicago Tribune,* August 11, 1877; *Pittsburgh Post,* August 10-12, 1877; *Reading Daily Eagle,* August 13, 1877; *Harrisburg Independent,* August 5, 1877; *St. Louis Globe-Democrat,* August 1, 2, 1877.

11. Burbank, *op. cit.,* p. 180.

12. *St. Louis Times,* August 4, 1877.

13. *National Labor Tribune,* August 18, 1877.

14. *St. Louis Globe-Democrat,* August 17, 18, 1877; *St. Louis Times,* August 17, 18, 1877; *Missouri Republican,* August 18, 19, 1877; Burbank, *op. cit.,* pp. 186-87.
Burbank points out that several historians, myself included, have incorrectly asserted that the members of the executive committee were sentenced to five years in the penitentiary and fined $200 each (p. 187). The reference in my case is to *History of the Labor Movement,* vol. I, p. 473.

15. *Chicago Tribune,* July 31, 1877.

16. George Frederick Howe, ed., "President Hayes' Notes of Four Cabinet Meetings," *American Historical Review,* vol. XXXVII, January 1932, p. 189.

17. *Ibid.*

18. Williams, *op. cit.,* vol. V, p. 440.

19. *Missouri Republican,* July 31, 1877. For concern about "financial people abroad," *see* letters to Carl Schurz, July 26, 1877, Carl Schurz Papers, Library of Congress, Manuscripts Division.

20. "Trade Union Fallacies," *Galveston Daily News,* August 1, 1877.

21. *Philadelphia Ledger,* August 3, 1877.

22. *Washington National Republican,* August 4, 1877.

23. *Pittsburgh Post,* August 5, 1877.

24. Robert B. Porter, "The Truth About the Strike," *Galaxy,* vol. XXIV,

December 1877, pp. 726-27. See also F. H. Heywood, "The Great Strike," *Radical Review,* vol. I, November 1877, p. 571.

25. W. M. Grosvener, "The Communist and the Railway," *International Review,* vol. IV, September 1877, pp. 585-86; A Red-Hot Striker of Scranton, Pa., "Do the Railway Kings Look For An Empire, Do They?" *Radical Review,* vol. I, November 1877, p. 527.

The article was reprinted as a pamphlet by Benjamin R. Tucker in 1880. Tucker, editor of the *Radical Review,* was a well-known philosophical anarchist.

26. *National Labor Tribune,* September 22, 1877. Emphasis added.

27. *Harper's Weekly,* vol. XXI, August 11, 1877, p. 617; Bruce, *op. cit.,* pp. 307-08; Louis Adamic, *Dynamite: The Story of Class Violence in America,* New York, 1936, p. 36.

28. Heywood, *op. cit.,* p. 575.

29. This figure is based on an estimate by William Riker, historian of the National Guard, who devotes one of the five chapters in his book, *Soldiers of the States: The Role of the National Guard in American Democracy* (Washington, D.C., 1957), to the militia 1877-1903. For the estimate *see* p. 47. However, Robert Reinders points out that since the strike spread over more than eleven states, more members of the militia were involved than indicated by Riker. ("Militia and Public Order in Nineteenth-Century America," *Journal of American Studies,* vol. XI, April 1977, p. 93.)

30. *New York Tribune,* August 3, 1877; Matthew Josephson, *The Politicos, 1865-1896,* New York, 1938, p. 255; *Nation,* vol. XXV, August 9, 1877, pp. 85-86; *The Commune in 1880, Downfall of the Republic,* New York, 1877, pp. 9-10.

31. *Locomotive Firemen's Magazine,* vol. I, August 1877, p. 276; *National Labor Tribune,* September 22, 1877; *Philadelphia Commonwealth,* reprinted in *Martinsburg Statesman,* August 28, 1877; *Pittsburgh Post,* July 30, 1877; *New York Sun,* August 12, 1877; *New York Tribune,* September 22, 1877; *Commercial and Financial Chronicle,* vol. XXV, July 28, 1877, pp. 73-74; *Cincinnati Enquirer,* August 28, 1877; Dixon Wecter, editor, *Mark Twain to Mrs. Fairbanks,* San Marino, Calif., p. 208.

32. Pierce, *op. cit.,* vol. III, pp. 252-54; Kann, *op. cit.,* pp. 97-98; Jack D. Foner, *The United States Soldier Between Two Wars,* New York, 1970, pp. 68-85.

33. "After the Battle," *Railroad Gazette,* August 12, 1877.

34. *Chicago Tribune,* August 4, 1877, September 12, 1878.

35. Thomas A. Scott, "The Recent Strikes," *North American Review,* vol. CCLVI, July-August 1877, p. 357.

36. Bruce, *op. cit.,* p. 303.

37. Thomas C. Cochran, *Railroad Leaders: 1845-1890,* Cambridge, Mass., 1953, p. 176.

38. Bruce, *op. cit.,* p. 304.

39. Cochran, *op. cit.,* pp. 176-77; Hoyt, *op. cit.,* pp. 230-31.

40. Edward McPherson, *A Hand-Book of Politics for 1877,* Washington, D.C., 1878, pp. 157-58; Hoyt, *op. cit.,* p. 231.

41. *Nation,* vol. XXV, August 16, 1877, p. 98; *Harper's Weekly,* vol. XXI, September 1877, pp. 678-79.

42. Gresham, *op. cit.,* vol. I, p. 408; Thompson to William Dennison, May 29, 1880, quoted and cited in Salvatore, unpublished manuscript on the life of Eugene V. Debs, p. 234.

43. Hoyt, *op. cit.,* p. 232.

44. *Chicago Tribune,* July 30, 1877.

45. Lucy Parsons, ed., *Life of Albert Parsons,* Chicago, 1889, p. xvii.

46. Scharnau, *op. cit.,* pp. 43-44; Kann, *op. cit.,* p. 101.

47. *Chicago Tribune,* July 25, 1877; *Labor Standard,* August 4, 1877.

48. Hillquit, *op. cit.,* pp. 200-201.

49. *Labor Standard,* August 4, 1877; *New York Times,* July 29, 1877.

50. *Labor Standard,* August 11, 18, 1877.

51. *Ibid.,* August 18, 1877.

52. *Arbeiterstimme,* August 12, 19, 26, 1877.

53. *Ibid.,* August 19, 26, 1877.

54. *Louisville Courier-Journal,* August 2, 5, 6, 1877; *New York Times,* August 12, 1877.

55. *Louisville Courier-Journal,* August 3, 5, 6, 7, 1877.

56. *Ibid.,* August 6, 7, 1877.

57. *Ibid.,* August 7, 10, 1877.

58. *Ibid.,* August 8, 1877.

59. *St. Louis Globe-Democrat,* August 7, 1877.

60. Burbank, *op. cit.,* p. 188.

61. *Martinsburg Independent,* reprinted in Bruce, *op. cit.,* p. 317; *St. Louis Globe-Democrat,* August 13, 1877.

62. *Emancipator,* August 18, 1877.

63. *Ibid.,* August 4, 1877.

64. *Labor Standard,* August 12, 19, 1877.

65. *Ibid.,* October 7, 1877; *Emancipator,* August 18, 1877.

66. *Emancipator,* August 4, 11, 18, 1877.

67. Hillquit, *op. cit.,* p. 203; Edward T. James, "American Labor and Political Action," unpublished Ph.D. thesis, Harvard University, 1954, pp. 128-30.

68. Burbank, *op. cit.,* p. 189.

69. *Scranton Republican,* July 30, August 8, 1877.
For the origins of the Greenback Party and its history before the election of 1877, *see* Foner, *History of the Labor Movement,* vol. I, pp. 475-79.

70. *New York Tribune,* September 16, 1877.

71. *Ibid.,* August 15, 28, 1877.

72. *Ibid.,* August 13-15, 1877.
The Civil War National Banking Act, by taxing currency issued by state banks, drove the note-issuing function of these banks out of existence, thus limiting currency in circulation. The Resumption Act of 1875 provided that, beginning on January 1, 1879, greenbacks would be redeemed in gold, thereby reducing the total amount in circulation.

73. *New York Times,* October 28, 1877.

74. *Ibid.*

75. *New York Tribune,* November 8-15, 1877; *New York Times,* November 8-15, 1877; *Rochester Union & Advertiser,* November 7, 1877; *The Path I Trod: The Autobiography of Terence V. Powderly,* ed. by Harry J. Carman, Henry David, and Paul N. Guthrie, New York, 1940, p. 204.

76. Hillquit, *op. cit.,* p. 226.

77. *Vorbote,* January 5, 1878; *New York Times,* December 31, 1877. The official name was the Sozialistiche Arbeiter-Partei, or, in its English version, the Socialistic Labor Party, a title which fifteen years later was revised to Socialist Labor Party.

78. *National Labor Tribune,* September 22, 1877.

79. *See* letter of P. M. Arthur in *St. Louis Globe-Democrat,* August 4, 1877.

80. *Ibid.,* August 12, 1877; Burbank, *op. cit.,* p. 177.

81. Bernard Mandel, "The 'Great Uprising' of 1877," *Cigar Makers' Official Journal,* September 1967, pp. 3-5; Samuel Gompers, *Seventy Years of Life and Labor,* vol. I, New York, 1925, pp. 142-54.

82. *Pittsburgh Telegraph,* August 12, 1877.

83. Foner, *History of the Labor Movement,* vol. I, pp. 438, 504-508.

84. *Ibid.,* pp. 500-503.

85. *Ibid.,* pp. 512-14; Gompers, *op. cit.,* vol. I, pp. 127, 210.

86. F. R. Plunkett to the Earl of Derby, Washington, July 31, 1877, *Reports of the Late Industrial Conflicts in the United States,* London, 1877, pp. 6-7.

87. *Labor Standard,* August 4, 1877.

88. Lucy Parsons, *op. cit.,* p. xvii; Kann, *op. cit.,* pp. 98-100.

89. Karl Marx to Friedrich Engels, July 24, 1877, Karl Marx, Friedrich Engels, *Werke,* Berlin, Band 34, p. 59.

90. Reprinted in *Martinsville Statesman,* September 4, 1877.

BIBLIOGRAPHY

Manuscript Collections

Chicago Historical Society
  Albert Day, "To My Children"
Rutherford B. Hayes Library, Fremont, Ohio
  Rutherford B. Hayes Papers
Kongelige Bibliothek, Copenhagen
  Studenterne Veal Kobenhavens 1829-1880
Library of Congress
  Walter Q. Gresham Papers
  Allan Pinkerton Papers
  Carl Schurz Papers
National Archives
  U.S. Army Signal Service Reports
  Adjutant General's Office, Letters Received, 1877, File #4042
  Military Division of the Atlantic Letters Sent and Received, 1877
  File RG393
    U.S. Troops at Scranton, Pa. Letter and Telegrams Sent and
      Received, 1877
    U.S. Troops at Reading, Pa. Post Letter Book, 1877
    U.S. Troops at Allegheny Arsenal, Pittsburgh, Pa. Letters Received,
      1877
    Military Division of the Missouri Letters Sent and Received, 1877
    U.S. Troops at Wilkesbarre, Pa. Letters Received, 1877
Tamiment Institute, Bobst Library, New York University
  "Philadelphia Tageblatt, Protokoll Buch de Verhandlunger Des Verwal-
    tungs Rathes, 1877"
Joseph A. Labadie Collection, University of Michigan Library
  "Protokoll Buch" of the Hoboken Section of the Workingmen's Party of
  the United States
State Historical Society of Wisconsin
  International Workingmen's Association Papers
  Workingmen's Party of the United States Material in Labor Collection

Unpublished Studies

Adler, Alan Drew, "Federal Courts and Railroad Receivership in the Late
  Nineteenth Century," Ph. D. thesis, University of Wisconsin, 1971

Anson, Charles Phillips, "A History of the Labor Movement in West Virginia," Ph.D. thesis, University of North Carolina, 1940

Behen, David M., "The Chicago Labor Movement, 1873-1896; Its Philosophical Bases," Ph.D. thesis, University of Chicago, 1953

Brown, Ray V., "The Erie Railroad Strike of 1877 in Hornellsville, New York," Senior Thesis, History, Princeton University, 1951

Cooper, Jean Marvin, "The Army and Civil Disorder: Federal Military Intervention in American Labor Disputes, 1877-1900," Ph.D. thesis, University of Wisconsin, 1971

Davis, George L., "Greater Pittsburgh's Commercial and Industrial Development, 1850-1900," Ph.D. thesis, University of Pittsburgh, 1952

Felton, Paul E., "The History of the Atlantic and Great Western Railroad," Ph.D. thesis, University of Pittsburgh, 1944

Gemorah, Solomon, "Laurence Gronlund's Ideas and Influence, 1877-1899," Ph.D. thesis, New York University, 1966.

Gutman, Herbert, "Social and Economic Structure and Depression: American Labor in 1873 and 1874," unpublished Ph.D. thesis, University of Wisconsin, 1959

Hoyt, Christopher, "The Labor Explosion of 1877: A Study of the Great Railroad Strike of 1877," Senior Thesis, History, Princeton University, 1960

James, Edward T., "American Labor and Political Action," Ph.D. thesis, Harvard University, 1954

Kann, Kenneth, "The Big City Riot: Chicago, Illinois," paper delivered at Annual Meeting, American Historical Association, Washington D.C., December 28, 1976

Kershner, Frederick D., "A Social and Cultural History of Indianapolis, 1860-1914," Ph.D. thesis, University of Wisconsin, 1950

Kuritz, Hyman, "The Pennsylvania Government and Labor Controls from 1865 to 1922," Ph.D. thesis, Columbia University, 1953

Reichley, Marlin S., "Federal Military Intervention in Civil Disturbances," Ph.D. thesis, Georgetown University, 1939

Ross, Marc, "John Swinton, Journalist and Reformer, The Active Years, 1857-1887," Ph.D. thesis, New York University 1969

Salvatore, Nicholas, "The Small Town Strike: Terre Haute, Indiana," paper delivered at Annual Meeting, American Historical Association, Washington D.C., December 28, 1976

Scharnau, David J., "Thomas J. Morgan, Chicago Socialist," Ph.D. thesis, University of Illinois, 1968

Stevenson, George J., "The Brotherhood of Locomotive Engineers and Its Leaders, 1863-1920," Ph.D. thesis, Vanderbilt University, 1954

Thompson, James H., "A Financial History of the City of Pittsburgh, 1816-1910," Ph.D. thesis, University of Pittsburgh, 1949

Whipple, James B., "Cleveland in Conflict: A Study in Urban Adolescence, 1876-1900," Ph.D. thesis, Western Reserve University, 1951

Government Documents

Adjutant General of Pennsylvania, *Annual Report, 1874*, Harrisburg, 1875

"Report of the Adjutant General of Pennsylvania for the year 1877," in *Governor's Message and Reports 1878*, Harrisburg, 1878, pp. 3-20

Biennial Message of Governor M. Mathews with Accompanying Documents to the Legislature of West Virginia, Wheeling, 1879

"Biennial Report of the Adjutant General of Illinois for 1877 and 1878," in *Reports of the General Assembly of Illinois*, Springfield, 1879, vol. II

Biennial Report of the Governor to the Legislature of Illinois, Springfield, 1879

Illinois Assembly, *Report of Special Committee on Labor*, Springfield, 1879

"Annual Report of the Adjutant General of Maryland for the year 1877," in *House and Senate Documents for Maryland, 1878*, Annapolis, 1878

Report of the Committee to Investigate the Railroad Riots in July, 1877, Harrisburg, 1878

Sixth, Seventh, Eighth and Ninth Reports of the (Massachusetts) Board of Railroad Commissioners, Boston, 1875, 1876, 1877

U.S. Commissioner of Labor, *Sixteenth Annual Report*, Washington D.C., 1901

Forty-Fifth Congress, 2d Session, House of Representatives, Executive Document L, Part II, "Report of the Secretary of War . . . Communicated to the Two Houses of Congress."

Journal of the Common Council of the City of Philadelphia for the Year 1877, Philadelphia, 1877, vol. II

Reports Respecting the Late Industrial Conflicts in the United States, London, 1877

Newspapers and Periodicals

Albany Journal (New York)
Altoona Mirror (Pennsylvania)
Arbeiter-Stimme (New York City)
Arbeiter-Zeitung (New York City)
Army Journal
Baltimore American
Baltimore Evening Bulletin
Baltimore Gazette
Baltimore News
Baltimore Sun
Boston Advertiser
Boston Globe
Boston Transcript
Brooklyn Daily Eagle
Buffalo Commercial Advertiser

Chicago Daily News
Chicago Inter-Ocean
Chicago Times
Chicago Tribune
Cigar Makers' Journal
Cincinnati Commercial
Cincinnati Daily Gazette
Cincinnati Enquirer
Cleveland Leader
Columbus Dispatch
Daily Ohio State Journal (Columbus)
Elmira Daily Advertiser (New York)
Frank Leslie's Weekly (New York)
Galveston Daily News
Harper's New Monthly Magazine
Harper's Weekly
Harrisburg Independent (Pennsylvania)
Hornellsville Tribune (New York)
Hornell Times (New York)
Indianapolis Sentinel
Irish World and Industrial Liberator (New York City)
Journal of the Brotherhood of Locomotive Engineers
Labor Standard (New York City)
Locomotive Firemen's Magazine
Louisville Courier-Journal
Martinsburg Statesman (West Virginia)
Missouri Republican (St. Louis)
National Labor Tribune (Pittsburgh)
National Republican (Washington, D.C.)
New Orleans Daily Picayune
New York Evening Post
New York Herald
New York Sun
New York Times
New York Tribune
New York World
Philadelphia Inquirer
Philadelphia North American
Philadelphia Record
Philadelphia Times
Pittsburgh Dispatch
Pittsburgh Leader
Pittsburgh Post
Pittsburgh Telegraph
Pittsburgh Times
Railroad Gazette
Reading Daily Eagle (Pennsylvania)
Rochester Union and Advertiser (New York)
St. Louis Daily Market Reporter

St. Louis Globe-Democrat
San Francisco Chronicle
San Francisco Mail
Scranton Republican (Pennsylvania)
Scranton Times (Pennsylvania)
Sozial-Demokrat (New York City)
Terre Haute Express (Indiana)
The Alarm (Chicago)
The Emancipator (Cincinnati)
The Independent (New York City)
The Nation (New York City)
The Socialist (New York City)
Toledo Commercial (Ohio)
Utica Observer (New York)
Vorbote (Chicago)
Weekly Miners' Journal (Pottsville, Pa.)
Wheeling Intelligencer (West Virginia)
Workingman's Advocate (Chicago)

Books and Pamphlets

Adamic, Louis, *Dynamite: The Story of Class Violence in America,* New York, 1936

Adams, Charles Francis, Jr., *Chapters of Erie and Other Essays,* New York, 1886

——, *Charles Francis Adams, 1835-1915, An Autobiography,* Boston, 1916

——, *Notes on Railroad Accidents,* New York, 1879

Aler, F. Vernon, *Aler's History of Martinsburg and Berkeley County, West Virginia,* Hagerstown, Maryland, 1888

"A Red-Hot Striker" of Scranton, Pa., *Do the Railway Kings Look For An Empire? Do They?* Boston, 1880

Barnard, Harry, *Rutherford B. Hayes and His America,* Indianapolis, 1954

Barrett, Thomas, *The Mollies Were Men,* New York, 1969

Bernstein, Samuel, *The First International in America,* New York, 1965

Bimba, Anthony, *The Molly Maguires,* New York, 1932

Bogen, Jules I., *The Anthracite Railroads,* New York, 1927

Boyle, O. D., *History of Railroad Strikes,* Washington, D.C., 1932

Brecher, Jeremy, *Strike,* Greenwich, Conn., 1972

Broehl, Wayne J., Jr., *The Molly Maguires,* Cambridge, Mass., 1964

Bruce, Robert V., *1877: Year of Violence,* Indianapolis, 1959

Burbank, David T., *City of Little Bread: The St. Louis General Strike of 1877,* St. Louis, 1957

——, *The Reign of the Rabble: The St. Louis General Strike of 1877,* New York, 1966

Burgess, George, and Kennedy, Mills C., *Centennial History of the Pennsylvania Railroad Company, 1846-1946,* Philadelphia, 1949

Burrows, Charles W., *William Evarts, Lawyer, Diplomat, Statesman,* Chapel Hill, N. Car., 1941

Calmer, Alan, *Labor Agitator: The Story of Albert R. Parsons,* New York, 1937

Carman, Harry J.; David, Henry; Guthrie, Paul W.; eds., *The Path I Trod: Autobiography of Terence V. Powderly,* New York, 1940

Chandler, Alfred D., *The Railroads: The Nation's First Big Business,* New York, 1965

Cochran, Thomas C., *Railroad Leaders: 1845-1890,* Cambridge, Mass., 1953

Cochran, Thomas C., and Miller, William, *Age of Enterprise,* New York, 1942

Commons, John R., and Associates, *History of Labor in the United States,* New York, 1918, vol. I

Commons, John R., ed., *A Documentary History of the American Industrial Society,* Cleveland, 1910, vol. X

Croffut, W. A., *The Vanderbilts,* Chicago, 1886.

Cross, Ira B., *A History of the Labor Movement in California,* Berkeley, 1935

Cullom, Shelby M., *Fifty Years of Public Service,* Chicago, 1911

Dacus, James A., *Annals of the Great Strikes,* St. Louis, 1877; repr. New York, 1969

David, Henry, *History of the Haymarket Affair,* New York, 1936; repr. New York, 1966

Dennett, Tyler, *John Hay,* New York, 1933

Dennis, Charles H., *Victor Lawson,* Chicago, 1935

Dictionary of American Biography, New York, 1957

Eckenrode, H. J., *Rutherford B. Hayes, Statesman of Reunion,* New York, 1930

Eggert, Gerald S., *Railroad Labor Disputes: The Beginnings of Federal Strike Policy,* Ann Arbor, Michigan, 1967

Flynn, Charles, *History of the Chicago Police,* Chicago, 1922

Foner, Jack D., *The United States Soldier Between Two Wars: Army Life and Reforms, 1865-1898,* New York, 1970

Foner, Philip S., *The Autobiographies of the Haymarket Martyrs,* New York, 1969

——, *History of the Labor Movement in the United States,* vol. I, New York, 1947; repr. 1972; vol. II, New York, 1955; repr. 1975

——, ed., *The Voice of Black America: Speeches by Blacks in the United States, 1797-1973,* New York, 1975, vol. I

——, ed., *The Formation of the Workingmen's Party of the United States: Proceedings of the Union Congress Held at Philadelphia, July 19-26,* New York, 1976

General Council of the First International 1864-1866: Minutes, Moscow, n.d.

Gompers, Samuel, *Seventy Years of Life and Labor,* New York, 1925, vol. I

Gowen, Franklin B., *To the Public,* n.p., 1877

Graham, Hugh Davis, and Carr, Ted Robert, *Violence in America: Historical and Comparative Perspectives,* New York, 1969

Greene, Victor R., *The Slavic Community on Strike: Immigrant Labor in*

Pennsylvania Anthracite, Notre Dame, Indiana, 1968

Gresham, Matilda, *The Life of Walter Quintin Gresham,* Chicago, 1919, vol. I

Hare, Maud Cuney, *Norris Wright Cuney,* New York, 1913

Hibben, Paxton, *Henry Ward Beecher, An American Portrait,* New York, 1927

Hillquit, Morris, *History of Socialism in the United States,* New York 1903

Hobsbawm, Eric, *Primitive Rebels: Studies in Archaic Forms of Social Movement in the 19th and 20th Centuries,* New York, 1959

Hofstadter, Richard, and Wallace, Michael, *American Violence: A Documentary History,* New York, 1970

Holbrook, Stewart, *The Story of American Railroads,* New York, 1947

Horowitz, Morton J., *The Transformation of American Law, 1780-1860,* Cambridge, Mass., 1977

Hungerford, Edward, *Men of Erie,* New York, 1946

——, *The Story of the Baltimore and Ohio Railroad, 1827-1927,* New York, 1928, vol. I

Hunter, Robert, *Violence and the Labor Movement,* New York, 1914

Josephson, Matthew, *The Politicos, 1865-1896,* New York, 1938

Kolko, Gabriel, *Main Currents in Modern History,* New York, 1976

Kross, Herman E., *American Economic Development,* Englewood Cliffs, N.J., 1955

Logan, Samuel C., *A City's Danger and Defense,* Scranton, 1887

McCabe, James D., (Edwin W. Martin, pseud.), *The History of the Great Riots,* Philadelphia, 1877

McCarthy, Charles, *The Great Molly Maguire Hoax,* Wyoming, Pa., 1969

McNeill, George E., ed., *The Labor Movement: The Problem of Today,* New York, 1891

McPherson, Edward, *A Hand Book of Politics,* Washington, D.C., 1878

Martin, Edwin Winslow. *See* McCabe, James D.

Marx, Karl and Engels, Frederick, *Letters to Americans, 1848-1895,* New York, 1953

——, *Werke,* Berlin, 1966, Band 34

Mason, Alpheus T., *Brandeis: A Free Man's Life,* New York, 1946

Mott, Edward H., *Between the Ocean and the Lakes: A History of the Erie,* New York, 1901

Nevins, Allan, *The Emergence of Modern America, 1865-1878,* New York, 1927

Oberholtzer, Ellis Paxson, *A History of the United States Since the Civil War,* New York, 1926, vol. IV

Parsons, Lucy E., *Life of Albert R. Parsons,* Chicago, 1889

Phillips, Clifton, Jr., *Indiana in Transition: The Emergence of an Industrial Commonwealth, 1880-1920,* Indianapolis, 1968

Pierce, Bessie Louise, *A History of Chicago, 1871-1893,* New York, 1957, vol. III

Pinkerton, Allan, *Strikers, Communists, Tramps and Detectives,* New York, 1878

Poor, Henry V., *Poor's Manual of the Railroads of the United States for 1877-1878*, New York, 1877; *for 1878-1879*, New York, 1878

Powderly, Terence V., *Thirty Years of Labor*, Columbus, Ohio, 1890

Quint, Howard H., *The Forging of American Socialism*, Columbia, S. Car., 1953

Rapport de Délégués des Ouvriers Mécaniciens de Paris à L'Exposition Universelle de Philadelphia, Paris, 1877

Reed, George Irving, *Encyclopedia Biography of Indiana*, Chicago, 1895

Rich, Bennett M., *The President and Civil Disorder*, Washington, D.C., 1941

Riker, William, *Soldiers of the States: The Role of the National Guard in American Democracy*, Washington, D.C., 1957.

Rudé, George, *The Crowd in History: A Study of Popular Disturbances in France and England, 1730-1848*, New York, 1964

Schlegel, Marvin E., *Ruler of the Reading: The Life of Franklin B. Gowen, 1836-1889*, Harrisburg, 1947

Schotter, H. W., *The Growth and Development of the Pennsylvania Railroad Company*, Philadelphia, 1927

Schurz, Carl, *The Reminiscences of Carl Schurz*, New York, 1907, vol. II

Sipes, William B., *The Pennsylvania Railroad, Its Origins, Construction, and Connections*, Philadelphia, 1875

Sorge, Friedrich A., *Socialism and the Worker*, New York, 1876

"Spectator," *The Commune in 1880: Downfall of the Republic*, New York, 1877

Stephenson, George, *The Brotherhood of Locomotive Engineers and Its Leaders*, Princeton, N.J., 1964

Taylor, George Rogers, *The Transportation Revolution, 1815-1860*, New York, 1951

Thayer, William Roscoe, *The Life and Letters of John Hay*, Boston, 1908, vol. I

Thompson, E. P., *The Making of the English Working Class*, New York, 1963

Tilly, Charles, and Louise, Richard, *The Rebellious Century, 1830-1930*, Cambridge, Mass., 1975

Ware, Norman J., *The Labor Movement in the United States, 1860-1895*, New York, 1929

Wecter, Dixon, editor, *Mark Twain to Mrs. Fairbanks*, San Marino, Calif., 1949

Williams, Charles R., ed., *Diary and Letters of Rutherford Birchard Hayes*, Columbus, Ohio, 1922-26, vol. III

——, *The Life of Rutherford Birchard Hayes*, Boston, 1914, vol. II

Wilson, James Harrison, *Under the Old Flag*, New York, 1912, vol. II

Wilson, William B., *History of the Pennsylvania Railroad*, Philadelphia, 1895, vol. II

Winchester, Paul, *The Baltimore and Ohio Railroad*, Baltimore, 1927

Woodward, C. Vann, *Reunion and Reaction: The Compromise of 1877 and the End of Reconstruction*, Boston, 1951

Yellen, Samuel, *American Labor Struggles*, New York, 1936

Articles

Abbott, Edith, "The Wages of Unskilled Labor in the United States," *Journal of Political Economy,* XIII, June 1950, 321-60

Adams, Charles Francis, "The Brotherhood of Locomotive Engineers," *The Nation,* XXIV, March 22, 1877, 173

Clark, Joseph S., Jr., "The Railroad Struggle for Pittsburgh," *Pennsylvania Magazine of History and Biography,* XLVIII, April 1924, 1-37

Cooper, Jerry M., "The Army As Strikebreaker—The Railroad Strike of 1877 and 1894," *Labor History,* vol. XVIII, Spring 1977, pp. 179-98

Filippelli, Ronald L., "The Great Railroad Strike of 1877," *Pennsylvania AFL-CIO News,* February 1973, 4

——,"The Railroad Strike of 1877 in Reading," *Historical Review of Berks County,* XXXVII, Spring 1972, 48-72.

Foner, Philip S., "The French Trade Union Delegation to the Philadelphia Centennial Exposition, 1876," *Science & Society,* XL, Fall 1976, 257-87

Garfield, James A., "The Army of the United States," *North American Review,* CXXVI, April 1878, 193-216

Grob, Gerald, "The Railroad Strike of 1877," *Midwest Journal,* VI, Winter 1954-55, 16-34

Grosvener, W. M., "The Communist and the Railway," *International Review,* IV, September 1877, 585-86

Gutman, Herbert G., "Trouble on the Railroads in 1873-1874: Prelude to the 1877 Crisis?" *Labor History,* II, Spring 1961, 215-35

——, "Peter H. Clark: Pioneer Negro Socialist, 1877," *Journal of Negro Education,* XXXIV, Fall 1965, 413-18

——, "The Worker's Search for Power," in Morgan, H. Wayne, ed., *The Gilded Age: A Reappraisal,* Syracuse, N.Y., 1968

——, "Work, Culture and Society in Industrializing America, 1865-1919," *American Historical Review,* LVI, June 1973, 531-87

Hacker, Barton C., "The U.S. Army as a National Police Force: Federal Policing of Labor Disputes, 1877-1898," *Military Affairs,* XXXIII, April 1969, 255-64

Henderson, James A., "The Railroad Riots in Pittsburgh: Saturday and Sunday, April 21st and 22nd, 1877," *Western Pennsylvania Historical Magazine,* XL, July 1928, 197-99

Heywood, F. H., "The Great Strike," *Radical Review,* I, November 1877, 1-25

Howe, George Frederick, ed., "President Hayes' Notes of Four Cabinet Meetings," *American Historical Review,* XXXVII, January 1932, 287-89

Jenks, Leland H., "Railroads as an Economic Force in American Development," *Journal of Economic History,* IV, May 1944, 12-26

Mackey, Philip English, "Law and Order, 1877: Philadelphia's Response to the Railroad Riots," *Pennsylvania Magazine of History and Biography,* XLVI, April 1972, 183-202

Mandel, Bernard, "The 'Great Uprising' of 1877," *Cigar Makers' Official Journal,* September 1967, 3-5

Morris, Richard B., "Andrew Jackson, Strikebreaker," *American Historical Review,* LV, October 1949, 54-68

Noelen, Russell M., "The Labor Movement in St. Louis from 1860 to 1890," *Missouri Historical Review,* XXIV, January 1940, 157-81

Otis, Col. Elwell S., "The Army in Connection with the Labor Riots of 1877," *Journal of the Military Service Institution of the United States,* V, September 1884, 292-325; VI, June 1885, 117-39

Parkman, Francis, "The Woman Question," *North American Review,* CCLXXV, October 1879, 316-24

Porter, Robert B., "The Truth About the Strike," *Galaxy,* XXIV, December 1877, 725-32

"Railroad Wages," *The Nation,* XXV, August 16, 1877, 99

Reinders, Robert, "Militia and Public Order in Nineteenth-Century America," *Journal of American Studies,* vol. XI, April 1977, 81-102

Schechter, Amy, "Labor Struggles in 1877,"*Daily Worker,* July 17, 1926, 7

Scott, Thomas A., "The Recent Strikes," *North American Review,*, September 1877, 351-62

Sigmund, Edwin W., "Railroad Strikers in Court: Unreported Contempt Cases in Illinois in 1877," *Illinois State Historical Journal,* XLI, Summer 1956, 190-209

Slaner, Philip A., "The Railroad Strikes of 1877," *Marxist Quarterly,* I, April-June 1937, 214-38

Smith, Goldwin, "The Labour War in the United States," *Contemporary Review,* XXX, September 1877, 529-41

Sorge, Friedrich A., "Die Arbeiterbewegung in den Vereinigten Staaten," *Die Neue Zeit,* Berlin, 1 Band, 1891-92, 112-25

Stitcher, George B., "The Schuylkill County Soldiers in the Industrial Disturbances in 1877, or the Railroad Riot War," *Publications of the Historical Society of Schuylkill County,* I, 1907, 193-215

Stone, Lucy, "The Strikers and the Mob," *Woman's Journal,* July 28, 1877, 236

Weaver, Bill I., "Louisville's Labor Disturbance, July, 1877," *Filson Club Historical Quarterly,* XLVIII, April 1974, 177-86

Whittaker, F., "The American Army," *The Galaxy,* XXIV, September 1877, 390-98

Wilson, James H., "The Size and Organization of Armies," *International Review,* July 1878, 514-29

Yearley, Clifton K., Jr., "The Baltimore and Ohio Railroad Strike of 1877," *Maryland Historical Magazine,* LI, April 1956, 191-212

Young, James D., "Scottish Labor and the American Railway Strike of 1877," *Labor History,* XII, Fall 1971, 603-4

INDEX

281

Fife, Hugh M., 58, 59, 60
Filipelli, Ronald I., 207
Finn, John, 175
Fischer, Adolph, 176
Fischer, William B., 176
Fisk, James, 13, 79
Flynn, John, 145-46
"Fort Schuler," 184-87
Fort Wayne, Ind., 98
Fraternization of militia with strikers, 83, 120
French, William H., 53, 142
French revolution, 167-68, 172, 216

Gabriel, Adolph, 110
Galaxy, 211
Galveston, Tex., 197-99, 266
Galveston Daily News, 198-99, 210
Garfield, James A., 41
Garrett, David, 58
Garrett, John W., 20, 32, 34, 36, 39-40, 42, 45, 46, 48, 52
Gemorah, Solomon, 261
General Council of the International Workingmen's Association, 167, 262
General Strike: almost one in Chicago, 145-46, 172; called in Kansas City, 157; in Philadelphia (1835), 261; in St. Louis, 158, 170-87; in Toledo, 157-58; meetings in support of, 166-74; number during Great Strike, 157; proclamation calling, 175-76
Germans, 129, 152-53, 159, 161, 214
Getty, William, 53
Glasgow Sentinel, 264
Glenn, Joseph N., 167-68, 208
Gould, James, 12, 41, 79, 143, 212
Government ownership of railroads, 115-16
Gowen, Franklin B., 26-27, 28, 70-75
"Grand Army of Starvation," 142-43
Grand Army of the Republic, 90
Grand Trunk Railroad, 14
Grant, Ulysses S., 217
Great Strike: as social revolution, 9, 161, 179; as a turning point for American workers, 229-30; attitude of railroad managers during, 51-52; beginning, 8, 9, 18, 34-35; Black and white unity during, 37, 72; building of armories after, 141-42, 192, 214; called "labor revolution," 157; calls for strengthening militia and U.S. Army, 212-13; calls for arbitration in, 67; cause of, 28, 32, 242; charge caused

by Communists, 104-5, 210-11; class harmony during, 100-101; crushed by troops, 201; discussion of, by historians, 9-11; discussions of remedies for, 209-17; effect of, on political upheaval of 1877, 226; end of, 188-201; ethnic differences disappear during, 153-54; and failure to rescind wage cuts, 204; first manifesto issued during, 44-45; fraternization of militia and strikers, 83, 120; and growth in influence of Lassalleans, 220-23; growth of Greenback-Labor Party, 224-26; guerrilla warfare during, 155-56; harassment of leaders of, 147-48; humor during, 203-4; illustrates theories of violence, 241; industrial unionism during, 163; industry paralyzed by, 189-90; leads to triumph of Lassalleans, 227; linked to Paris Commune, 103-4; Marx evaluates, 230; meetings in support of, 70, 117-25, 170, 178-79; miners in, 57; number of strikers during, 8, 186; offers to end by compromise rejected, 194; on Baltimore & Ohio, 33-54; on Erie, 79-89; on Lake Shore, 89; on New York Central, 89-94; on Pennsylvania, 55-78; on Philadelphia & Reading, 70-75; on Vandalia, 95-101; opposition to strengthening of army after, 213-14; power amassed against strikers during, 192; and precedents dangerous to labor, 195-98; railroads affected by, 10; rescinding of wage cuts during, 164; spread of, 8, 189-90; strikes of miners during, 75-77; strikers defended, 173-74; sympathy of public for strikers, 35-36, 59, 71, 76; and trade unions, 218-19, 228-29; use of federal troops in, 8, 38-43; warning against imprisonment of strikers, 205-6; wealthy frightened by, 9, 190; Workingmen's Party role in, 105-6, 113-14, 116, 218. *See also* Deaths; Demands of strikers; Press; Railroad workers; Slogans; Women; various cities and states
"Great Uprising of 1877," 228
Greenback-Labor Party, 224-26
Gresham, Walter Quintin, 90-99, 100, 104, 194, 195, 196
Grievances: of miners, 75-76; of railroad workers, 17-20, 28-29, 33-34, 45-46, 55-56, 81-82, 88

Lessons for today's fighters

Teamster Rebellion ($14.95), **Teamster Power** ($16.95),
Teamster Politics ($16.95), **Teamster Bureaucracy** ($17.95)
Farrell Dobbs

The 1985-86 Hormel Meat-Packers Strike in Austin, Minnesota
Fred Halstead, $2.50

Labor's Giant Step
Twenty Years of the CIO
Art Preis, $23.95

"Opening Guns of World War III: Washington's Assault on Iraq"
Jack Barnes
in *New International* 7, $10.00

COINTELPRO: The FBI's Secret War on Political Freedom
Nelson Blackstock, $14.95

The Frame-Up of Mark Curtis
A Packinghouse Worker's Fight for Justice
Margaret Jayko, $5.00

Out Now!
*A Participant's Account of the Movement in
the United States against the Vietnam War*
Fred Halstead, $29.95

Revolutionary Continuity
Birth of the Communist Movement: 1918-1922
Farrell Dobbs, $15.95

The Communist Manifesto
Karl Marx, Frederick Engels, $2.50

In Defense of Socialism
Fidel Castro, $12.95

Nelson Mandela: Speeches 1990
'Intensify the Struggle to Abolish Apartheid,' $5.00

The Revolution Betrayed
What Is the Soviet Union and Where Is It Going?
Leon Trotsky, $18.95

Cosmetics, Fashions, and the Exploitation of Women
Joseph Hansen, Evelyn Reed
Introduction by Mary-Alice Waters, $11.95

ORDER FROM PATHFINDER. SEE FRONT OF BOOK FOR ADDRESSES.

from Pathfinder

Teamster Rebellion
Farrell Dobbs
First of a four-volume series on the 1930s strikes and organizing drives that transformed the Teamsters union in Minneapolis into a fighting industrial union movement. 195 pp., $14.95

The Changing Face of U.S. Politics
The Proletarian Party and the Trade Unions
Jack Barnes
Building a party of socialist workers in a world of imperialist wars, economic crises, and assaults on the unions—a world where the battles by the rank and file play an increasingly central role. 346 pp., $18.95

The Eastern Airlines Strike
Ernie Mailhot and others
The story of the 22-month strike that blocked the building of a profitable nonunion Eastern Airlines and brought down notorious union buster Frank Lorenzo. 91 pp., $8.95

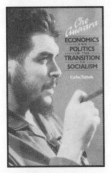

Che Guevara: Economics and Politics in the Transition to Socialism
Carlos Tablada
For Che Guevara, the key to the building of socialism is growing political consciousness and control by working people. 286 pp., $16.95

Malcolm X Talks to Young People
Malcolm X denounces U.S.-organized wars against national liberation struggles in Vietnam and Africa and describes the challenges young people face in the fight for a just world. A new collection. 110 pp., $9.95